MEDICAL CONCEPTS AND PENAL POLICY

Gerry Johnstone, BA (Hons) (NUI)
MSc in Legal Studies (Criminology) (Edin),
PhD (Edin),
Lecturer in Law, University of Hull

Cavendish
Publishing
Limited

First published in Great Britain 1996 by Cavendish Publishing Limited,
The Glass House, Wharton Street, London WC1X 9PX
Telephone: 0171-278 8000   Facsimile: 0171-278 8080

British Library Cataloguing-in-Publication Data A catalogue record for
this book is available from the British Library.

Johnstone, Gerry
Medical Concepts and Penal Policy
(Medico-Legal Series)
I Title II Series
344.20441

ISBN 1-85941-021-9

Printed and bound in Great Britain by
Biddles Ltd, Guildford and King's Lynn

To

Brigid and Eleanor

ACKNOWLEDGMENTS

I am indebted to David Garland for his invaluable help and advice during the planning, researching and writing of this book. I am also grateful to friends who have read and commented on earlier drafts of all or part of the manuscript and offered much useful advice, especially Beverley Brown, William Lucy, Jessica Penn, Peter Rush, Stuart Toddington and Peter Young.

I would like to thank the University of Edinburgh, Law Faculty, for its financial support while I carried out the research. I also thank the University of Hull Research Support Fund for a small grant in aid of publication. I am very grateful to my colleagues in the Law School, University of Hull, for generously allowing me a term of study leave and reductions in my teaching and administrative duties while completing the manuscript. I am grateful to the publishers of Social and Legal Studies for permission to use passages previously published in 'From Vice to Disease' (Vol 5.i), in Chapters 3 and 4.

Special thanks are due to Mary and (the late) Pearse McInerney for their support and encouragement at an early, and vital, stage of my academic career. I am most grateful, however, to my wife Brigid for her whole-hearted help and encouragement at every stage of the preparation of this book. I am delighted to be able to dedicate this book to her and my daughter, Eleanor.

CONTENTS

Contents

CHAPTER 1

INTRODUCTION

During the 1970s and 1980s the medical model of crime was subjected to severe criticism by philosophers, social scientists and legal scholars.[1] This criticism had a dramatic impact upon the attitudes of 'liberal' and 'radical' thinkers towards therapeutic interventions into the lives of offenders and towards the medical and psychiatric discourses on crime that inform these interventions. Largely as a result of these criticisms, what was previously regarded as a progressive way of thinking about and dealing with offenders came to be seen as a reactionary and dangerous approach to the problem of crime. Since the middle of the 1980s, certain aspects of the critical work on the medical model of crime have in turn been subjected to criticism and the debate about the medicalisation of deviance and social control has taken some new turns.[2] However, the fundamental objections to the medical model, raised during the 1970s and 1980s, are still widely regarded as valid, and therapeutic interventions into the lives of offenders still tend to be viewed with profound distrust by progressive thinkers who express an interest in crime and punishment.

I start this book by arguing that much of the critical literature on the medical model of crime produced during the 1970s and 1980s is of limited value for understanding and assessing *actual* therapeutic interventions into the lives of offenders. I argue that this criticism was directed not at actual therapeutic interventions or at the ideas and principles embodied in these interventions, but at a set of abstract philosophical ideas, ideals, and arguments, *viz* the 'medical model' of crime. This body of criticism may, therefore, be useful for understanding the weaknesses of the medical model of crime and for grasping the problems and dangers that would follow, logically, from the implementation of this model in its pure form. I argue, however, that it is of little use for assessing concrete therapeutic interventions into the lives of offenders or the substantive discourses that inform these interventions. I argue further that this limitation was seldom acknowledged and is still seldom recognised. There is a tendency to presume that criticisms directed at

---

1   See, in particular, Kittrie (1973), Balch (1975), Bean (1976), Moran (1978), Murphy (1979, pt 3), Box (1980), Conrad and Schneider (1980), Conrad (1981), and O'Donovan (1984). For useful discussions of the intellectual and cultural currents which gave rise to this body of criticism, see Pearson (1975: chapter 2) and Hirst and Woolley (1982: chapter 10).

2   See, in particular, the works of Peter Miller and Nikolas Rose (listed in the bibliography) who, inspired by the researches of Michel Foucault, have led the way in rethinking the role of the medical, the psychiatric and the psychological in regulating conduct. See also Nye (1984), Mort (1987), Pick (1989) and Sim (1990). For a fairly useful guide to the differences between 'critical psychiatry' and 'poststructuralist approaches' see Ingleby (1985).

the 'medical model' – which is an abstract programme for viewing and dealing with the problem of crime – are applicable to the actual practices and discourses that constitute therapeutic interventions into the lives of offenders. I will put forward a number of reasons why criticisms of the former cannot be extended to the latter.

I draw two implications from this argument. First, therapeutic interventions into the lives of offenders have been rejected by progressive thinkers as conservative and hazardous, on mistaken grounds. It has been assumed that the shortcomings and dangers which critics identified in the medical model of crime are also present in actual therapeutic interventions. However, before we could justifiably make such an assumption we would have to examine the nature of these interventions. Such an examination might reveal that, in practice, therapeutic interventions avoid many of the problems and dangers which critics of the medical model identified. Secondly, in focusing critical attention upon the medical model of crime, the existing body of critical literature neglected actual therapeutic interventions into the lives of offenders. These interventions, and the discourses that inform them, have yet to be subjected to critical scrutiny in their own right. The abstract ideal of modelling interventions into the lives of offenders upon medical interventions into the lives of the sick has been thoroughly analysed and its weaknesses and dangers exposed. But actual therapeutic practices, and the ideas implicit in them, have been largely ignored by critical theorists.

I argue, therefore, that it is necessary to examine the nature of therapeutic interventions into the lives of offenders and to re-open the prematurely closed debate about their meaning and consequences. In the rest of the book, I try to make a small but significant contribution to that task. Drawing upon some detailed 'case studies' which I have undertaken of the practical discourse of those who initiated and carried out therapeutic interventions into the lives of offenders in Britain since about 1850, I try to describe the nature of these interventions and of the ideas and principles which they embody.[3] Without ever aspiring to construct a comprehensive history of the therapeutic approach to crime, I try to rectify some common mistakes about the nature of therapeutic interventions. These mistakes have arisen, mainly, from the tendency to regard them as the practical realisation of the medical model of crime.

One of the main arguments I make is that, contrary to what is often assumed, therapeutic interventions into the lives of offenders are not usually modelled on *medical* treatment of either the physically or mentally ill. Rather,

---

3   The studies are of therapeutic interventions into the lives of 'alcoholic' and 'psychopathic' offenders and of the discourses which inform these interventions. Whilst I focus on developments in the British penal systems, and especially that of England and Wales, much of the argument may be applicable to our understanding of therapeutic interventions in other penal systems. Of course, as with any generalisations derived from cases studies, those drawn from this work must be regarded as provisional.

they tend to be much closer in their nature to *moral management*, which was advocated and practised in some 19th century lunatic asylums as an alternative to medical-style treatment (see Skultans 1975: chapter 4), and *social therapy*, which has been advocated and practised in some areas of modern psychiatry again as an alternative to medical-style treatment (see Clark 1981). The practices of 'moral management' and 'social therapy' with offenders do require critical scrutiny. But criticisms directed at medical-style treatment are of little value for assessing these practices.

A second argument I make is that therapeutic interventions into the lives of offenders tend to be informed, not by a narrow, 'technical' medical-somatic view of offender-patients, similar to that found in surgery for example, but by much broader moral-environmentalist and social-psychological 'focuses', similar to those found in some areas of 19th century public health programmes (see Mort 1987), 19th century psychiatry (see Skultans 1975), and the modern psychological complex (see Rose 1985 and 1989). These moral-environmentalist and social-psychological perceptions of offender-patients encompass moral and social dimensions of 'criminality' that would be excluded from a medical-somatic gaze, which tended to be the target of critics of the medical model of crime.

A third argument of this book is that the procedures used to admit offenders to therapeutic programmes are quite different from those that were targeted for criticism by most critics of the medical model. Critics of the medical model tended to object to 'despotic' procedures such as enforced treatment of offenders against their wishes, compulsory hospitalisation, indeterminate detention of offenders for therapeutic purposes without the protection of ordinary criminal justice proceedings, and the screening and testing of children to determine whether they have criminal or violent tendencies and the compulsory treatment of those who test 'positive' (Kittrie 1973; Moran 1978). I try to show that relatively few treatment professionals actually advocate or employ such procedures. The procedures which they use are much less extreme, and a great deal more complex, than was implied by critics of the medical model. These procedures do require careful critical examination, but such an examination must be based upon a proper understanding of them.

A fourth argument concerns the scope of therapeutic interventions into the lives of offenders. Critics of the medical model tended to imply that those who promote therapeutic interventions see them as applicable to almost all offenders. I show in this book that the ambitions of treatment professionals tend to be much more modest. For a number of reasons, they tend to regard therapeutic interventions as appropriate for relatively few offenders.

THE MEDICAL MODEL OF CRIME

Since the late 19th century, it has been frequently suggested that our interventions into the lives of offenders should be modelled on medical interventions into the lives of the sick.[4] The sentiments behind this idea are partly humanitarian: medical interventions often ameliorate the lives of sick people whereas punitive interventions seem to be designed to worsen the lives of offenders. However, some criminologists and penologists have been attracted to the medical model because of the *effectiveness* of medical interventions in achieving their objective of conquering illness. Whilst medical doctors and their allies enjoy great success in their battles against disease and illness, penal policy makers and practitioners tend to experience dismal failure in their war against crime. With the aid of scientific medicine our society has, for example, defeated many infectious diseases which, until quite recently, posed a serious threat to it. Moreover, we seem to have developed a framework which allows us to be confident that, in time, we can gain control over those diseases which continue to plague us. However, in the fight against crime we have not advanced at all. In this struggle, we seem to be no further on than we were decades or even centuries ago.

The following quotations from the early decades of the 20th century, which we can perhaps regard as the 'golden age' of the medical model of crime, might help to impart something of the flavour of this ideal. The first, from a 1901 lecture by Enrico Ferri, one of the founding fathers of scientific criminology, compared our success in the battle against contagious diseases with our failure in the war against crime and other 'moral diseases':

> The 19th century has won a great victory over mortality and infectious diseases by means of the masterful progress of physiology and natural science. But while contagious diseases have gradually diminished, we see on the other hand that moral diseases are growing more numerous in our so-called civilisation. While typhoid fever, smallpox, cholera and diphtheria retreated before the remedies which enlightened science applied ... we see on the other hand that insanity, suicide and crime, that painful trinity, are growing apace (Ferri 1913: 7–8).

The second quotation, equally as strong in its rhetoric, is from a 1928 article by a psychiatrist, A Gardner, called 'Science Approaches the Lawbreaker'. Gardner argued for a scientific revolution in the penal system similar to that which had occurred, long ago, in medicine:

> ... the methods employed by the Man of Science should be extended from the care and treatment of the body to the care and treatment of the soul ... Science has already rescued the body of man from the unscientific hands of the medieval practitioner who, ignorant of the true causes of the maladies he has

---

4   See, for example, Menninger (1968). For a critique of the views expressed by Menninger see Murphy (1979: 147–64).

sought to cure, had recourse to remedies which we now see were not calculated to produce the desired results ... All that now remains is to allow the Men of Science in a similar manner to rescue the soul of man out of the hands of the medieval psychologist – whose way of thinking underlies and is exemplified by our present penal methods (Gardner 1928: 205).

It is fairly easy to see why some criminologists and penologists have been attracted to the medical model. It is a model of scientific rationalism, which contrasts starkly with the ignorant emotionalism which seems to play such a major role in guiding penal interventions. What is less clear is what this ideal means in more specific terms. Medicine is, after all, a very diverse field. Public health interventions, surgery, general practice, and psychiatry, to mention just some of the main areas of medical intervention, might share certain core characteristics, but otherwise they differ considerably from each other. And, even within each of these areas of medical practice, practitioners often adhere to quite different 'working ideologies'. One would therefore expect those who advocate – and also those who criticise – the idea of modelling interventions into the lives of offenders upon medical interventions into the lives of the sick to specify, in a little more detail, precisely what they have in mind. However, those who discuss the medical model of crime – whether they are fervent supporters, sceptics, or outright critics – share in common a tendency to be quite vague about what the medical model looks like.[5] In what follows I will try to give some idea of what people might mean when they advocate the medicalisation of crime by identifying a number of core features that most people would include within the medical model of crime. It must be made clear, however, that this description does not, and probably could not, include all of the assumptions, principles, ideas and procedures which various participants in the debate have in mind when they refer to the medical model of crime.

Advocates – as well as critics – of the medical model of crime tend to explain what it is by contrasting it with the dominant 'legal' or 'penal' model of crime. Before we can identify the core distinctive features of the medical model of crime it is necessary, therefore, to identify some key characteristics of the penal model, to which it is usually opposed.

The penal model

In the penal model, interventions into the lives of offenders are informed by the assumption that people freely choose to become offenders. It is assumed,

---

5   This vagueness provoked one commentator to announce: 'I am distressed at the naive and cavalier way in which psychobiological insights may be dismissed because they are associated with the "medical model". There should, in my opinion, be a special place in purgatory for those who use the term "medical model" without defining it' (Halleck 1979: 148).

in other words, that offenders have full control over their conduct and that, using this capacity, they could, if they so wished, have avoided committing crime. Offenders are therefore deemed to be fully responsible and culpable for their wrongdoing. A closely related assumption is that offenders, and others who are tempted to offend, can be dissuaded from crime by the threat of punishment. According to this assumption offenders have the ability to control the course of their conduct and to act in accordance with self-interest; hence, they will not offend if it is demonstrated to them that the commission of crime will be followed by the infliction of punishment which will offset any pleasure they gain from the crime.

In the penal model, interventions are informed also by the 'moral' (and perhaps sociological) assumption that offenders ought to be punished. It is assumed that it is necessary for society to punish offenders in order to express disapproval of their wrongdoing and to ensure that they receive their just desert (as well as to deter the offender – and others with similar motives and opportunities – from committing further offences).

In the penal model, it is acknowledged that punishment is harmful to those who receive it. Punishment 'involves a deliberate and avoidable infliction of suffering' (Honderich 1971: 11). Hence, it is assumed that people would prefer not to be punished and that whilst society must punish offenders, the use of punishment must be regulated and limited. It is important that punishment is inflicted only on those who merit it, and that people receive only the amount of punishment which their behaviour deserves. There are, therefore, a number of 'limiting principles' which guide, or at least restrict, penal policy makers, sentencers and penal administrators. These include the principles that punishment must be inflicted only in response to a definite criminal act (or acts); the severity of punishment should not be wholly disproportionate to the gravity of the offence; and, as far as is reasonable, the severity of the punishment for a particular type of offence should be determined and made known in advance.

Some distinctive features of the medical model

The medical model tends to be defined in terms of certain assumptions that inform modern medicine's response to sickness. It is useful first to identify these assumptions and then to look at how they might be applied to offenders.

In the medical model, it is assumed that people do not choose to become sick. Sickness arises from causes and processes which lie beyond the afflicted person's control. Whilst persons can take some precautionary measures to avoid sickness, for the most part sickness results from forces over which the afflicted person is powerless (see Porter 1987a: 25). Hence, it is assumed that persons are not responsible or to be blamed for becoming sick. It is also assumed that persons who have fallen sick cannot make themselves better through an act of will. They cannot be persuaded or threatened into becoming better, because they have no control over the process. In order to make sick persons better it is necessary to repair the parts or functions of the body that have been damaged. This task can be performed only by medical experts: people with special knowledge and distinctive skills that enable them to understand the workings of the body and to 'tinker' with it safely and effectively.[6]

In the medical model, it is assumed that people do not deserve to be censured or punished for becoming sick, or for displaying symptoms of sickness, even if by becoming sick they become a nuisance or a danger to other people. To the contrary, it is assumed that sick people merit sympathy, help and compassion. Sick people are regarded as victims of misfortune – misfortune which strikes people more or less randomly. What sick people do require is medical care and treatment. They need to be cared for whilst they suffer from and are incapacitated by their sickness. And they require medical treatment which will remedy their ailment.

Medical care and treatment are regarded as beneficial to those who receive it. It is therefore assumed that whilst some forms of medical treatment may be onerous or even painful, people who are sick want medical care and treatment. Indeed, one of the main problems facing those responsible for the allocation of medical treatment is that the demand for it tends to exceed what is available. Occasionally, however, people may be sick and be deemed – by medical professionals and by others who come into contact with them – to require medical care and treatment, but may refuse to seek treatment voluntarily and may refuse to cooperate with attempts to treat them. An open question within the medical model is whether, and to what extent, such people should be treated against their wishes and be detained against their will in order to ensure that they receive the treatment which they are deemed to require. We need to discuss this issue briefly here as those who advocate a medical model of crime usually envisage offenders being subjected to compulsory hospitalisation and obliged to undergo treatment.

As a general rule, our society has decided that persons who suffer from physical sickness should not be compelled to undergo treatment. As Anthony Clare (1980: chapter 8) puts it, in his very informative discussion of the issue of involuntary mental hospitalisation and compulsory psychiatric care,[7] 'someone suffering from a physical illness, even a lethal one, is free to disregard medical advice, refuse treatment, and risk his own life in the process' (*ibid*: 341). The exception, of course, is where persons suffer from serious diseases which are highly contagious. But even in such cases our society has tended to be hesitant about compulsory medical interventions (see

---

6   See Goffman (1968) who describes medicine as a 'tinkering trade'.

7   There have, however, been profound changes in the law relating to compulsory psychiatric care since the publication of Clare's discussion.

Mort 1987). In the area of mental illness, however, for a variety of reasons, our society has tended to allow compulsory hospitalisation and treatment: 'a mentally ill person may be legally deprived of his rights and his liberty and be detained, against his wishes, for observation and treatment in hospital' (Clare 1980: 341). Such powers have been opposed (Szasz 1974), although some have conceded that they are justifiable but have argued that their use needs to be carefully regulated and limited to prevent their abuse. Others, however, place their trust in medical professionals not to abuse these powers and oppose all but minimal legal control on the ground that over-regulation will prevent people who need treatment from receiving it. Those who are most enthusiastic about compulsory treatment[8] assume that the question of whether a person requires it should be decided by medical doctors and that its duration should not be determined in advance by legal means, but that it should continue for as long as medical experts think it is required.

The medical model as applied to offenders

What would it mean to apply the medical model, as described above, to offenders? First, it would mean that our dealings with offenders would be based upon an assumption that offenders do not freely choose to become offenders, ie that their behaviour is in some way caused by forces beyond their conscious control. Offenders would be seen as not personally responsible or culpable for their behaviour. It would also mean assuming that offenders could not change their behaviour through acts of will, ie that even if they made a conscious effort to obey the law, they would nevertheless be propelled towards crime by forces over which they have no control. It would be pointless to try to dissuade such persons from offending through the threat of punishment. The logic of punitive deterrence is that the threat of punishment will influence the choices made by those tempted to commit crime – that it will discourage such people from actually breaking the law. The concept of deterrence assumes that offenders have a choice about whether or not to offend. If we assume, on the other hand, that offenders commit crime not because they choose to but because they must – ie that they act under compulsion – then we must conclude that punishment can make no impact upon their behaviour.

Applying the medical model to offenders would mean assuming that, in order to stop offenders from re-offending, it is necessary physically to restrain them or to remedy the disorder which drives them to offend. The task of 'curing' offenders would be performed by experts, ie by people with special

---

8   Clare provides the following quotation from a lecture by L Birley: 'Compulsory psychiatric care is not a threat but a right. Every citizen should have the right to be admitted against his will to the care of a first-class psychiatric service' (quoted in Clare 1980: 341).

knowledge and distinctive skills that enable them to understand the complex processes that produce 'criminality' and to reverse their effects.

Applying the medical model to offenders would lead to a radical alteration in assumptions about what should be done with offenders. On the negative side, it would mean assuming that it is *unfair* to punish them, since this would amount to censuring and harming them for doing things which they could not avoid doing. On the positive side, it would mean assuming that we should be sympathetic towards offenders and offer them care and treatment.

Of course, many offenders who are deemed to require treatment will not avail themselves of it voluntarily. Many will receive the treatment they require only if they are compelled or at least pressured into accepting it. Hence, if the medical model is applied to offenders the question of compulsory hospitalisation and enforced treatment is raised. Few proponents of the medical model of crime address the issue of whether compulsory hospitalisation and treatment are justified, even if offenders are ill. Most seem to assume that offenders will be deprived of their freedom anyway, and that compulsory hospitalisation instead of compulsory imprisonment requires little justification.[9]

Applying the medical model to offending would mean that compulsory hospitalisation would be distinguished from imprisonment for the purposes of punishment. The former would be conceived as a means of ensuring that offenders receive the treatment which they need, and are incapacitated from doing harm whilst they remain ill. It would not be seen as a method of punishing offenders for the wrongs which they have done. Hence, the 'limiting principles' which apply to imprisonment as punishment would not be applicable to compulsory hospitalisation for purposes of treatment and incapacitation. It would not be necessary, before an order of compulsory hospitalisation was made, to establish that the person had committed a definite criminal act. Rather, it would be sufficient to show that the person has an illness which requires treatment, that if the illness is untreated the person will probably commit offences, and that the person will not voluntarily undergo treatment. The duration of compulsory hospitalisation would not be determined by reference to the gravity of the offence. Rather, it would be determined by the offender's treatment needs. And, since it is difficult to predict, precisely, the course of an illness or the results of a treatment programme, the duration of compulsory hospitalisation would not be determined in advance. Rather, hospitalisation would cease when it was decided by medical experts that the offender no longer required it.

---

9   We might note that even if this assumption is correct, it would still be necessary to justify enforced treatment, where treatment consists of more than mere hospitalisation.

THE CRITIQUE OF THE MEDICAL MODEL OF CRIME

For many people, the medicalisation of offending, as described above, would be a progressive development which would benefit both offenders themselves and the wider community. Offenders would no longer be regarded as 'bad people' and would avoid the censure and punishment which they now receive. Instead, they would be regarded as people deserving of sympathy. And perhaps most importantly, they would be able to avail themselves of treatment facilities currently denied to them. The community would benefit also by the fact that, instead of being returned to society after being punished to commit further offences, offenders would be cured of the illness that makes them offend. Hence, 'medicalisation' would mean less crime. However, as I have indicated, during the 1970s and 1980s, the medical model of crime was subjected to a harsh and very influential critique. Critics of the medical model of crime questioned the appropriateness of medical interventions as a model for interventions into the lives of offenders and argued that, although 'medicalisation' might have had some beneficial consequences for offenders, it also had a whole range of more deleterious consequences (see note 1).

Criticism of the medical model of crime frequently takes the form of a demonstration that there are fundamental differences between the nature of illness and the nature of crime, followed by an argument that the model which has been used successfully to understand and deal with the former is inappropriate for understanding and dealing with the latter. It is then argued that the actual application of this inappropriate model has led to a whole range of deleterious consequences for offenders. I will look first at the fundamental differences between illness and crime, according to critics of the medical model.

The inappropriateness of the medical model

According to Balch (1975), there is a fundamental difference between physical illness on the one hand and deviance, delinquency and crime on the other. Because of this difference, he argues, the framework used for understanding the former cannot be used for making sense of the latter. Physical illnesses, he contends, exist independently of the *judgments* people make about them. Delinquency, on the other hand, has no existence apart from the judgments people make about particular kinds of behaviour. In order to get this point across, he uses the example of a physical disease which, like delinquency, is judged to be shameful: venereal disease.

> VD is more than physical illness – there is a powerful social stigma attached to it. But remove the social stigma, even make VD a prestigious thing to have, and the physical disorder remains. Venereal diseases exist independently of the judgments we make about them (Balch 1975: 117).

If, on the other hand, we take away the opprobrium from types of behaviour which we judge to be criminal, certain crimes would no longer exist. Or, as Balch puts it: 'Remove the condemnation of all those things we call juvenile misbehaviour and delinquency would cease to exist' (*ibid*).

One obvious inference from this argument, if it is right,[10] is that we have an option in dealing with crimes which we do not have in dealing with illnesses: we can simply define certain types of crime out of existence. If people decide to tolerate behaviour which they previously condemned and prohibited, such behaviour would cease to be a problem, or so the argument runs. One problem with the analogy between illness and crime, according to critics of the medical model, is that it obscures this option.

However, Balch also draws a more subtle inference from his argument. He suggests that, since physical illness has an independent existence we can ignore the social judgments people make about it and still explain it. To use Balch's example of venereal diseases, we can explain how they come into existence by identifying their material causes and modes of transmission. We can ignore the judgments which people make about venereal diseases and still produce a sensible and fruitful explanatory account. In order to explain delinquency, however, we need a theoretical framework which includes, indeed focuses upon, the social reaction to different types of behaviour: 'The critical variable in the study of deviance ... is the social audience ... since it is the audience which eventually determines whether or not any episode of behaviour ... is labelled deviant' (Balch 1975: 118). Hence, for Balch, the medical perspective on offending, which ignores the critical role played by social audiences in defining behaviour as deviant, is a 'theoretical blind alley' (*ibid*: 116).

A second fundamental difference between illness and crime, according to some critics of the medical model, is that – contrary to the assumptions of some proponents of medicalisation – offending behaviour usually is the result of intentional, deliberate choices made by the offender (see Cohen 1971: 19–20). Whereas illness is something that happens to people – that strikes them for no particular reason – crime is something which people choose to do, even if those choices are constrained and influenced by cultural values and socio-economic circumstances over which individual offenders have no personal control. Hence, it is argued, explanations of crime must take into account the motives, intentions, reasons, etc of the offender. The medical model, which focuses only on the 'objective', 'material' world of cause and effect and excludes from the frame the inner subjective world of the offender, therefore misses a vital part of the explanation of offending.

10 See Sedgwick (1982), who criticises such arguments by pointing to the subjective, value-laden nature of the concept of illness, and Clare (1980: chapter 1) for a discussion of the complexity of this issue.

A third difference between illness and crime, according to some critics of the medical model, is that they have different determinants. Illness has physical determinants. It is caused, for example, by germs, viruses or harmful bacteria somehow entering the body and damaging its organs or tissues. Criminal behaviour, on the other hand, to the extent that it has 'external' determinants, is caused by social forces, such as sub-cultural values or socio-economic circumstances (see Greenwood and Young 1980: 158). Accordingly, it is argued, the medical model leads to a fruitless search for physical causes of crime and to the neglect of its social causes.

If the analogy between illness and crime is seriously misleading, as the critics of the medical model suggest, it follows, or so it is often argued, that medical solutions to the problem of offending cannot work. Hence, critics of the medical model suggest that treatment programmes for offenders which are based on the assumptions, (a) that the problem of crime can be solved by eliminating or controlling the factors which cause criminal behaviour, and (b) that these causes are objective physical forces, are bound to fail. Instead, the critics imply, a proper solution to the problem of offending behaviour is one that is as much concerned with questioning and perhaps altering the judgments which people make about certain types of behaviour as with stopping the behaviour itself. Also, to the extent that the aim is to stop the behaviour itself, this requires addressing the offender as a rational subject, whose behaviour is to be understood as intentional and as arising from conscious reasons and motives, rather than treating him or her as an object whose behaviour is the determined result of impersonal forces. And, to the extent that it is possible to prevent crime by eliminating its objective determinants, these determinants have to be understood as 'social' rather than biological.

The harmful consequences of the medical model

So far, I have indicated the position of the critics as being that the problem of crime – unlike the problem of physical sickness – cannot be solved within the medical model. Rather, according to the critics of the medical model, a much broader framework is required. Many critics go further than this, however, by arguing that not only is the medical model inappropriate for crime, but that the introduction of this inappropriate model into practice results in a whole range of deleterious consequences. The problem with the medical model in practice, according to many critics, is not only that it leads to the wasting of considerable resources on misconceived attempts to find the physical causes of crime and to treat offenders by medical means. Nor is it only that it deflects attention away from the social causes of crime, or from the fact that to call something a crime involves making a moral judgment. In addition, many critics suggest, the modelling of interventions into the lives of offenders upon medical interventions into the lives of the sick has direct harmful effects for offenders. The portrayal of offenders as sick people, the actual treatment of offenders, and the procedures adopted as a result of the medical model, are all criticised because of their deleterious impact upon offenders.

First, critics of the medical model questioned the widespread assumption that offenders only benefit from being defined as 'sick people' rather than as 'bad people'. For example, Gusfield (1980) suggests that to label a person as 'sick' is, in many ways, more disparaging than labelling them as 'bad' since, to classify offenders as sick is to suggest that they are helpless and pitiful people. It implies:

> ... helplessness and loss of control that is itself an unflattering self-portrait to which many object. Better to be thought a sinner, but responsible for myself, than to be a victim of the fates! There is a moral connotation to sickness that underlies the humanitarian perception of the deviant as victim (Gusfield 1980: vii).[11]

A somewhat related criticism of the analogy between illness and crime is that it leads to offenders being regarded and treated as objects – propelled to crime by impersonal forces over which they had no control – rather than as subjects who had behaved intentionally, with motives that were usually intelligible, often rational, and occasionally honourable. There is something dehumanising, the critics suggested, about being regarded in this way.

Secondly, critics denounced as dangerous and inhumane the practice of treating offenders. In practice, some critics suggested, the treatment of offenders included hazardous and dehumanising procedures such as psychosurgery, electric shock treatments, the implantation of electrodes into the brain, the administration of nausea-producing drugs, and brain-washing techniques (Moran 1980). These methods, it is suggested, are hazardous in a straightforward sense. Moreover, it is argued, to the extent that they succeeded in their objective of changing the personalities of offenders, they constituted a threat to the right to be different (Kittrie 1973) – a human right that is regarded as so precious that, according to many, not even the most dangerous and heinous of offenders should be deprived of it.

Third, critics argued that the procedures introduced under the influence of the medical model constitute a serious threat to the liberty of offenders and also, indeed, to the liberty of many non-offenders. It was argued that no matter how benevolent the *intentions* of the therapists, the compulsory detention and treatment of offenders does, like punishment, constitute an interference with the liberty (Kittrie 1973). Or as Allen put it:

---

11 Gusfield also questions the assumption that medical definitions of offending are morally neutral. He contends that they embody *disguised* moral judgments. Whilst the medicalisation of offending behaviour indicates that the offenders themselves are not bad, it corroborates the moral-political judgment that the medicalised *behaviour* is pathological. Hence, many offenders are extremely irritated by medical definitions of their behaviour because, in their eyes, their behaviour is normal and perhaps even preferable to so-called normal behaviour (Gusfield 1980: vii–viii).

Measures which subject individuals to the substantial and involuntary deprivation of their liberty are essentially punitive in character, and this reality is not altered by the facts that the motivations that prompt incarceration are to provide therapy or otherwise contribute to the person's well-being or reform (Allen 1973: 181).

However, whereas explicit punishment was carefully regulated and subject to a number of limiting principles, compulsory hospitalisation and treatment were not. An offender who was defined as ill could be committed to a 'hospital' and subjected to treatment for indeterminate periods, without the protection of 'due process' (*ibid*). Moreover, the medical analogy had led to many deviants who had not committed any actual crimes being subjected to 'preventative treatment' on the same basis as actual offenders. Indeed, even those who had done nothing wrong, but merely tested positive on tests designed to identify criminal tendencies, were being deprived of their liberty, according to critics of the medical model, and treated as if they were actual offenders.

Medicalisation as a conspiracy

We could accept these criticisms as valid and conclude that the application of the medical model to the problem of crime was a mistake, ie that those who promoted a medical model were blind to its latent dangers. It is easy to see how such a mistake could have been made. By rejecting antiquated ideas about, and 'remedies' for, sickness and adopting modern medical knowledges, procedures and forms of treatment, doctors had made dramatic advances in their battle against disease. It is likely that those who promoted the medicalisation of official responses to offending genuinely believed that, by taking a similar approach to offending, they could achieve a similar level of success in the area of 'moral disease'. The problem was that, in their enthusiasm, they failed to consider the crucial differences between the nature of illness and the nature of offending. Consequently, they failed to realise that, not only would the procedures and methods which were successfully used for dealing with the problem of illness not work with the problem of offending, but that the extension of these procedures and methods from the problem of illness to quite different types of social problem would have pernicious effects

However, during the 1980s, many critics of the medical model began to imply that medicalisation was less a mistake, more a conspiracy. According to this radical view, the medical model of crime was promoted and supported, despite its obvious problems and dangers, because it facilitated the repression and control of deviance. Radical critics of the medical model contend that it was favoured because it helped to produce 'civil tranquillity and social harmony' (Box 1980: 96) in a number of ways.

As we have seen, some critics of medicalisation had argued that the disease analogy obscured the true nature of offending by neglecting both the role that social audiences played in defining behaviour as delinquent and the role which cultural and socio-economic factors played in producing criminal behaviour. The more radical critics suggest that it suits the state to obscure the true nature of offending in this way. The notion that certain types of conduct are pathological, rather than simply *judged* to be offensive, helps to block challenges to the existing set of prohibitions and to the cultural values which produce them. As Box puts it, medical experts propose:

> definitional shifts in moral, ethical and political problems into medical conditions, so that the conflicts, disputes and disagreements implicit in the former can be avoided by systematically labelling some of the antagonists, usually the least powerful, as diseased (Box 1980: 96).

Radical critics of 'medicalisation' argue that the medical model's neglect of the social causes of offending is also ideologically useful for the state (see Ramon 1986). They argue that by representing offending behaviour as the product of individual sickness, medical definitions of deviance deflect attention away from the socio-economic causes of crime. They thereby divert attention from the state's, or society's, responsibility for crime. The idea that people commit crime because they have illnesses which are often inborn implies that changes to social structures and policies can do little to prevent offending. The medical model implies that individual treatment and segregation are the solutions and that the problem can be solved without changing social policies or structures. Such a notion, the critics point out, is very useful for those who benefit from current social policies and structures.

With regard to treatment, we have seen that 'early' critics of medicalisation suggested that the move from a penal to a medical model resulted in offenders being subjected to unbridled 'therapeutic' interventions which were more burdensome than punishment, which was surrounded by legal limitations and safeguards. The radical critics of medicalisation took this objection a stage further, arguing that the powers of compulsory hospitalisation, enforced treatment, and indeterminate detention which had been awarded to 'therapists' were quite useful from the point of view of social control. However, such powers could not be justified in penal terms; such extensive intrusions into the lives of 'ill offenders' were seldom warranted by their offences. Hence, these radical critics argued, the language of treatment was employed to throw a cloak of medical respectability around what was, nakedly, an apparatus of social control (Ramon 1986).

Other radical critics of medicalisation present an even more sinister image of treatment. Focusing on the actual methods of treatment employed (methods which earlier critics had denounced as perilous and dehumanising) radical critics argue that, although treatment is not effective as a means of preventing crime (which will continue to occur until its social causes are removed), it is effective as a form of social control. Some forms of treatment, such as psychosurgery of pharmacological treatments, do serve to subdue rebellious individuals: 'A generation of urban poor, many of them on prescribed drugs since their infancy, are hardly going to transcend their medication and revolt' (Box 1980: 121). Other forms, such as behavioural therapies, do succeed in repressing deviant behaviour. And, some types of therapy, they suggested, do produce real personality changes, rendering individuals more docile. Treatment does not *accidentally* infringe the right to be different, radical critics argue. Rather, its very *purpose* is to stifle individual difference and to crush rebelliousness.

THE LIMITATIONS OF THIS CRITIQUE

I do not question, at least not here, the fairness or validity of these criticisms of the medical model of crime. I argue, however, that these criticisms are limited in their scope. They apply only to a particular *model* of crime – ie to a set of abstract philosophical assumptions, ideas and ideals concerning how we should understand and respond to criminal lawbreakers – and to the *logical* consequences of implementing this model in its pure form. Since such a model frequently has been advocated, it is important to identify its weaknesses and to expose the undesirable consequences that would be likely to follow its implementation. Hence, the critics of the medical model – whatever exaggerations some of them indulged in – should be recognised as having made an important contribution to the philosophy and sociology of punishment. The critics should have made it clear, however, that most of their criticism applies only to the medical model and that it does not necessarily apply to those concrete practices and substantive discourses which make up the therapeutic response to offenders. However, the critics usually failed to make this clear. Instead, they tended to allow their arguments to be read as if they were applicable to actual therapeutic interventions. One consequence of this is that the nature of actual therapeutic interventions has seldom been understood, still less subjected to critical scrutiny.

I argue here that it is mistaken to assume that criticisms directed at the medical model of crime apply to actual therapeutic interventions into the lives of offenders. The medical model must be understood as a highly general orientation towards the problem of crime. It is not at all clear what this general orientation means in terms of specific practices. The aim of 'medicalising' crime can be interpreted in a variety of ways. And, just as important, a variety of quite different types of intervention can be justified as realisations of the medical model. For example, the segregation or sterilisation of habitual offenders to prevent them from breeding, on the assumption that 'criminality' is an hereditary psychological disease, could be justified by reference to the medical model. But, arguably, attempts to 'educate' those who drink and drive, on the assumption that such behaviour results from insensibility to its consequences, can also be justified by reference to the medical model. These programmes certainly share some basic assumptions and some basic problems, eg both focus upon the deviant individual and ignore the social-structural causes of problem behaviour.[12] However, the character of these programmes clearly differ in fundamental ways. The two very different types of intervention, and the two very different ideas which inform them, need to be distinguished for purposes of critical assessment. However, many critics of the medical model of crime would object to both in the same terms (just as many supporters of the medical model would support both in the same terms).

One reason why the precise practical meaning of the medical model of crime is unclear is that it is an abstract ideal. Even if we agreed about the nature of the ideal, there would still be considerable scope for disagreement about what the ideal means in terms of substantive practices. To take just one example, we might agree that a central assumption of the medical model of crime is that offenders should not be punished but should be given treatment. However, 'treatment' can mean a variety of quite different things. As Halleck (1979: 152) points out, there is not even a consensus about whether the word refers to activities or objectives: 'Treatment can be defined either as certain activities one person engages in while trying to influence another, or the specific goals of the activity'. Further, as Halleck points out, if we define 'treatment' in terms of goals, there are a number of conceivable goals in 'treating' an offender (*ibid*). These range from doing 'something to an offender that will diminish the probability of his committing crimes' even if this is painful to him or compromises his future potentialities, to doing something to the offender that will make him 'more comfortable and effective' regardless of whether the intervention has any effect upon the offender's subsequent criminal behaviour (*ibid*). Halleck points out that the four different goals of treatment which he identifies each 'have profoundly different ethical meanings and consequences for the offender' (*ibid*). Yet, he indicates, when people talk about treatment they seldom specify which goal they have in mind. This applies, he suggests, to practitioners of treatment and also to fervent supporters and critics of therapeutic interventions. Clearly, if the debate about treatment is to become more meaningful, those who object to therapeutic interventions need to clarify what it is they object to (just as supporters need to clarify what it is they support). However, in my view, the most important implication of this argument is that before we engage in debate about actual therapeutic interventions into the lives of offenders, we need to find out in what sense these are intended as 'therapeutic'. We need to find out what the precise, practical objectives of these interventions are and what methods are used to achieve these objectives.

Another reason why the practical meaning of the ideal of modelling interventions into the lives of offenders upon medical interventions is so

---

12   See Gusfield (1980) on the individualistic assumptions of treatment programmes for drink-drivers.

unclear is that the nature of medical intervention is itself unclear. Medical interventions are not all similar in their objectives and underlying assumptions. Rather, there is considerable diversity within the field of medical interventions. Public health interventions – which some early proponents of the medical model of crime seemed to have in mind – are quite different in their operational principles from surgical operations. Does adopting a medical model of crime involve attempting to isolate the moral equivalent of viruses and bacteria which cause diseases and establishing a system of administrative, medical and educative interventions to eliminate or control these causes? Or, does it mean repairing damaged organs which produce a criminal disposition?

An even deeper problem is that within particular branches of medicine, there is often no consensus about the best mode of intervention and often no consensus about the nature of the problem which is to be solved. Rather, there are often two or more competing frameworks. This diversity of 'working ideologies' is most obvious in psychiatry (see Clare 1980). In psychiatry, there is considerable disagreement about the very scope of the category mental illness, about what mental illness is, about what causes it, and about how the mentally ill should be handled. Yet, it is to psychiatry – rather than to physical medicine – that most penal treatment professionals have looked for a model for their interventions. For many treatment professionals, the medical model means regarding and treating offenders as mentally abnormal people, ie – as individuals who suffer from some kind of mental abnormality which renders them excessively impulsive, anti-social, or violent. Hence, many treatment professionals have looked to psychiatry for ideas about how to understand, process and treat offenders. However, in psychiatry they have found not a single approach to mental disorder but a variety of competing approaches. So, in order to understand the nature of therapeutic interventions it is necessary to ask which of the various psychiatric frameworks has been most influential upon the *practice* of treatment in penal settings.

In what follows, I outline the key distinctive features of two quite different approaches to psychiatric disorder: the medical-somatic approach and the social-psychological approach. I will show that these approaches differ significantly in their operational principles and underlying assumptions about the nature and causes of psychiatric disorder. I will then pose the question, 'to which of these approaches are actual therapeutic interventions into the lives of offenders closest'? In the rest of the book, I will show that therapeutic interventions into the lives of offenders tend to be modelled on the social-psychological side of psychiatric practice, rather than on the medical-somatic side.

APPROACHES TO PSYCHIATRIC DISORDER

Psychiatry seeks to understand, help and treat people who are deemed to have mental problems. However, within psychiatry there a number of different, and often competing, orientations towards mental suffering (see Clare 1980). Controversy within psychiatry starts with the basic question of what type of problems fall within the concerns and expertise of professional psychiatrists. Some would restrict the discipline to severe disorders of the recognised mental functions (*ibid*: chapter 1). Others include a much wider range of disorders of personality, feelings, and conduct within the scope of psychiatry's legitimate concerns and expertise. There are also fundamental disputes over how psychiatric disorder, however it is defined, can best be conceptualised, interpreted, explained and remedied. In what follows I make no attempt to summarise the controversies within psychiatry. Rather, I highlight some key differences between two rival approaches to explaining and treating psychiatric disorder: the 'medical-somatic' approach and the 'social-psychological' approach.

One of the most obvious differences between these two approaches is in their assumptions about the causes of psychiatric disorder. The medical-somatic approach, regarding the mind as the product of its material base, focuses upon material or organic causes of psychiatric disorder. Within this approach, psychiatric disorder is regarded as a result of brain disorder, whether inborn (perhaps due to hereditary disease) or acquired as the result of disease or injury (Clare 1980: 43–6).[13] In the social-psychological approach, on the other hand, psychiatric disorder tends to be attributed to environmental causes. Those who adhere to a social-psychological approach regard most psychiatrically disordered persons as physically healthy people who, in response to problems in their environments, have developed mental or personality disorders (*ibid*: 46–71).

A less noticed, but equally important, difference between the two approaches lies in their assumptions about the role of the subject in becoming psychiatrically disordered. In the medical-somatic approach, the process of becoming psychiatrically disordered is conceived in 'objective' terms and as 'external' to the person. It is assumed that the subject has no control over the process of becoming psychiatrically disordered. Psychiatric disorder is understood to be like physical sickness in that it strikes at random and for no particular reason. In the social-psychological approach, on the other hand, the

---

13 The following quotation from Maudsley, a staunch 'materialist' and one of the founders of modern British psychiatry, illustrates this orientation: 'Insanity is in fact disorder of the brain producing disorder of mind; or to define its nature in greater detail, it is a disorder of the supreme nerve-centres of the brain – the special organs of mind – producing derangements of thought, feeling and action, together or separately, of such degree or kind as to incapacitate the individual for the relations of life' (H Maudsley, quoted in Clare 1980: 52).

process of becoming psychiatrically disordered is conceived in more 'subjective' terms and as 'internal' to the person. It is assumed that the person to some extent plays an active role in becoming psychiatrically disordered (cf Figlio 1987).

To turn to treatment, in the medical-somatic approach to psychiatric disorder treatment tends to be closely modelled on treatment in physical medicine. In other words, treatment consists of some means of 'tinkering' with the body of the patient by, for example, administering drugs or carrying out surgical operations (see Goffman 1968). One important feature of the medical-somatic approach is that this 'tinkering' is done by medical experts: people who possess a high level of anatomical, physiological and biological knowledge and highly technical skills which enable them to operate very complex or precise tools and to manipulate safely the body's processes. One crucial implication of this is that patients tend to play a passive role in medical-somatic treatment – they receive treatment. Medical experts play a highly active role – they carry out treatment. Treatment is something done *to* the patient *by* medical professionals.

A less noticed but crucially important assumption of the medical-somatic approach to treatment is that, in it, a sharp distinction is usually perceived between treatment and non-treatment (see Nokes 1967: chapter 6). This distinction is often both spatial and temporal. Treatment usually takes place in spaces which are set aside for the specific purpose of treatment and during distinct periods. So, whilst other things may happen in the spaces, these other things are generally regarded as quite distinct from and secondary to treatment. For instance, during a stay in hospital, a patient may receive visits from friends and relatives, may develop relationships and friendships with other patients and members of staff, and might undertake various activities and hobbies in order to pass the time. Such activities tend to be viewed as important and beneficial by medical staff. But, they are usually distinguished sharply from actual treatment.

Finally, in the medical-somatic approach, treatment usually has a quite specific objective or set of objectives. It is aimed at repairing specific organs or functions which are deemed to be damaged or at suppressing specific symptoms. The achievement of these specific objectives tends to be regarded as cure.

Before looking at how the social-psychological approach to treatment differs from the medical-somatic approach, it is worthwhile looking briefly at some distinctive features of psychotherapy, as compared with medical-somatic treatment, since psychotherapy might be understood as occupying a position somewhere in between the medical-somatic and social-psychological approaches to treatment.

Psychotherapy consists, not of physical tinkering, but of talk – albeit a special type of talk – which the therapist uses as an instrument of personal influence. Through dialogue the therapist tries to help the patient to clarify 'the meaning of events, feelings, impulses and behaviour in the context of past and often forgotten or repressed events and experiences' (Clare 1980: 47). There is an important difference between the role of the patient in medical-somatic treatment and in psychotherapy. In psychotherapy, the patient is an active participant in the therapeutic process. For psychotherapy to take place the patient must talk to the therapist, indeed must enter into a dialogue with the therapist. Psychotherapy is not possible without the patient's cooperation. The high level of cooperation required means that a genuinely psychotherapeutic conversation can only take place if the patient decides to participate.

Another important difference between medical-somatic treatment and psychotherapy, is that in the latter it is not quite so easy to distinguish treatment from non-treatment. Of course, psychotherapy is to some extent modelled on medical-somatic treatment in that it usually takes place in formally time-tabled sessions and in a place set aside for therapy. However, in psychotherapy the border between treatment and non-treatment can become blurred. The line between ordinary conversation and the special form of dialogue that is psychotherapy often seems far from clear. Since talk is the instrument of psychotherapy, but also a means of non-therapeutic conversation, there is a tendency for therapy and ordinary talk to shade into each other.

I turn now to the distinctive characteristics of the social-psychological approach to treatment. In the social-psychological approach, treatment consists of the use of environmental, organisational and personal influences. Social-psychological treatment is based upon the principle that impaired people will be shaped by their environment for better or worse and that those who deal with them should recognise this and endeavour to create a therapeutic environment – one which will enable the ill person to become healed (Clark 1981). Accordingly, there is little need for those who carry out or organise social-psychological therapy programmes to possess medical expertise. A much wider range of people can become involved in treatment programmes. What participants in treatment programmes require is an understanding of and commitment to the principles of social-psychological treatment and the appropriate inter-personal skills. It is assumed that medical professionals do not necessarily possess the appropriate understanding or skills. It is also assumed that many people who have no medical training can acquire the understanding and skills required to become involved in social therapy.

Perhaps the key distinctive feature of treatment in the social-psychological approach is that the 'patient' plays an active role in the process. The core principle of social-psychological treatment is that the patient participates in his or her own recovery. This principle is linked to the subjective conception of illness outlined earlier. Just as becoming ill is partly a subjective process, so becoming healed is also a partly subjective process. A crucial step on the road to recovery in the social-psychological approach to treatment is that the patient himself or herself decides not to be ill. Cure in social-psychological treatment is similar in many respects to conversion to a different view of oneself and one's role in the world.

This conception of treatment as involving patient activity has implications for assumptions about the relationship between treatment and non-treatment activities. As I have indicated, in the medical-somatic approach, treatment is distinguished sharply from non-treatment activities. In the social-psychological approach, the opposite is the case. Finding ways of helping and encouraging patients to become active, to interact with people, to participate in life, to take on social responsibilities, etc are all part of treatment. Treatment is conceived, in the social-psychological approach, not as a segregated activity which takes place in special places set aside for it. Rather, treatment is something that shades into and is continuous with everyday social interaction and activities.

Finally, in the social-psychological approach to treatment, the objectives tend to be much more general than in the medical-somatic approach. What social-psychological treatment aims at is not the repair of any specific organ or function, but rather the general socialisation (or re-socialisation) of the person. This involves bringing about a general change in the person's subjective state and social performance.

I have simplified greatly what is actually a quite complex distinction between two overlapping but distinct approaches to understanding and dealing with psychiatric disorder. However, from the above it should be clear that if we are to understand the nature of actual therapeutic interventions into the lives of offenders it is necessary to ask to which of these approaches they are nearest. Do therapeutic interventions into the lives of offenders resemble medical-somatic treatment and do they embody the assumption that offenders suffer from 'objective', organic-based psychiatric disorders? Or, do they resemble more closely social-psychological treatment and embody the assumption that offenders suffer from 'subjective', environmentally caused psychiatric disorders? We need to answer this, and a number of other questions, before we can properly assess therapeutic interventions into the lives of offenders and before we can begin to understand the meaning and consequences of the partial shift from a punitive to a therapeutic approach to crime which has taken place.

UNDERSTANDING THE NATURE OF THERAPEUTIC INTERVENTIONS

The general thrust of my argument in this chapter is that in order to understand and assess the meaning and consequences of the rise of therapeutic responses to offenders we need to shift, or at least expand, the *focus* of inquiry and debate. As well as focusing upon the advantages, shortcomings, problems and dangers of the abstract medical model of crime, we need to examine the nature of concrete therapeutic interventions into the lives of offenders, and of the substantive objectives, ideas and operational principles that are embodied in and which inform these interventions. Hence, the rest of this book will consist of some detailed studies of the nature of actual therapeutic interventions into the lives of offenders.

These studies will be undertaken through detailed readings of the *practical discourse* of reformers and treatment professionals who initiate and undertake therapeutic interventions into the lives of offenders. The main sources of this practical discourse are evidence given to official inquiries and contributions to practitioner's journals. In these forums, reformers and treatment professionals have occasionally presented highly general, rhetorical and idealistic appeals for the adoption of a medical model of crime. However, they have also specified, often in considerable detail, what they mean by this at the level of concrete practices. They often explain, in minute detail, among other things:

- what the activities that constitute 'treatment' consist of;
- when and where these activities take place;
- where treatment institutions are located;
- how these institutions are designed;
- what the daily routines of these institutions are;
- how these institutions are managed and financed;
- how these institutions are staffed and what criteria are used for selecting suitable staff;
- what types of offenders are admitted to these institutions;
- how these offenders are regarded;
- what it is that renders these offenders ill or disordered in the eyes of those who deal professionally with them;
- how these offenders became ill or disordered;
- what procedures are used to admit offenders to therapeutic institutions and programmes;
- what procedures are used to discharge offenders from therapeutic institutions and programmes; and
- what counts as a successful therapeutic intervention.

Through a close and careful reading of this practical discourse of treatment professionals it is possible to construct a much richer and more nuanced image and understanding of the nature of therapeutic interventions into the lives of offenders than the one relied upon by participants in the debate about the medical model of crime. We can reach a fairly sophisticated understanding of what the operational objectives of therapeutic interventions are, what means are used to achieve these objectives, and what theories of offending behaviour inform these interventions. Such an image, I suggest, will be a much more adequate and accurate basis for debate about the meaning and consequences of 'medicalisation' than that drawn only from a reading of the abstract philosophical ideas and ideals that make up the medical model of crime.

Since what I am after is not a comprehensive history of therapeutic responses to offenders, but rather an understanding of what is *distinctive* about these responses, what is required are detailed studies of some areas of practical discourse of treatment professionals, rather than a more complete but more superficial study of this discourse. Hence, I proceed through two 'case studies' of therapeutic interventions. The first examines therapeutic interventions into the lives of 'alcoholic' offenders from around 1860 to the 1970s and focuses more on institutional practices. The second examines interventions into the lives of 'psychopathic' offenders since around 1860 and focuses more on the understandings of offenders which inform those practices.

INTRODUCTION TO STUDY A

Every year, the British police make thousands of arrests for 'drunk and incapable' or 'drunk and disorderly' behaviour, or for related 'drunkenness offences'.[1] Some of those arrested are 'one time' or occasional offenders. However, many are 'habitual drunken offenders', ie people who regularly appear in the courts because of 'drunkenness offences' and are repeatedly cycled through the criminal justice system (Tether and Robinson 1986: 284). The processing of such offenders is largely a matter of routine. They are charged,[2] appear in the magistrates' courts, plead or are found 'guilty', and are fined, put on probation, or sentenced to a short term of imprisonment. Many of those who are fined end up in prison as defaulters. Whatever way they are disposed of, habitual drunken offenders are usually restored to 'freedom' fairly soon after their arrest, to continue with their lifestyle and pattern of behaviour.

Since the 1860s, numerous attempts have been made to divert habitual drunkards away from the criminal justice system and to establish an alternative system of dealing with them. In the second half of the 19th century, a network of retreats and reformatories was established for the treatment of 'inebriates'. Legislation was passed enabling the courts to commit those classified as 'habitual drunkards' to these institutions for reformatory treatment, in some cases for up to three years, and allowing the superintendents of these institutions to detain inmates against their wishes. Those who campaigned for the establishment of these inebriate institutions and laws supported their proposals with the claim that, in many cases, habitual drunkenness was not a simple vice but was the result of a disease, called 'inebriety' or 'dipsomania'. They argued that penal measures designed for the control of simple vice were inappropriate for checking the spread of a disease which left those affected with an irresistible craving for intoxicating beverages. The inebriate institutions and laws that were established in the second half of the 19th century fell into disuse during World War I. However, the notions that many habitual drunken offenders drank, not out of choice but out of compulsion, and that what they required was not punishment but treatment, became firmly established amongst criminal justice and treatment professionals.

---

1 For England and Wales see Tether and Robinson (1986: chapter 10). For Scotland, see McLaughlin (1985). In England and Wales the total findings of guilt and cautions per year is generally over 100,000. In Scotland the number of arrests per year is about 15,000. These figures do not include drink-driving offences. It is worth noting that the police seldom intervene solely on the ground of a person's being found drunk in public. Rather, as Tether and Robinson point out: 'The police exercise considerable discretion in their approach to simple drunkenness. In general, inebriates in the company of sober friends or who are not a danger to themselves or others will not usually attract police attention. The association of disorderly behaviour with public drunkenness considerably reduces the scope for police discretion but even 'disorderliness' is open to interpretation' (Tether and Robinson 1986: 284).

2 Since 1973, cautioning schemes have been used widely in the area of drunkenness offences. However, many 'habitual drunken offenders' exceed the 'cautioning threshold' (see Tether and Robinson 1986: 286–7).

In the 1960s, amidst a dramatic growth in the number of arrests for habitual drunkenness,[3] fresh attempts were made to establish a therapeutic alternative to the penal response to habitual drunken offenders. Habitual drunken offenders, it was argued, were not the immoral, dissolute people which the general public perceived them to be. Rather, they were sick people who suffered from a serious illness called alcoholism. This illness was recognised by the medical profession and by the World Health Organisation (see Kessel and Walton 1965). It was argued that, with appropriate treatment many of these people could recover from this illness and could lead normal lives.

The resulting campaign made some impact upon penal and social policy. The Criminal Justice Act 1967 provided for the abolition of the short period of imprisonment that could be imposed for being 'drunk and disorderly' (but this provision was not to be activated until alternative 'services' for those convicted were available – Tether and Robinson 1986: 285).[4] In 1971, a Home Office working party recommended the establishment of a range of treatment facilities for habitual drunken offenders, including detoxification centres, hostels and advice centres (ibid). In 1973, responsibility for the rehabilitation of habitual drunken offenders was vested in the Department of Health and Social Security (DHSS), which in turn urged local government and health authorities to provide treatment facilities (ibid). And, in 1978 the abolition of imprisonment for drunk and disorderly behaviour came into effect.

Despite these initiatives, most habitual drunken offenders continue to be processed as ordinary criminal justice cases. The Criminal Law Act 1977, which abolished imprisonment for being drunk and disorderly, also increased the fines for drunkenness offences (ibid: 286). As a result, a few thousand 'drunkenness offenders' are sent to prison each year for non-payment of fines. Moreover, the treatment facilities which many envisaged either failed to materialise or failed to survive for very long (ibid).

These attempts to replace the penal response to habitual drunken offenders with a therapeutic response were once conventionally portrayed as progressive. In a 1967 essay on the attempts to establish treatment facilities for inebriates in the last half of the 19th century, the historian, Roy MacLeod, took it for granted that the proponents of a therapeutic response were on the side of 'progress' and 'reform'. This is made clear in the very first sentence of the essay:

> The progress of British legislation for inebriates illustrates one classic form of the struggle waged by Victorian professional men and social reformers against

---

3   See the *Report of the Home Office Working Party on Habitual Drunken Offenders*, 1971, app D, para 21.

4   See Nimmer (1971: 3–4) for criticism of the widespread assumption that abolition of the penal response to habitual drunkards must be conditional upon the establishment of some alternative system for dealing with them.

public apathy, parliamentary ignorance, and resistance from self-appointed advocates of 'individual liberty' (MacLeod 1967: 215).

Later he states:

Not until the last half of the 19th century did the scientific appreciation of alcoholism become general. Only then, under the guidance of a few doctors and reformers, was the image of the drunkard as a disorderly, ill-disposed social unit gradually transformed into one of a neglected patient suffering from a mental disease with well-marked clinical features. Reformers who sought to remove the stigma from alcoholism, and to treat the alcoholic by medical means, led the advance guard of a movement to promote prevention and cure on a public basis (MacLeod 1967: 217).

The move towards the decriminalisation and concomitant 'medicalisation' of habitual drunken offenders in the 1960s and 1970s was also celebrated as a progressive reform. In opening a symposium on the drunkenness offence at the Institute of Psychiatry in 1968, the Hon S C Silkin, QC, MP, declared:

Informed opinion is today prepared to accept that intoxication and alcoholism are not to be regarded as crimes to be punished, so much as diseases to be cured if possible. In the field of alcoholism we are witnessing the same transition as we saw, not so long ago, in the field of mental illness; the alcoholic is moving away from the position of social outcast to the position of ordinary patient who can and should receive treatment. Even our criminal law, so often the last refuge of conservatism, has at last taken a timid step along the road of progress. But with our prisons still containing a substantial proportion of men and women whose predominant problem is alcoholism, it is clear that we have not travelled nearly far enough (Silkin 1969: xiv).

In the 1970s, however, more critical views of the medicalisation of habitual drunkenness began to emerge. In 1972, a leading medical journal, *The Lancet*, published an article by Thomas Szasz called, 'Bad Habits are Not Diseases: A Refutation of the Claim that Alcoholism is a Disease'. Szasz dismissed the notion that alcoholism was a disease and criticised medical interventions into the problem as a threat to freedom and to the concept of personal responsibility:

In my judgment, the view that alcoholism is a disease is false; and the programmes sponsored by the State and supported by tax moneys to 'cure' it are immoral and inconsistent with our political commitment to individual freedom and responsibility (Szasz 1972: 83).

Applying his radical liberal views to the debate about alcoholism, Szasz argued that alcoholics should be regarded as normal citizens, with the same responsibilities and rights as other citizens. On the one hand, this meant that they should not be able to avoid responsibility and punishment for criminal behaviour by pleading that they suffered from an illness called alcoholism. But on the other hand, it meant that provided they stayed within the law they should not be interfered with, against their wishes, by the State or the medical profession. Hence, Szasz attacked proposals that some alcoholics might be given compulsory treatment as a serious threat to human freedom.

In 1979, the *British Medical Journal* published a less vitriolic, but much more persuasive, critique of the medical model of alcoholism by R Kendell. In a paper called, 'Alcoholism: a Medical or a Political Problem', Kendell argued that, although it had produced some beneficial consequences, the disease concept of alcoholism acted as a barrier to the development of a more intelligent and effective approach to the problem (1979: 367). During the 1950s and 1960s, Kendell pointed out:

> ... much research was done in an attempt to show that those who became dependent on alcohol and incapable of drinking in moderation differed in some way from their fellow men, either in their personality structure or in the manner in which they metabolised alcohol. The results were meagre ... the putative abnormality predisposing some people to alcoholism remains elusive (Kendell 1979: 368).

What the clinical evidence did establish, Kendell stated, was that what determined whether a person became physically dependent on alcohol was, 'how much he drinks and for how long, rather than his personality, psychodynamics, or biochemistry' (*ibid*). In short, any person who drank excessively for a long period would eventually become physically dependent on alcohol. The key to preventing alcoholism was therefore to prevent excessive drinking.

Kendell went on to argue, drawing upon statistical research, that within any society there is a fixed relation between average and excessive consumption of alcohol (*ibid*: 368–9). Put simply, his argument was that an increase in average consumption of alcohol would lead to a higher incidence of excessive consumption, which would in turn lead to a higher incidence of physical dependence upon alcohol, and vice versa.[5] The incidence of alcoholism could therefore be reduced by decreasing average consumption of alcohol in the society. The radical implication of this argument is that alcohol prevention strategies should be aimed at changing the drinking habits of all of us, rather than being focused upon a small core of problem drinkers. Responsibility for the problem of alcoholism is shifted from the individual to the society.

Kendell, again drawing upon statistical evidence, also challenged the assumption that medical treatment, or any other form of treatment, was effective in 'curing' alcoholics of their dependence (*ibid*: 369). This assumption, he argued, was not only mistaken, it was also a block to the development of more effective prevention strategies. The problem with the assumption that treatment was effective was not only that it led to scarce resources being used

---

5   The actual statistical argument is more complex than I have indicated here. Kendell's argument was based upon the 'Ledermann hypothesis', developed in France by Sully Ledermann.

on relatively ineffective treatment programmes. In addition, and more seriously, the assumption helped to cement the notion that the problem of alcoholism could be understood and solved at the level of the individual, ie without major changes in the drinking behaviour of the society in general. The only effective solution to the problem of alcoholism, Kendell insisted, was a 'political' one. Legislative and fiscal measures had to be used to restrict the supply of alcohol and a massive public education programme aimed at the whole community must be established (*ibid*: 369–70). Also, Kendell argued, society had to decide: 'how much damage and suffering it is prepared to tolerate for the sake of how much enjoyment' (*ibid*: 371).[6]

Another critical perspective on the therapeutic response to habitual drunkenness which is worth mentioning briefly is that developed by Peter Archard in his book, *Vagrancy, Alcoholism and Social Control* (1979). Archard presents an interesting account of the social organisation of vagrant alcoholics and of how they perceive and interpret their world and especially the various official agencies whom they encounter. Like similar studies – such as that by Phillimore (1979) and Wiseman's excellent *Stations of the Lost* (1970) – Archard's work uncovers complexities of the lives of vagrant alcoholics to which professionals who deal with them are generally blind. However, unlike Phillimore or Wiseman, Archard also presents an explicit critique of therapeutic interventions into the lives of vagrant alcoholics. Drawing upon the theories of radical criminologists, Archard suggests that the sole purpose of 'therapeutic interventions' is to contain and control, on behalf of society, a group who are a considered to be a nuisance. Treatment professionals, he contends, conceal their real functions by disguising what they do as humanitarian help (*ibid*: chapter 8). The implication seems to be that if, as radicals, we want to take the side of the underdogs in this conflict, we should oppose the development of therapeutic interventions into the lives of vagrant alcoholics and expose their true purpose, which is social control.

For the most part, the criticisms which I have outlined are directed at an abstract model: the medical model of alcoholism. In this model it is assumed: (1) that habitual drunkenness is often caused by a medical condition, called alcoholism, which renders those affected incapable of drinking in moderation; and (2) that the solution to the problem of alcoholism is to give treatment to those affected by this illness. In addition, some proponents of such a model advocate compulsory treatment in cases where the alcoholic refuses to recognise that he or she is ill and refuses to undergo treatment. The critics argue that this model is wrong, that it hinders our understanding of the causes of habitual drunkenness, that it hampers the development of more effective responses to the problem, and that it leads to unjustifiable interference with the liberty of habitual drunkards – interference which is disguised as humanitarian care and treatment.

---

6   For a critical discussion of this type of perspective on alcoholism see Bunton (1989).

In what follows, I attempt to shift the focus of debate away from the medical model of alcoholism, and its alleged shortcomings and dangers, and focus instead upon the nature of *actual* therapeutic interventions into the lives of habitual drunken offenders and upon the ideas about habitual drunkards which are embodied in those interventions. In doing so, I will suggest that the nature of these interventions cannot be 'read off' from the medical model of alcoholism. Indeed, in many ways, these interventions must be understood as alternatives to those which are informed by a medical model of alcoholism.

In chapters 2 and 3 I study the therapeutic response to 'inebriate' offenders in the second half of the 19th century. In these chapters, I explore three main sets of issues. First, I look at how the concept of inebriety was applied in practice and at how those labelled as inebriates were processed. I ask: What types of persons were included in the category of inebriates? What types of persons were sent to retreats and reformatories? What procedures were used to commit people to and detain them in these institutions? How long did people spend in these institutions? Second, I look at how treatment professionals perceived and make sense of those whom they classified as inebriates. I ask: What did they mean when they described inebriates as ill? How, in their view, did inebriates become ill? What was their position on the question of the responsibility of inebriates for their condition and their behaviour? Third, I look at the nature of the practice of treatment in the inebriate reformatories and retreats. I ask: What were the 'operational objectives' of treatment? What methods were used to obtain these objectives? How did the practice of reformatory treatment differ from other ways of handling habitual drunkards? In chapter 4, I turn to the attempts to establish a network of treatment facilities for habitual drunken offenders in the 1960s and 1970s. I look at what those who dealt professionally with habitual drunken offenders actually meant when they described them as 'alcoholics' and I describe in detail the nature of the system of treatment which they sought to establish.

CHAPTER 2

TREATMENT AND INDIVIDUAL LIBERTY
A NEW POLICY FOR HABITUAL DRUNKEN OFFENDERS, c 1860–c 1908

INTRODUCTION

Until near the end of the 19th century, people who were arrested for drunkenness offences could expect to be ordered to pay a small fine or, if their offence was deemed to be serious, sent to prison for a few weeks. Towards the end of the 19th century, however, a new policy for those repeatedly convicted of drunkenness offences came into effect. Under the new policy, habitual drunken offenders could be sent to a reformatory for treatment for up to three years. This new policy towards habitual drunken offenders was just one of those recommended by reformers and medical professionals to counter the apparently growing problem of habitual drunkenness. Reformers and professionals had also proposed that 'non-criminal inebriates' – ie people who suffered from the disease of inebriety but managed to avoid trouble with the law – should be committed to inebriate retreats, through a civil procedure and detained until they were cured.

There is no doubt that the new policies towards habitual drunkards (both those implemented and those proposed but not accepted by Parliament) had serious implications for the liberty of habitual drunkards. Indeed, as MacLeod (1967) points out in his sympathetic account of the reformers, one of the main sources of opposition to the new policy were 'advocates of individual liberty'. They regarded the new policy as an interference with the right to drink and enjoy oneself, and as part of a more general drift towards state interference in matters of private morality that were outside of its legitimate concern.[1] MacLeod quotes from an editorial in *The Times* which, when such proposals were first made public, responded:

> All through the debates on the Licensing Bill it was persistently agreed that man could never be made sober by Act of Parliament, but here is the project of an Act for making us all sober with a vengeance. It was rather fancied that legislation must be practically limited to the prevention of disorderly conduct or public indecency, but these notions are now left far away in the rear ... Alas for the 'amiable weaknesses' of youths and poets, the 'glow of soul' and all other pictures of conviviality and good fellowship ... Imprisonment may come from a picnic, and hard labour from a Conservative festival (*The Times*, 27 June 1872, quoted in MacLeod 1967).

---

1   The other main reason for opposition to the new policy was the financial cost of the proposed institutions. For more sceptical accounts of the 'inebriate reformatory experiment' see Radzinowicz and Hood (1990: chapter 9) and Harding and Wilkin (1988).

Similarly, the Vigilance Association for the Defence of Personal Rights opposed a Bill to introduce the new policy in terms which would later be echoed by many opponents of the disease concept of alcoholism:

> We do not believe that it is possible to check the spread of drunkenness by violent methods, such as this Bill proposes; whilst the inroads thus made upon personal rights introduce dangers of the most real, and palpable kind (quoted in MacLeod 1967: 222).

Whilst opponents of the new policy probably overstated its dangers, the policy clearly did involve a reduction of individual liberty. Nor is there any doubt that a medical model of habitual drunkenness was used to justify this encroachment upon the liberty of habitual drunkards. The main argument used to justify the compulsory confinement of habitual drunkards was that it was necessary in order to cure them of the illness which caused their iniquitous behaviour. Those who proposed new laws and new methods for dealing with habitual drunkards supported their proposals with the relatively novel claim that, in many cases, habitual drunkenness was not a simple vice but was the result of a disease. Many habitual drunkards, it was claimed, suffered from a medical condition, called inebriety or dipsomania, which gave them an insatiable thirst for intoxicating drinks or rendered them unable to control the impulse to get drunk. Until this illness was cured, it was argued, such people would drink to excess whenever they had the opportunity to do so. Neither 'moral suasion' nor the threat of criminal punishment could influence their behaviour. Until they were cured, only physical restraint could prevent them from getting drunk. Hence, 'inebriates' or 'dipsomaniacs' had to be confined and treated, and released only when cure was achieved. Such cure, it was suggested, would take at least six months and could take as long as three years.

This seems to confirm the claim made by many critics of the medical model of crime, ie that it invariably results, not in a relaxation of social control, but in a much greater intrusion upon the freedom of deviants. If all of the proposals of those who initiated the new policy towards habitual drunkards had been accepted, the state's powers of detention would have been expanded in two ways. First, those who were already subject to confinement, ie habitual drunken offenders, would be confined for much longer periods than before. Secondly, those who were not already subject to confinement, ie 'non-criminal inebriates', would be confined against their wishes through a civil procedure. In other words, under the new policy, more people would be incarcerated and for much longer periods. As it transpired, only the first of these expansions took place – the power to confine non-criminal inebriates was not awarded by Parliament.[2] Nevertheless, as Garland has pointed out, even this 'took

---

2 Parliament did create the power to detain, against their will, people who committed themselves voluntarily to inebriate retreats. However, few people availed themselves of this opportunity to commit themselves voluntarily to what would then be compulsory detention (see Radzinowicz and Hood 1990: 299).

penality a first step beyond the normal constraints of criminal law' and 'amounted to an important extension of the powers of detention beyond the offence itself' (Garland 1985: 217–8).

It would be wholly inadequate, however, to criticise this policy development simply by showing that it led to an extension of the state's powers of detention. In the first place, this would only be a criticism if we accepted, without question, the classic liberal doctrines that individuals should be deprived of their liberty only in return for the commission of a definite criminal act and that interference with the liberty of individuals cannot be justified on paternalistic grounds, ie on the ground that it is for the detained person's own good (Mill 1859). Many reject these doctrines. Some, for instance, would regard detention as justifiable if it is necessary in order to restore seriously incapacitated subjects to a state more tolerable to themselves and others. If we adopt the latter view, which is at least as reasonable as the classic liberal position, we would have to look much closer at the confinement of 'inebriates' and ask how it was meant to and actually did affect their lives. If compulsory treatment could and did change inebriates from people who were slaves to a debilitating habit into people who were capable of choosing when and how much to drink, and if the social and economic costs of compulsory treatment were reasonable, then it might well be a policy that 'progressives' and 'radicals' can and should support.

Secondly, to focus on the mere fact of compulsory confinement would be to miss much of what was distinctive about the new policy towards habitual drunkards. The policy was informed by new concerns, new objectives, new ways of making sense of 'pathological' behaviour, and new ideas about how to alter the behaviour of troublesome people. These broader aspects of the new policy must be subject to critical scrutiny. However, their nature cannot be inferred from the medical model of alcoholism. Rather, it is necessary to look closely at the discourse of the 'inebriety reformers' in order to decipher the rationale of the new policy towards habitual drunkards.

In this chapter, I start this investigation of the therapeutic response to habitual drunkards by looking, in detail, at the types of person who were included in the category of 'inebriates' and sent to the inebriate institutions. The main finding of this investigation is that the concern of those who initiated the new policy was with a much smaller group than habitual drunkards. The 'inebriety reformers' did not include *all* habitual drunkards within the categories of dipsomaniacs or inebriates. To the contrary, they insisted that most of those who frequently got drunk did so by choice. According to the reformers, these voluntary drunkards could be handled as ordinary criminal justice cases if they broke the law, or be left 'untouched by legislative restraint' if they stayed out of trouble with the police. The inebriety reformers applied the concepts of dipsomania and inebriety to only a small minority of habitual drunkards: those whose inability to resist the desire for intoxicants rendered them unable to discharge their obligations to their families and to society. This finding has important implications for our understanding of the concerns of those who initiated the new policy. It suggests, I argue, that their concern was not with immorality *per se*, but rather with social inefficiency. The reformers were concerned with drunkenness to the extent that it was one important cause of social inefficiency. They were not, as their liberal critics alleged, directly attacking the right of people to live and behave as they liked provided they remained within the boundaries of public order and decency. Like their liberal critics, the inebriety reformers were content, for the most part, to regard drunkenness as a matter of private morality. They proposed to interfere with the liberty of habitual drunkards only if they were unable to contain the social costs of their bad habit.

A second theme of this chapter concerns the gap between the powers of compulsory treatment which the reformers sought and those which they actually obtained. As I have indicated, the reformers sought, but did not obtain, the power to commit non-criminal inebriates to inebriate retreats for treatment. The failure to obtain this power led to a class discrepancy in the use of compulsory treatment. 'Poor' habitual drunkards, who often got into trouble with the police, were confined against their will. 'Rich' habitual drunkards, on the other hand, avoided trouble with the police and so were immune from compulsory treatment. They could be detained only if they first committed themselves voluntarily to an inebriate retreat. There is no doubt, then, that as it *actually* operated, the inebriate reformatory experiment was biased against the poor. However, it is important to understand the reasons for this. This bias against the poor, I will suggest, was not the result of a deliberate policy. The reformers saw the disease of inebriety as prevalent in all sections of society and were as deeply concerned about middle class drunkards who were ruining their family businesses as with working class drunkards who were failing to provide for their families. Their proposals to create powers of detention for non-offenders, as well as for offenders, were a direct response to the realisation that habitual drunkards from the higher ranks of society were only rarely arrested for drunkenness offences. The failure to obtain the power to detain 'non-criminal inebriates' was due, mainly, to libertarian resistance. Parliament would not sanction interference with the liberty of non-criminal middle class people. It was far less resistant, however, to proposals to extend the confinement of criminals. Hence, I will suggest, there are important lessons to be learned from this about the impact of libertarian arguments upon social policy proposals.

A third theme of this chapter concerns the gender imbalance in reformatory committals. One of the surprising findings of my inquiry into who actually was sent to reformatories is that the vast majority of those committed were women. Some feminist critics of the medical model would no doubt see this as confirming the view that the medical model of crime is ideologically biased against women; that female offenders are more likely to be seen as sick, irrational, and as bound by their biological make-up than are male offenders.[3] However, as I show, the gender imbalance in committals to inebriate reformatories was due to different factors: the convenience of reformatories for clearing the streets of prostitutes, a campaign conducted by the National Association for the Prevention of Cruelty to Children against drunken mothers, and the idea that women were more amenable than men to environmentalist methods of treatment.

THE CATEGORY OF INEBRIATES

In this section, I argue that the inebriety reformers applied the concepts of dipsomania and inebriety, not to all of those who frequently got drunk, but only to those whose craving for intoxicants led them to neglect their social responsibilities. Hence, the inebriety reformers did not seek to 'medicalise' all habitual drunkards, but only those who could not contain the social costs of their habit. The argument is developed in two stages. The first looks at the inebriety reformers' campaign for the creation of legal powers and institutional facilities to confine and treat inebriates. The second looks at the use which the inebriety reformers made of the powers which they eventually obtained.

Defining the target of 'medical' control

In 1860, Alexander Peddie published a lecture in which he advocated the creation of legal powers to confine dipsomaniacs in inebriate 'asylums' for a period long enough to cure them of their habit. One of the obstacles to the creation of such powers, he pointed out, was a widespread misunderstanding of against whom they would be used (Peddie 1860: 538). He therefore stressed that 'it is not, as some seem to suppose, every drunkard, or every habitual or inveterate tippler, for whom we wish legal restraint' (*ibid*). For one thing, 'to raise asylums for all such would indeed be a formidable undertaking' (*ibid*). Rather, Peddie proposed to deal with a much smaller group of 'insane drinkers' or dipsomaniacs.

Before looking at how Peddie drew the distinction between 'ordinary drunkards' and dipsomaniacs, it is worthwhile looking briefly at why he felt the need to clarify this issue. At the time, the Temperance Movement was beginning to campaign for a radical restriction (or even a total prohibition) of the sale, production and importation of alcoholic drinks. This attack upon the 'liberty' to drink alcohol was highly unpopular and was resisted by powerful groups in society (see Harrison 1971). Peddie undoubtedly feared that his concerns would be confused with those of the Temperance Movement and

---

3   For a discussion of these theories see Allen (1987).

that his proposals would consequently meet with similar resistance. It seems, therefore, that he was trying to distinguish his concern, which was with a relatively small group of mischievous and dangerous drunkards, from the much wider concerns of the Temperance Movement, which not only opposed *all* drunkenness but was increasingly turning against even moderate drinking. Hence, it was important for Peddie to allay the fears of those who imagined that he was hostile towards drink as such and that, if he had his way, all those who enjoyed drinking would be imprisoned. He had to convince potential critics that the powers he sought would not be used against all of those who enjoyed hard drinking, but would be applied to only a small minority of mischievous and irresponsible drunkards – those whom he described as dipsomaniacs. If he was to have any chance of success in his attempts to establish a more stringent policing of inebriates, he had to convince powerful groups in society that he was not a moral crusader, intent on attacking the freedom to drink, and that his proposals would affect only those habitual drunkards who neglected their social obligations by committing crime, failing to provide for themselves and their families, and so on.

Peddie insisted that it was easy to draw a distinction between the 'ordinary drunkard', in whom drinking was a simple vice, and 'the insane constitutional drunkard' or 'dipsomaniac', in whom drinking was a disease (Peddie 1860: 538). Although he implied that this distinction was a medical one, the actual criteria which he used to draw the distinction were mostly *behavioural*. In the category of 'ordinary drunkards' he included a variety of more specific types:

> ... the social, jolly after-dinner drinker; the go-to-bed-drunk but rise-again-sober drinker; and the systematic morning dram drinker. We have also the occasional 'go-on-the-spree', or paroxysmal drinker; and the habitually imbibing but never thoroughly intoxicated drunkard (Peddie 1860: 538).

All of these types were excluded by Peddie from the category of dipsomaniacs – and moreover, could be left untouched by legislative restraint despite the fact that their behaviour was deplorable and even though they occasionally brutalised and disgraced themselves (*ibid*: 538–9). What distinguished these types from dipsomaniacs, who did require legislative control, was their ability to contain the *effects* of their drinking. *Despite their drinking habits, they were able to do their jobs properly, discharge their duties to family and society, and maintain a respectable appearance*:

> ... they are on the whole able to perform their usual duties tolerably well; some, though drunk at night, can face the world pretty respectably next morning, and not only eat a good breakfast, but do duty or give good advice in the shop, counting-room, or chambers. Many hard drinkers can exercise wonderful control over themselves, choosing the time to drink and the time to keep sober; and while sober, can discharge all their family, professional, social, or even religious duties – so far, at least, as outward observances go (Peddie 1860: 538).

Peddie claimed, however, that what started out as a mere vice was occasionally transformed into a disease, a 'vicious habit' became an 'insane impulsive propensity', and the ordinary drunkard became a dipsomaniac. Peddie called this condition 'acquired dipsomania' (*ibid*: 539). In addition, he claimed, dipsomania was often met as an hereditary affection: ie some people inherited an irresistible craving for alcohol from their parents (*ibid*: 539–40). Peddie did not actually specify the processes by which ordinary drunkards became dipsomaniacs, or by which parents transmitted dipsomania to their offspring. He did, however, present a description of the appearance and behaviour of the dipsomaniac. He described the dipsomaniac as a physical wreck:

> Physically, the dipsomaniac is truly lamentable to behold, with his general broken-down aspect, feeble tremulous limbs, pale or leaden-coloured visage, and watery, lustreless eye (Peddie 1860: 539).

Dipsomaniacs could also be recognised by their tendency towards solitary, rather than social, drinking (*ibid*). But, for Peddie, the most salient characteristic of dipsomaniacs was their inability to manage their affairs or to behave properly:

> He cannot now control his conduct, or manage his affairs; he is useless or dangerous to himself or others; disqualified for social and civil duties, a wreck of humanity, and a burden on society (Peddie 1860: 539).

So, from the outset, the inebriety reformers applied the concept of dipsomania or inebriety, not to all regular drunkards, but only to those whose propensity to drunkenness led them to lose all sense of responsibility and all self-control, not only over their drinking but over their conduct in general (*ibid*: 539–41). The concept was to be applied, in short, to those whose craving for alcohol rendered them 'insensible of [their] obligations to God and man' (*ibid*: 541).

The campaign to provide legal recognition and institutional treatment for inebriates gained momentum in the late 1860s when Dr Donald Dalrymple, one of the leading campaigners, was elected to Parliament (see MacLeod 1967: 218–20). Dalrymple moved a resolution on the subject of habitual drunkards (Hansard 1870: vol 199, cc 1241–8) and introduced a private Bill to license inebriate reformatories, asylums and refuges and to allow the compulsory confinement of 'habitual drunkards' in these institutions for as long as was 'necessary for the due protection and more complete restoration of the mind and health of such persons' (Bill No 197 of Session 1870, s 2). The Bill defined the habitual drunkard, for whom special powers and institutional provision was sought, as 'any person who, by reason of frequent, excessive, or constant use of intoxicating drinks, is incapable of self-control, and of proper attention to and care of his affairs and family, or is dangerous to himself or others' (s 1). As we can see, Dalrymple's category of 'habitual drunkards' was similar to Peddie's category of 'dipsomaniacs'. The category did not include everyone who habitually got drunk, but only those who – by reason of habitual drunkenness – were unable to perform their obligations or became dangerous.

Dalrymple made this point clear in the parliamentary debate on his resolution, in which he tried to convince his critics that he did not 'propose to deal with ordinary cases of intemperance' and nor did he 'seek to interfere with the convivial proclivities or social enjoyments of anyone'. He advocated 'interference' only in cases where drunkenness led to crime and other behavioural problems. His concern was limited to the habitual drunkard who, for example, 'pawned for liquor, engaged in wife-beating', or whose home was 'a hell on earth' (Hansard 1870: vol 199, cc 1241–8).

Dalrymple's Bill failed to obtain a second reading on two occasions, but he did succeed in having it referred to a Select Committee, chaired by himself, which reported in 1872 (*The Report of the Select Committee on Habitual Drunkards, 1872*, hereinafter referred to as the '1872 Report'). The members of the Select Committee, and those who gave evidence to it, were mostly either closely involved in the inebriety reform movement or sympathetic towards it. Hence, the Committee's report and the minutes of evidence provide us with useful material for a study of the inebriety reformers' assumptions, concerns and objectives. In particular, they provide us with a clear image of the types of person which the inebriety reformers regarded as inebriates.

Many witnesses made it clear, as Peddie and Dalrymple had done, that their concern was not with 'regular drunkards', but only with those who could not control the mischievous effects of their habit. These concerns are reflected in the Committee's recommendations concerning the type of evidence which was required to support an 'accusation' that a person was an habitual drunkard. Before a person could be officially registered as an habitual drunkard, it would have to be established that he had been repeatedly convicted of drink-related offences (1872 Report: para's. 15–18) or proof would have to be given that he was unable to control himself, incapable of managing his affairs, or that he was dangerous to himself or others, and that this was due to abuse of alcoholic drinks or sedatives (1872 Report: recommendation 3). Hence, the drinking behaviour of the person 'accused' of being an habitual drunkard was regarded as of secondary importance. What was deemed to be of primary importance was his competency and conduct in general. People could get drunk as often as they pleased, without risking being labelled an 'habitual drunkard' and without being subjected to 'legislative interference', provided their drunkenness didn't interfere with their ability to perform their duties or make them an annoyance or a threat to the public. So long as drunkards did not commit crimes, did not neglect their obligations to their families and to the rest of the community, and did not make themselves a burden on society in other ways, they would be defined as normal people who had a mere vice and would not be interfered with. What mattered was not drunkenness or morality as such, but the ability to contain the costs of one's drunkenness and immorality. So, those drunkards who could not stay out of trouble with the law, no matter how many times they were punished, or those who squandered their family fortunes or ruined their businesses, were to be labelled as 'habitual drunkards' and subjected to stringent forms of institutional control.

Committals to inebriate reformatories

Following the 1872 Report, Dr Dalrymple introduced a Bill to carry out the Committee's recommendations (No 279 of Session 1872), but failed to get it beyond the second reading. In 1877 a new Habitual Drunkards Bill was introduced which eventually became law in 1879, but only after the proposals contained in the original Bill were greatly diluted through amendments.[4] The 1879 Act created the power to detain those who had first voluntarily entered an inebriate 'retreat'. It was not until 1898 that the inebriety reformers obtained the power to actually commit 'criminal inebriates' to inebriate 'reformatories'. The Inebriates Act 1898 provided the power to commit two classes of inebriates to detention in an inebriate reformatory for up to three years: inebriates convicted of a crime caused by, or contributed to by, drink (s 1) and those who had been convicted summarily of drunkenness four times within one year (s 2) (see *The Report of the Departmental Committee on the Operation of the Law relating to Inebriates and to their Detention in Reformatories and Retreats, 1908* – hereinafter referred to as the '1908 Report' – chapter 3; Kelynack 1904/5: 118). Subsequently, the Licensing Act of 1902 enabled a magistrate to send an inebriate wife to a retreat in lieu of a separation order (see the 1908 Report: q 278) and the Provision of Meals Act 1903 and the Prevention of Cruelty to Children Act 1904 provided for the detention in inebriate reformatories of those found guilty of child neglect or cruelty to children, where such neglect or cruelty was deemed to be due to inebriety. The inebriety reformers never obtained the power to commit and detain those inebriates who managed to stay out of trouble with the criminal law (see the 1908 Report: para 18).

Against whom were these legal powers used? To whom was the concept of inebriety applied in practice? In what follows I will show that the concept was indeed applied in practice, not to all habitual drunkards, but only to those whose drinking habits led them to neglect their obligations to their families

---

4   A summary of these Bills is presented in appendix 6 of the *Report from the Departmental Committee on the Treatment of Inebriates*, 1893/4 (hereinafter the '1893 Report'). The Habitual Drunkards Act 1879 made provision only for the licensing of retreats, established as 'private speculations', to which habitual drunkards could be admitted on their own application (*ibid*). The original Bill had also proposed the establishment of *reformatories*, funded by local rates with contributions from the Treasury, to which criminal and non-criminal habitual drunkards could be committed. These compulsory procedures were dropped, as were proposals to create powers to 'recover patients who have escaped'. Hence, the 1879 Act did not provide the legal powers or institutional provision which the reformers had sought; rather, it led only to the establishment of 'temporary refuges for gentlemen alcoholics' (Radzinowicz and Hood 1990: 294–300). By 1891 there were only seven inebriate retreats operating, and on 31 December 1891 only 62 patients were 'legally amenable to the discipline of the retreat' (1893 Report: para 6).

and to the rest of the community. The powers to commit persons to reformatories as inebriates were used against three main types of 'habitual drunkard': women who neglected their children; prostitutes; and men from the poorest and roughest sections of society.

Child neglecters

More than 70 per cent of those committed for offences which were caused, or contributed to, by drink (ie s 1 committals) were women who had been convicted of neglect or cruelty to children under the 1903 and 1904 Acts (see above). The committal of child neglecters to inebriate reformatories was the result of a campaign by the National Society for the Prevention of Cruelty to Children (NSPCC), which proudly claimed responsibility for 316 committals. In their study of the inebriate reformatories, Harding and Wilkin conclude from this that the powers to confine inebriates were used in a way which had not been envisaged by the inebriety reformers.

> ... the legislation came to perform a function that had not been envisaged by its proponents or drafters: the protection of children from violent parents, particularly their mothers, as well as the reform of those parents (Harding and Wilkin 1988: 198).

This conclusion is based on the mistaken assumption that the primary concern of the inebriety reformers was with drunkenness in itself. It is probably true that the inebriety reformers had not envisaged the 'inebriety powers' being so heavily used in child neglect and cruelty cases. But, the use of the inebriety powers to commit mothers who neglected their children, or were cruel to them, was quite consistent with their original objective which was to control those who, by reason of habitual drunkenness, neglected their obligations to their families or to the wider community.

Prostitutes

The majority of those committed after four drunkenness offences within 12 months (ie s 2 committals) were also women (see Harding and Wilkin 1988: 198–9). There is some evidence to suggest that most of these were sent to inebriate reformatories, less because of their drinking habits, more because of their involvement in prostitution. Once again, this might seem like an inappropriate use of the 'inebriety powers'. But, as I have suggested, a close reading of the inebriety reformers' discourse shows that it was quite consistent to use these powers to control those who behaved scandalously or annoyed the public, where this behaviour was thought to be the result of habitual drunkenness.

The link between the concerns with inebriety and prostitution was raised, implicitly or explicitly, by many of those who dealt professionally with inebriate offenders in their evidence to the Departmental Committee on the

Law relating to Inebriates which reported in 1908. For instance, a magistrate, Mr E Baggallay, remarked, in a thinly veiled reference to prostitution:

> ... we should keep the streets and other public places free from habitual drunkards, and particularly women, who are a great trouble; and there is no doubt with regard to women that they influence others. As I understand it, at the time the 1898 Act was passed it was very largely supported on the ground that it would assist the magistrates and the police in keeping the streets clear (1908 Report: q 302).

The connection between inebriety and prostitution was made most explicit, though, in the evidence of Thomas Holmes, a police court Missionary and Secretary of the influential penal reform body, the Howard Association. He declared:

> The police court inebriates who come under that Act are first immoral ... The women who come within this Act and who so frequently appear at the police courts are simply absolute prostitutes and nothing else – that is eighty per cent of them ... the whole bulk of young women that are charged in police courts are activated first by lust (1908 Report: q 1488).

Holmes in fact spent most of his testimony moralising about prostitution. The first impression one gets from reading his testimony is that he has made a mistake about which problem the inquiry is addressing. Indeed, his questioners found it necessary to remind him that the concern of the committee was with inebriety, and not with prostitution (*ibid*: q 1511). To this, Holmes replied that with most arrests of women for drunkenness offences, and subsequently with most of the committals of women to inebriate reformatories, drink was only the surface reason for arrest and committal. The real underlying reason, he claimed, was prostitution (1908 Report: qq 1489–1518).[5]

'Rough' drunkards

Finally in this section, I look at the inebriety reformers' perceptions of the men that were labelled as inebriates and sent to inebriate reformatories. It seems clear that the concept was applied to those habitual drunkards who came from the poorest and most troublesome sections of the 'labouring classes': the 'residuum' of unemployed and vagrants or tramps who were widely regarded as a specific and dangerous class (Stedman Jones 1971; Garland 1985: chapter 2). To quote from W Byrne, who was under-secretary of State at the Home Office:

> I may now say that the scum of the gutters and of the streets has been sent to these reformatories; in many instances with the excellent object of removing the scandal and danger which their life of freedom entailed (1908 Report: q 21).

---

5   I will return to the issue of gender imbalance in committals to reformatories towards the end of this chapter.

Others also described those who were sent to inebriate reformatories in terms which went far beyond a specific concern with habitual drunkenness. The following is from Branthwaite, the inspector of the reformatories:

> ... irreformable inebriates are persistently drunken when not in prison, commit wilful damage, attack policemen, or are publicly disorderly and indecent. They gain no benefit from repeated prison punishment; but, on the other hand, exhibit progressive physical deterioration, steady decline of mental power, and finally become hopeless mental and moral degenerates. During periods of liberty between imprisonment such persons create disturbances without number by fighting, disorderly conduct and obscene language, behaving indecently, and causing obstruction. They are responsible for assaults, wounding ... and wilful damage. They are also the cause of considerable expense to public funds without adequate return ... They bring into the world ill-fed, uncared-for and mentally useless children, who provide the mass from which the future criminal, drunken, and lunatic army is recruited, and finally they themselves become in later years chargeable to the rates as paupers or lunatics (1908 Report: q 209).

Hence, just as the early inebriety reformers had asserted that those who could manage their affairs, and not become a nuisance or a danger to the public, would not be defined as inebriates whatever their drinking habits, the later inebriety reformers made it clear that their criterion for interference was not drunkenness as such, but rather the irresponsible behaviour which often resulted from it. Of course, although the inebriety reformers insisted that their concern was only with irresponsible and dangerous drunkards, their policy clearly did have implications for all of those who got drunk. The distinction between ordinary drunkards and dipsomaniacs was a flexible one, and was based on *judgments* of social worth rather than upon medical diagnosis of disease. Therefore all drunkards were in danger of being classified as inebriates if they got into trouble with the law, or simply failed to manage their affairs or to look after their homes and children. The confinement of inebriates was clearly intended to have a deterrent effect on all drunkards and even on moderate drinkers – it would be a powerful reminder of the consequences of letting their bad habits get out of hand (cf Foucault 1977, especially part 4).

NON-CRIMINAL INEBRIATES

As I indicated earlier, the inebriety reformers proposed to extend compulsory treatment to all of those whom they considered to be inebriates, even if they had not broken any specific criminal law. For the reformers, a policy which dealt with 'criminal inebriates' alone would be insufficient to prevent the spread of the disease of inebriety. According to the reformers, many inebriates in need of treatment – perhaps the majority – were never convicted of drunkenness offences. There were a number of reasons for this. One was the use of police discretion. There was evidence that only one in 20 of those found drunk in public by the police were actually brought to the police station (1872 Report: qq 1469–1510). In addition, many drunkards were discharged by the officer on duty – in contravention of official policy – without being charged and brought before the magistrates (*ibid*: q 1792 and 2462–5). The reformers suggested, however, that even if the existing laws were enforced more consistently they would have no impact upon the majority of inebriates because most inebriates managed to avoid being found drunk in public. Hence, the 1872 Select Committee sought to highlight the problem of:

> ... a very large amount of drunkenness ... which never becomes public ... but which is probably even a more fertile source of misery, poverty, and degradation than that which comes before the police courts; for this no legal remedy exists, and without further legislation it must go unchecked (1872 Report: para 9).

Or, as one reformer put it:

> The habitual drunkard whom we wish to treat ... very rarely comes before the Justices; he is cunning enough to keep out of the way; it is the ordinary drunkard who comes before the justices (1872 Report: q 889).

The procedures proposed for committing non-criminal inebriates to inebriate institutions were modelled on those used for committing the insane to asylums. It was proposed that a person could be committed:

> ... on the application of their friends and relatives, under proper legal restrictions, or by the decision of a local Court of Inquiry, established under proper safeguards, before which, on the application of a near relative or guardian, or a parish or other local authority, or other authorised persons, proof shall be given that the party cited is unable to control himself, and incapable of managing his affairs, or that his habits are such as to render him dangerous to himself or others; that this arises from the abuse of alcoholic drinks or sedatives; and he is therefore deemed to be an habitual drunkard (1872 report: rec'n. 3).

It was proposed that such persons be confined for a period not exceeding 12 months and that control of their property should be placed with a trustee or guardian. (*ibid*: rec'n. 4). In addition, it was proposed that persons could voluntarily declare themselves to be habitual drunkards and enter an inebriate retreat. However, having done so, they would then be liable to detention as if they had been committed (*ibid*: rec'n. 2–3).[6]

Of course, there could be no question of sending non-criminal inebriates to the same institutions as criminal inebriates, or of subjecting them to harsh treatment.[7] As we shall see in the next chapter, inebriate retreats would not be

---

6   There was a precedent for this in the procedures of the Contagious Diseases Commission (see 1872 Report: q 729).

7   The proposed institutional routines of inebriate reformatories and retreats are described in detail in chapter 3.

attached to prisons or workhouses (1872 Report: q 649, 669) but were to be established as totally separate institutions in rural districts and would employ some of the gentler methods of 'moral treatment'. Nevertheless, the proposal to subject non-criminal inebriates to compulsory detention and treatment was heavily resisted. This proposal was far more controversial than the proposal to confine habitual drunken offenders for longer than was warranted by their specific offence. It would involve a radical departure from the 'liberal' principle that individuals could be deprived of their liberty only on the ground that they had committed a definite illegal act (see Dicey 1962: chapter 5). Hence, this proposal was opposed by powerful individuals and groups who regarded it as a dangerous extension of the state's power over the individual (see MacLeod 1967). The proposal provoked Lord Salisbury, the Conservative Prime Minister in 1895, to respond:

> Here you give power over the liberty of men that you have never given before. You allow a single judge, without appeal, without a jury on an occasion obviously vague, obviously incapable of being reduced to a definite statement – you allow him to deprive a man of his liberty for two years, practically to confine him to prison ... My Lords, you are meddling with edged tools' (Salisbury, quoted in MacLeod 1967: 235).

As a result of this resistance, the proposal that non-criminal inebriates could be committed to inebriate retreats without their consent, through a civil procedure, was never implemented. The reformers did obtain the power to detain inebriates who committed themselves voluntarily, even if – as a result of an attack of temptation – they subsequently tried to leave the retreat. However, as Radzinowicz and Hood (1990: 299) point out, 'habitual drunkards could rarely be persuaded to commit themselves, for that involved the stigma of a public hearing and the humiliation of self-denunciation'.

As a result of their failure to get this aspect of their proposed policy implemented, the reformers' policy *as it operated* was biased against inebriates from the lower orders of society. Lower class persons who developed the inebriate habit were likely to find themselves repeatedly convicted of drunkenness offences and ran a high risk of being committed to an inebriate reformatory for three years. Higher class persons who developed the habit were unlikely to find themselves convicted of drunkenness offences. They were unlikely to be found drunk in 'public' places, ie places subject to police supervision. Even if they were found to be drunk in public by the police, there was very little likelihood of their being arrested and charged. The more likely outcome of such an encounter was that they would be escorted home by the police officer in order to ensure that they were not attacked. Hence, as long as numerous convictions for drunkenness offences were required before one could be compelled to undergo treatment, such persons would remain beyond the reach of compulsory therapeutic interventions.

It is important to emphasise that the class discrepancy in the policy of compulsory treatment of inebriates was *not intended* by the reformers and professionals who implemented the policy. They were deeply concerned with the problem of inebriety amongst the middle classes. They were particularly concerned to detain and treat those wayward members of respectable families who were squandering their families' 'fortunes' or who were ruining family businesses. The class discrepancy in the policy as it operated was due to the differential impact of libertarian resistance. This resistance did little to check the extension of the state's powers of detention over the lower classes. However, it did prevent attempts to extend compulsory treatment to the middle and upper classes. I suggest therefore that the ideology of the defenders of liberty requires as much critical scrutiny as that of the proponents of compulsory treatment.

THE GENDER IMBALANCE

As I indicated earlier, there was a striking gender imbalance in committals to inebriate reformatories (see also Harding and Wilkin 1988: 188–9). The following figures give some indication of the extent of this imbalance. In the inebriate reformatories established under the 1898 Act there was accommodation for 165 males and 1,021 females (1908 Report: q 92). In the Marlborough Street court, for the nine years to April 1908, 140 persons were committed as habitual drunkards; of these 17 were men and 123 were women. In the Tower Bridge court, for the same period, the figures were 15 men and 123 women (*ibid*: q 304). This gender imbalance is all the more surprising in that it does not appear to have been the result of a deliberate policy. The inebriety reformers had, if anything, given the impression that reformatories were intended for men rather than for women. For instance, of all those who gave evidence to the 1872 Committee, the only one to declare a special interest in female inebriates was Dr Druitt. Unlike most of the other witnesses, he was concerned primarily with the problem of secret drinking amongst upper class women. However, as we have seen, it was not upper class women, but prostitutes and other women from the lowest social classes who were sent to reformatories. So it seems that, as with the class discrepancy, the gender imbalance in reformatory committals was not due to a deliberate policy, but was an unintended outcome.

Feminist critics of the medical model would probably interpret this gender imbalance as confirming their suspicions that female deviance is far more likely than male deviance to be interpreted as arising from illness and that women are far more likely than men to be diverted from punishment into treatment.[8] This phenomenon is usually explained in terms of a neat

---

8   For discussions of this issue see Allen (1987), Smart (1989: 94ff) and Williams (1991: chapter 16). For critical studies of medical discourse on female deviants see Todd (1983), O'Donovan (1984), Mort (1987) and Sim (1990: chapter 6).

correspondence between cultural stereotypes of women and the assumptions of the medical model of crime. Women, it is suggested, tend to be seen as closer to nature and as overdetermined by nature (Smith 1981: chapter 7; Smart 1989: 94). Medical discourses, which regard people as part of nature, are therefore deemed to be more appropriate to women's lives than to men's lives. Men tend to be regarded as active, rational, and hence responsible. Women tend to be regarded as passive, irrational and irresponsible. Also, it tends to be assumed that it is normal for men to participate in crime and deviance, whereas it is abnormal for women to offend. Hence, women's deviance is more likely to be regarded as indicative of abnormality, madness and sickness.

I do not question the claim that the medical model tends to be applied more to female deviance than to male deviance, or that this is both due to and perpetuates cultural stereotypes of women. What I do argue, however, is that the gender imbalance in committals to inebriate reformatories cannot be explained in these terms. In some respects, the explanation for this gender imbalance is more simple than feminist theories would suggest, in other respects it is more complex.

First, as we have seen, the gender imbalance was due to two quite contingent factors. First, some people regarded the power to confine people to inebriate reformatories as a useful means of managing the quite different problem of prostitution. It seems strange to us today that the courts could send people who were regarded as troublesome because of their involvement in prostitution to institutions which were established for the treatment of habitual drunkards. And, no doubt, many of those who initiated the inebriate reformatory experiment were irritated about the reformatories being used for this purpose. However, we should note, as Nye (1984: 144) points out, that late 19th century medical men hardly distinguished between the various 'social pathologies', tending to see them as different aspects of the one social problem. The link between one problem, such as inebriety, and others – such as prostitution, crime, pauperism, madness and suicide – was easily made. The following statement from the Departmental Committee on Inebriates, 1908, is an example of how various types of troublesome behaviour were attributed to the same underlying pathology: lack of self-control:

> Many inebriates exhibit lack of self-control, not only in indulgence in drink,
> but also in abhorrence of steady employment, in excessive sexual indulgence,
> in violence of temper, and in other ways (1908 Report: 6).

One of those who gave evidence to the 1908 Committee linked inebriety and prostitution in a more direct way by suggesting that, for many women, the road to prostitution started with inebriety. Inebriate women, it was suggested:

> pawn their children's or husband's clothes, and eventually the man gets a
> separation, and then that woman, what happens to her – the street' (*ibid*: q
> 1476).

A second 'contingent' reason for the gender imbalance in reformatory committals was, as we have seen, that the NSPCC regarded the powers to commit inebriates to a reformatory as an opportunity to do something about the problem of mothers who neglected and abused their children. Once again, it should be made clear that this was by no means a misuse of the powers. Rather, for the NSPCC, the problems of cruelty to and neglect of children were usually inextricably linked with the problem of inebriety. The following, for example, is how R J Parr, Director of the NSPCC, described one woman who – as a result of his efforts – was sent to an inebriate reformatory:

> Age 36, started to drink to excess 14 years ago, continued 7 years, then for 3 years was steady, afterwards relapsed, and for 3 years had been drunken. She frequently accosted men in the street in order to obtain drink. There were six children involved, the oldest 13 years, the youngest one month (this child was blind with gonorrheal opthalmia).

> The husband was a respectable, hard-working man. Average earnings 28 shillings weekly. The woman had pawned the clothing and household goods as far as possible; the other furniture and windows broken. Rooms dirty; bedding black with dirt.

> The children were fairly nourished, but they were very dirty, as was their clothing. That their condition was not more deplorable was due to the efforts of the mother's sisters.

> Committed for three years' detention on 18 October 1907, the previous convictions were:

> October 1904 – Woman reprimanded by magistrates and given a chance to reform.

> November 1904 – Husband got a separation; remained apart for a few months.

> February 1906 – Six months for neglect.

> 1906–7 – Several fines for being drunk and disorderly (1908 Report, evidence of R J Parr).

From this description, it seems fair to conclude that Parr genuinely believed that the woman's neglect of her children was due to her inebriate habit and that, if her drink problem was cured, she would become a better mother. It is this assumption, rather than a general assumption that women are close to nature or that female deviance is a sign of abnormality, which explains why, in the case of the inebriate reformatory experiment, therapeutic interventions were directed mainly at women.

The third possible reason for the gender imbalance in reformatory committals is more complex and is difficult to explain at this stage, since I have not yet described the nature of reformatory treatment. Some of those who established inebriate retreats and reformatories thought that women were more easily shaped by the *environment* than were men (1908 Report: qq 700–704). As one reformer put it: 'I think the environment of a woman is very important because she seems to take on the colour of her environment more than men do' (*ibid*: q 700). This assumption was important, not because it was used to explain why women became inebriates, but because it led people to believe that women were more amenable than men to reformatory treatment, which consisted of the use of environmental influences to change the character and habits of inmates. Men, it was assumed, would be less likely than women to respond to good environmental influences, because men were less influenced than women by their environment. Hence, the gender imbalance may have been due, in part, to a general cultural stereotype of women. But this cultural stereotype is quite different from the one that feminist critics of the medical model have criticised. It was not that women were seen as closer to nature than men, and hence more influenced by their biology. Rather, it was thought that women were more shaped by their social environment than men and that they were therefore more susceptible to reformatory treatment, which consisted of environmental influences.

CONCLUSION

I have shown that the emergence of a therapeutic response to the problem of habitual drunkards in the second half of the 19th century had important implications for personal liberty. The inebriety reformers adhered to the view that treatment could and should be imposed upon inebriates against their wishes. Indeed, they assumed that without compulsory powers the treatment of inebriates would be impossible. However, not everyone was affected by the new policy towards habitual drunkards in the same way. The poor and women were much more likely to be certified and incarcerated as inebriates than were the rich and men. Hence, my study partly confirms the claims made by some critics of the medical model of crime, but it does so in quite different terms and for very different reasons.

In addition, in this chapter I have uncovered some important facets of the therapeutic policy towards habitual drunkards that until now have not been noticed. First, the medical campaign against the habit of inebriety was directed at only certain types of habitual drunkard: those who, as a result of their habit, became incapable of performing their obligations or of behaving responsibly. Medical professionals did not seek to 'medicalise' the whole problem of habitual drunkenness. As far as the inebriety reformers were concerned, habitual drunkenness could, for the most part, continue to be regarded and handled as a simple vice. For the inebriety reformers, most habitual drunkards who broke the law could be processed as ordinary criminal justice cases. And while most inebriety reformers were sympathetic towards the efforts of moral reformers to persuade people to give up the vice of drunkenness, few allied themselves formally to the Temperance

Movement.[9] For the inebriety reformers, so long as hard drinkers could perform their social obligations they were immune from compulsory therapeutic interventions no matter how immoral their behaviour. Interference with liberty was a 'penalty', not for immorality, but for failing to control its effects – for neglecting one's obligations to family and society.

Hence, liberal claims that the new policy towards habitual drunkards amounted to a dangerous encroachment upon personal freedom were only partly justified. The inebriety reformers had no intention of locking people up simply because they indulged in vice. They proposed to interfere with liberty only where immorality led to social inefficiency. Had the liberal opponents of the new policy understood its aims better, they might well have been less resistant towards it. However, it must be remembered that the inebriate reformatory experiment was launched at a time when the medical press, which had once portrayed alcohol as necessary for good health, was becoming increasingly hostile towards drink (Lowerson and Myerscough 1977: 70) and in which Temperance reformers were beginning to advocate prohibition. In such a climate, any policy that had the declared purpose of checking the spread of the habit of drunkenness – and especially one proposed by medical professionals – was likely to meet with over-reaction from defenders of personal rights.

Finally, I have tried to show that whilst those on the receiving end of the new policy were mostly lower class people and women, this discrepancy was not an inevitable result of an attempt to apply the medical model to a social problem. Rather, the discrepancy resulted, for the most part, from contingent historical factors which affected the way the policy was implemented in practice. There are lessons to be learned from a study of the 'gap' between the original intentions of the reformers and the actual outcome. But we can learn little about the problems of therapeutic interventions, in this case at least, if we attribute such discrepancies to ideological biases implicit in the medical model of crime.

---

9   Many temperance reformers were hostile towards the inebriate reformatory experiment. In their view it was the drink rather than the drunkard which needed to be locked away.

CHAPTER 3

UNDERSTANDING AND TREATING THE INEBRIATE

INTRODUCTION

In the previous chapter, I looked at one aspect of the therapeutic response to habitual drunkards in the late 19th and early 20th centuries: the question of how people were selected for compulsory treatment as inebriates. In this chapter, I turn to examine the nature of therapeutic interventions into the lives of those who were classified as inebriates. Since therapeutic interventions were guided by a set of relatively novel ideas about how people became afflicted by the illness of inebriety, and about how they could recover from the condition, I start by looking at how the inebriety reformers understood the inebriate habit.

As I explained in the previous chapter, the inebriety reformers drew a distinction between the 'ordinary drunkard' and the inebriate. This distinction was drawn, partly, in terms of the individual's capacity to control his or her drinking behaviour. The ordinary drunkard could choose when to get drunk and when to stay sober. Inebriates, on the other hand, had no self-control over their drinking behaviour. As Peddie put it, the inebriate 'cannot overcome the desire for spirituous liquors which burns within him ...' (Peddie 1860: 541). In this chapter, I look at how the inebriety reformers understood and explained this condition. Why, in their view, did some people lack or lose the power to control their drinking behaviour? One answer the reformers gave was that inebriates had become afflicted by a disease called 'inebriety' or 'dipsomania'. But, what did they mean by this? In what sense did they regard inebriates as 'ill'?

These issues – and in particular the issue of what the inebriate reformers meant by the terms 'disease' and 'illness' – tend not to be analysed in existing historical accounts of the inebriate reformatory experiment.[1] Rather, it tends to be taken for granted that the reformers regarded inebriates as ill in a frankly medical sense. For instance, in what is probably the widest read account of the inebriate reformatory experiment, Radzinowicz and Hood suggest that the reformers regarded inebriety as disease with a physical origin and that some of the leading reformers viewed it as an hereditary disease of the brain (pp 289–91):

> In the middle of the 19th century the view gained acceptance among certain medical authorities that habitual drunkenness was a disease ... An excessive

---

1   MacLeod (1967), Radzinowicz and Hood (1990: chapter 9) and Harding and Wilkin (1988).

and uncontrollable desire for intoxicating drinks was 'symptomatic of some abnormal cerebral condition which gives it the character of a form of insanity' (Radzinowicz and Hood 1990: 289).

Accordingly, it tends to be assumed that the logic of treatment was 'somatic', ie that its objective was to cure inebriates of their craving for alcohol by facilitating the repair of body tissue:

> This concept of drunkenness led to the conclusion that the patient should be detained until he was cured. And cure could be achieved only when 'The time arrives at which all the tissues of the body have been changed, and a new tissue laid down in its place (Radzinowicz and Hood 1990: 292).

In this chapter I show that, although some reformers did seem to expound such a theory of inebriety, their actual understanding of the condition was more complex. A close scrutiny of their discourse on the problem shows that the reformers tended to regard inebriety, not as a physical disease, but as a moral disorder, or more specifically as a disorder of the *moral will*, and therefore not as an 'illness' in the strict sense in which we usually understand the term. The reformers conceived of the mind as an entity composed of different segments. One of these segments was the will; others were the passions or desires. They conceived of all people as engaged in an internal moral struggle in which the will was used to control the passions. They regarded inebriates as people who, for some reason, had feeble wills and who were therefore unable to control their passions and desires. Such weakness of will was occasionally explained as an hereditary defect, but it was often attributed to indulgence in vice. It was contended that habitual indulgence in vice both weakened the will and strengthened the passions, so that what started as a vicious but controllable habit eventually became an uncontrollable compulsion.

The remedy for this 'disease', according to the reformers, was not medical-somatic treatment but *moral* treatment.[2] Indeed, the reformers were highly dismissive of medical-somatic treatments for inebriety and regarded the purveyors of medical-somatic cures as quacks. According to the reformers, if the inebriate was to recover, his or her will had to be strengthened and restored. This could be achieved only through the disciplinary methods of moral treatment. Inebriates had to subject themselves to, or have imposed upon them, a moral environment of order and industry. The logic of reformatory treatment was therefore not medical-somatic but disciplinary. The objective of treatment was to restore the will of inebriates by surrounding them with moral influences and by training them in the arts of self-government.

---

2   Digby (1985) provides an invaluable analysis of moral treatment as it was practised at the 'Retreat', a small psychiatric institution in York run by Quakers. Skultans (1975: chapter 4) is a very useful collection of excerpts from 19th century representations of moral treatment. Useful critical analyses of the practice include Castel (1980), Fears (1977) and Foucault (1967: chapter 9).

UNDERSTANDINGS AND EXPLANATIONS OF THE INEBRIATE HABIT

How did the inebriety reformers make sense of the inebriate habit? In this section I argue that although they persistently referred to inebriety as a disease – and often as a disease of the brain – the inebriety reformers did not mean that inebriates suffered from a disease in the ordinary sense of the word. Rather, they meant that inebriates suffered from a disorder of the 'will'.

I start, once again, with the views of Alexander Peddie (1860), one of the initiators of the inebriate reformatory experiment. Peddie maintained that dipsomaniacs suffered from a disease of the brain. However, a careful reading of his lecture shows that he qualified this claim considerably, by stating that in cases of dipsomania it was the 'action', rather than the 'nutrition', of the cerebral matter that was perverted (*ibid*: 539). His implication was that the brain tissue of dipsomaniacs was not necessarily abnormal, rather there was something wrong with the way in which their minds functioned. More specifically, the portions of the mind which were impaired were the 'moral feelings' and 'volitions' (*ibid*: 539, 540, and 543).

So how did one's moral feelings and volitions become perverted, so that the person became a dipsomaniac? According to Peddie there were two ways in which one could become a dipsomaniac. First, those who repeatedly indulged in the vice of habitual drunkenness could, especially if they had a 'nervous or sanguine temperament', become dipsomaniacs (*ibid*: 539). Crucially, Peddie did *not* represent this as a physiological process, ie he did not suggest that the habitual drinker eventually became physiologically dependent upon alcohol. Rather, he presented the process more as one in which habitual indulgence in the vice of drunkenness led to *moral disintegration*, so that the drunkard eventually became unconcerned about his or her responsibilities or duties (*ibid*: 539). Secondly, Peddie argued that people could inherit a tendency towards dipsomania from their parents. He *implied* that the transmission of dipsomania from parents to their offspring was a physiological process by claiming that, as an hereditary affection, dipsomania resembled other constitutional diseases such as gout, rheumatism or heart disease (*ibid*). But, other than this, he said nothing about the process of transmission. And indeed, his tone became much more moralistic when he suggested that dipsomania was 'frequently visited on children for the sins of their parents' (*ibid*: 540).

For Peddie, dipsomania – whether acquired or inherited – had the same consequence: a complete loss of control over one's behaviour (*ibid*). The dipsomaniac was unable to resist the desire for alcohol: 'He [was] destitute of any command over his own will – of all ability to resist the craving, and he [was] the involuntary slave of an insane propensity' (*ibid*: 539). Peddie emphatically spelled out the practical consequences of this. First, it meant that the ordinary methods used to influence conduct could make no impact upon the behaviour of dipsomaniacs:

> The motives presented by religion and morality have no sway over him, the ties of nearest and dearest kin have no hold on him. Medical advice is still less availing without the power of enforcing restraint; the criminal law holds no terrors to him (Peddie 1860: 541).

Secondly, Peddie argued that dipsomaniacs would stop at nothing to satisfy their desire for alcohol and that, once under its influence, they lacked all control over their conduct. This was what made the dipsomaniac such a dangerous person:

> He cannot overcome the desire for spirituous liquors which burns within him, which excites him to mischievous, sometimes theftuous actions, or sudden fits of violent conduct, or to suicide, or murder (Peddie 1860: 541).

The conception of inebriety as a disease of the *will* and *moral sense* was elaborated by many of those who gave evidence to the Select Committee on Habitual Drunkards of 1872. The issue generally arose during questions about the relationship of inebriety to insanity. Most witnesses insisted that inebriety was similar to insanity, yet distinct from it; or as one witness put it: 'inebriety is like a twin-brother of insanity' (1872 Report: q 3096). The consensus seems to have been that whereas insanity affected the intellect, inebriety affected the will and moral power.[3]

Many witnesses *seemed* to propose medical-somatic explanations for this 'morbid state of the will'. However, if we closely examine these explanations we find that 'physicalism' was nearly always compromised by moral-social explanations. A striking example of this was the claim that inebriety could be caused by a 'blow on the head'. Many of the witnesses suggested that there were cases in which a previously sober person became an habitual drunkard after receiving a blow on the head. They concluded from this that habitual drunkenness could result from brain damage (*ibid*: q 595). However, in his evidence to the Committee, Dr Peddie explained the connection between blows on the head and inebriety in rather different terms: persons who received blows on the head often sought relief from the discomfort by drinking, they then developed a desire for drink, and eventually became dipsomaniacs (q 943). Similarly, the notion that the disease of inebriety could be inherited from parents seems to have become firmly entrenched by this time. Many witnesses insisted that drunkenness was hereditary (eg 1872 Report: qq 562–5). However, if we look very closely at their utterances on this matter, we find that what many of them meant was that the children of habitual drunkards themselves became inebriates because they were neglected and ill-treated (*ibid*: q 158 – see the discussion in chapter 2 of the reformers' concern with child neglect). So, in the words of one committee

---

3 See Ackroyd's draft report, para 15; minutes of evidence, qq 939, 2659–66. On the related concepts of 'moral insanity' and 'moral imbecility' see chapters 5 and 6 of this book.

member, they attributed the phenomenon 'more to the moral conditions into which the drunkard's child is thrown, than to the inheritance of any particular tendency' (*ibid*: q 159). And, in arguing for hereditarianism, witnesses tended to appeal less to contemporary biological theories, more to the 'Aristotelian maxim' that, 'drunken parents beget drunken children' (*ibid*: q 581). More generally, the tendency to insist that habitual drunkenness was a disease did not prevent many witnesses pointing to *social and psychological* causes of habitual drunkenness. The 1872 Report itself attributed the growth of habitual drunkenness to 'higher wages and shortened working hours' (*ibid*: para 2) and many witnesses pointed to the proliferation of beerhouses and other drinking places (eg q 219).

For most of the remainder of the 19th century there was little change in this understanding of inebriety. The Departmental Committee on Inebriates of 1893 tended to avoid the issue of the nature and causes of the condition altogether; it simply took it for granted that inebriety was a disease and concentrated on the question of legislative reform and institutional provision (1893 Report: para 18). However, in the 1908 Report the disease concept of inebriety was heavily qualified and a more complex view of the nature of the phenomenon was proposed.

In its 'general observations on the nature of inebriety', the 1908 Report started by describing, in familiar terms, the controversy between two seemingly 'irreconcilable' attitudes towards inebriety: as a vice to be met with punishment and as a disease to be met with medical treatment:

> There is no general consensus on the nature of inebriety. Some regard it as an exaggeration of ordinary self-indulgent drunkenness, and, therefore, a vice, which should be dealt with by punishment alone. Others consider it a disease allied to insanity, to be treated by medical measures, and not by punishment (1908 Report: 3).

However, the report then went on to sketch a model of inebriety which fell somewhere between these, apparently irreconcilable, positions and which was more complex than either of them. It contended that the craving or desire for intoxicants was innate in human nature (*ibid*). However, it argued, people also had other desires which conflicted with the passion for drink, especially the desire for self-respect and to retain the respect of others (*ibid*: 4). Exercising their will or volition, most people stopped drinking before they became drunk so that the desire for respect could be satisfied (*ibid*). If, however, the strength of the desire for drink was stronger than either the desire for respect or the powers of self-control, they became drunk (*ibid*).

The report went on to explain the categories of inherited and acquired inebriety in these terms. Some people had an inborn 'constitutional susceptibility' to inebriety because they had inherited either an extraordinarily strong impulse to drink or a weak will (*ibid*: 4–5). However, others could acquire a susceptibility to inebriety by 'vicious indulgence', ie habitually giving in to the desire for intoxicants (*ibid*).

> By continually yielding to desire, and continual failure to exert self-control, not only is desire strengthened, but self-control is weakened, until it is reduced permanently below the point necessary to overcome the desire; and thus inebriety is established (1908 Report: 5).

The Committee concluded that inebriety was undoubtedly an inborn or acquired 'constitutional peculiarity' (*ibid*). Whether one called it a disease or not was – the committee at one point insinuated – simply a matter of nomenclature.

Crucially, however, the committee warned that calling inebriety a disease could be misleading, given the popular understanding of the term, and it argued that there were 'cogent reasons why the term disease should *not* be used to characterise the inebriate habit' (*ibid*, emphasis added). For the committee, the problem with the term disease was its implication that inebriates bore no responsibility for developing the condition and that recovery through voluntary effort by the inebriate was impossible. The report argued – contrary to the rhetoric of some earlier inebriety reformers – that such a doctrine was both false and counter-productive.

> By disease is popularly understood a state of things for which the diseased person is not responsible, which he cannot alter except by the use of remedies from without, whose action is obscure, and cannot be influenced by exertions of his own. But if, as is unquestionably true, inebriety can be induced by cultivation; if the desire for drink can be increased by indulgence, and self-control diminished by lack of exercise; it is manifest that reverse effects can be produced by *voluntary effort*; and that the desire for drink may be diminished by abstinence, and self-control, like any other faculty, can be strengthened by exercise. It is erroneous and disastrous to inculcate the doctrine that inebriety, once established, is to be accepted with fatalistic resignation, and that the inebriate is not to be encouraged to make any effort to mend his ways. It is more so, since inebriety is in many cases recovered from, in many diminished, and since the cases which recover or amend are those in which the inebriate himself desires and strives for recovery (1908 Report: 5–6, emphasis added).

At first sight this looks like a simple volte-face. In one respect it was – whereas earlier inebriety reformers had argued that the defining feature of inebriety was a loss of all self-control or an inability to resist the desire for intoxicants, those who prepared the 1908 report were arguing that the inebriate could resort to self-help as a means of recovery. However, we should not see the 1908 Report as a simple return to a traditional, voluntaristic view of the habitual drunkard. Whilst their emphasis on the capacity of inebriates to help themselves contrasted sharply with the earlier insistence that inebriates were unable to resist the craving for intoxicants, their actual characterisation of the phenomenon of inebriety was – at a deeper level – quite consistent with the views of earlier inebriety reformers.

For the authors of the 1908 Report, the characteristic feature of inebriety was a lack of self-control or an impairment of that portion of the mind known as the 'will'. In this respect, the 1908 Report developed and elaborated the idea which earlier inebriety reformers had proposed. What was different about the analysis of inebriety presented in the 1908 report was that it referred not to a total annihilation of the power of self-control, but rather to a *weakening* of the will to such an extent that it was unable to overcome the desire for drink. Hence, for the 1908 Report, the inebriate retained some powers of self-control. These powers could be strengthened – through exercising them – and hence inebriates could restore a healthy ratio between the desire for drink and the capacity to control that desire. In order to strengthen the will, the inebriate had to struggle against the desire for drink and submit to a regime of disciplinary treatment (1908 Report: 6).

It is inaccurate and misleading to describe this mode of conceptualising the inebriate habit as a 'disease concept'. It would be far more accurate to describe it as a moral-psychological concept. For the inebriety reformers, habitual drunkenness did not result from a physical disease over which the person had no control. Rather, it resulted from a want of discipline. The inebriety reformers, in typically Victorian fashion (see Wiener 1990), perceived individuals as engaged in a constant battle with their immoral desires, such as the desire to indulge in drunkenness, fornication, etc. Most people, they contended, could moderate their behaviour, despite these desires, through the use of the mental capacity known as 'will' or 'self-control'. However, some people seemed to be unable to regulate their behaviour. The inebriety reformers tried to understand why this was so. Their answer was that these people – for various reasons – had either abnormally strong desires or abnormally weak wills. In either event, the implication was that if individuals were to regain mastery over their behaviour, they had to exercise their wills so that they became stronger and therefore capable of controlling desire. The way in which one exercised one's will was through disciplinary techniques: the practice of abstinence, living according to a strict timetable, submitting to the routines of regular work, and so on. For the inebriety reformers, the solution to the 'disease' of inebriety was not medical-somatic treatment, but *moral* or *disciplinary* 'treatment'. So, a close examination of what the inebriety reformers actually meant by 'inebriety' shows that what appears at first to be a radically new medical conception of the inebriate habit, is actually a much older 'moral' notion of the individual engaged in a constant struggle between good and evil, and of the will becoming enslaved by habit and a want of discipline.[4]

---

4   This notion goes back at least as far as St Augustine's *Confessions*, where it is stated: 'From a perverted act of will desire had grown, and when desire is given satisfaction, habit is forged; and when habit passes unresisted, a compulsive urge sets in' (quoted in Hearnshaw 1987: p 40).

THE REFORMERS' CRITICISMS OF EXISTING RESPONSES TO INEBRIATES

I turn now to the reformers' proposals for dealing with inebriates. The inebriety reformers were highly critical of the existing official responses to the problem of habitual drunkenness. The current penal methods of dealing with habitual drunkards, they argued, were neither checking the spread of the inebriate habit nor correcting confirmed inebriates. The reformers proposed, therefore, to replace or supplement the existing penal responses with therapeutic interventions. Before looking at the nature of these therapeutic interventions it is worthwhile looking briefly at the character of the reformers' criticisms of the existing penal methods of dealing with inebriates. These criticisms, I suggest, were more limited in their scope and of a quite different kind than is implied by available historical accounts of the inebriate reformatory experiment. The reformers did not object to the criminalisation and punishment of habitual drunkenness *per se*. They did not regard the punishment of habitual drunkards as unjust or as totally pointless. Rather they argued that the existing penal methods of fines and short imprisonments were ineffective as means of reforming the inebriate. It is important to understand the scope and nature of these criticisms since, as we shall see, the reformers proposed that the new policy of treating inebriates should contain a strong penal element. We can only make sense to this proposal if we realise that the inebriety reformers were not opposed to the 'penal model' of habitual drunkenness in its entirety. Rather, they objected only to certain penal methods and only on the ground that they were ineffective as methods of reforming inebriate offenders.

I have already discussed, in chapter 2, one aspect of the reformers' critique of the existing penal response to habitual drunkards: that many inebriates avoided penal sanctions either because they managed to stay out of trouble with the police or because criminal sanctions were inconsistently enforced. Here, I focus on the criticisms that were aimed at the actual penal methods employed by the criminal justice system, mainly small fines and short periods of imprisonment. The reformers argued that these sanctions were ineffective from the point of view of reforming inebriates. This was proved, they contended, by 'the fact that the same individual is convicted over and over again, to even more than 100 times' (*ibid*: para 3).

The reformers argued that small fines, even if they were enforced,[5] contributed nothing to reformation and that prison sentences, when they were

---

5   One of the criticisms made by reformers was that many of those fined for drunkenness offences did not pay the fine and, since many of them had no fixed abode, suffered no further consequences (1872 Report: q 1469). The reformers also complained that the magistrates' courts did not record their proceedings, which made it difficult to determine whether an offender had previous convictions for drink-related offences (*ibid*: q 1480).

imposed, were actually counter-productive (*ibid*: para 3 and q 533). Those who were sentenced to imprisonment usually received a seven-day sentence, which the reformers considered far too short for reformative purposes (*ibid*: q 139). Moreover, this expensive policy actually made things worse, they argued, since it led to inebriates meeting 'real criminals' and being sucked into the criminal class (*ibid*: q 150 and 853–55). It was also argued that habitual drunkards who received short prison sentences were not taught any trade or skills, so that on release they had no way of earning a living (*ibid*: appendix No 7). These criticisms of imprisonment were supported by prison governors who, eager to rid themselves of responsibility for the social management of this group, argued that habitual drunkards were not fit for the hard labour of prisons and made unprofitable and disorderly prisoners (*ibid*: qq 47 and 139). The implication, then, was that inebriates required longer sentences, but in different institutions.

To conclude this section we should note that the reformers also objected to the once prevalent but increasingly uncommon practice – which was of dubious legality – of sending habitual drunkards to lunatic asylums (*ibid*: qq 452–79). They maintained, as we shall see later, that asylums were inappropriate institutions for the treatment of inebriates. They also argued that asylum keepers had no legal power to detain inebriates against their will, and that they were therefore unable to hold inebriates who attempted to leave without rendering themselves liable to legal action on the ground of false imprisonment.

TREATMENT: MEDICAL OR MORAL?

Historical accounts of the inebriate reformatory experiment assume and suggest that when the inebriety reformers proposed to supplement the existing penal response to inebriates with 'treatment' they had medical-somatic treatment in mind. For instance, although he tells us very little about the nature of the proposed 'treatment' programme, MacLeod (1967) suggests that the inebriety reformers advocated a system of treatment 'by medical means' (*ibid*: 217). Similarly, Radzinowicz and Hood (1990), as we have seen, described the logic of treatment, as proposed by the inebriety reformers, as being to heal diseased internal tissues of the body thereby removing the physical craving for alcohol. Hence, in explaining the reformers' ideas they quote the following statement from one of the leading inebriety reformers, Dr Norman Kerr: 'There has been a degeneration of brain tissue, and time must be given for a new and ample supply of healthy brain and nerve substance' (*ibid*). Moreover, throughout their chapter on the inebriate reformatory experiment, Radzinowicz and Hood frequently refer to the 'medical treatment' of inebriates (eg p 307).

In what follows I look more closely at the nature of the practices which the inebriety reformers described as 'treatment'. I show that the reformers did *not* conceive of treatment as medical-somatic treatment. Indeed, they were much concerned to dispel the popular impression that there was a medical remedy for habitual drunkenness which could bring about a 'radical cure' (see 1872 Report: q 2717). The reformers conceived of treatment as *moral* treatment. The logic of moral treatment was not to heal diseased tissues of the body thereby removing the physical craving for alcohol, but to train inebriates in habits of self-discipline so that, through force of will, they could overcome the temptation to drink. I will also show in this chapter that the inebriety reformers applied the concept of treatment to a set of interventions which had penal as well as therapeutic objectives, and that they often distinguished the treatment of inebriates from the treatment of the insane by pointing out that the former had a penal element to it which was absent from the latter.

On this basis I argue that the reformers' proposals were more modest, yet more complex, than has hitherto been realised. The reformers did not propose a radical change in the status of habitual drunkards: from offenders to medical patients. Rather, they proposed a more subtle change in their status: from ordinary offenders to offender-patients. And the reformers did not propose a radical change in the methods of intervention: from punishment to medical treatment. Rather, they proposed a more subtle change: from ordinary criminal sanctions to a system of moral management which incorporated penal and reformative goals.

In this discussion, I also look at the aims of treatment. I show that the aim was not just to help inebriates achieve sobriety or to prevent them from re-offending. Rather, it was to lead the inebriate into a new life as a useful and responsible individual. Treatment aimed to enhance the social usefulness of its recipients, rather than simply to cure them of their drinking habits. What this meant in practice depended upon the inebriate's station in life.

THE TREATMENT OF INEBRIATE OFFENDERS

The inebriety reformers proposed to remedy the problems they identified in the existing official response to habitual drunken offenders by supplementing the system of criminal sanctions with a system of 'treatment' for all confirmed inebriates. The proposed treatment system would deal with two classes of inebriate: habitual drunken offenders and non-offender inebriates. In this section I will describe the reformers proposals regarding habitual drunken offenders, ie persons who were repeatedly convicted of any of a variety of drunkenness offences and found by the judge or magistrate to be habitual drunkards.[6] In the next section I look at their proposals regarding 'non-criminal inebriates'.

The reformers proposed that, instead of being given a fine or a short prison sentence, habitual drunken offenders should be sent to an inebriate 'asylum' or 'reformatory' for a period long enough to effect their cure (1872 Report: q 462).[7] There was much debate amongst the reformers about how long habitual drunken offenders should spend in reformatories. In the early years of the campaign the vast majority of inebriety reformers recommended that habitual drunkards be detained for up to 12 months (1872 Report: rec'n. 4). However, a small minority of reformers proposed that the maximum period be two years (*ibid*: discussion of amendments). In the event, the Inebriates Act 1898 provided for a maximum of three years' detention (see Radzinowicz and Hood 1990: 305). I suggest, however, that the move to three year 'sentences' was prompted not by therapeutic but by penal concerns – an issue to which I will now turn.

The penal element in treatment

The main declared purpose of reformatory treatment was the 'reformation' or 'cure' of inebriates. However, from the outset of their campaign some inebriety reformers also highlighted the deterrent and 'educational' value of inebriate reformatories. Others explained that the proposed institutions were meant to perform penal as well as therapeutic functions. And, especially as the campaign developed, many reformers portrayed reformatories as a means of incapacitating an annoying and potentially dangerous group of individuals. It is important to realise this since many of the repressive features of reformatory treatment, which might be seen as latent aspects of therapeutic aspirations, were due as much to the reformers' therapeutic aspirations being blended with penal concerns.

The following statement is an example of the reformers' concern with deterrence and the moral education of drunkards *outside* the inebriate 'asylums':

---

6   The reformers expressed a variety of views on the question of how many drunkenness offences had to be committed before one could be registered as an habitual drunkard. In the event, the Inebriates Act 1898 provided that those convicted three times within the year preceding the current offence could be registered. The procedure, which also involved proposals for recording of convictions and identifying recidivists, is described in more detail in Radzinowicz and Hood (1990: 305). As we saw in the previous chapter, the Inebriates Act 1898 also provided that those who were found guilty of serious offences which were attributed to the habit of drunkenness could be committed to inebriate reformatories. Radzinowicz and Hood state that 'this category had appeared out of the blue, without any prior recommendation by committees or the medical profession' (*ibid*).

7   The early inebriety reformers tended to describe these institutions as 'asylums'. This was the term used to describe the inebriate institutions in the United States which served as models for the British inebriety reformers. Later, they were officially described as 'reformatories'.

the advantage of the inebriate asylums is much wider and greater than in the mere restoration of individuals ... My own impression is, that if they were very numerous and not very large, scattered all through the country, the deterrent influence upon inebriates who are outside would be very strong. I think that institutions of this class, properly conducted, with suitable men at the head of them, would be centres of a great deal of information and light. That would go very much to the formation of a proper public sentiment, and modify the estimate which people have of drunkards themselves (1872 Report: Ackroyd's draft report, para 16).

As I have indicated, some of the early inebriety reformers also envisaged the reformatories as a means of ridding society of a public nuisance (*ibid*: q 79). This justification became more prominent as the campaign progressed, so that by the time of the 1908 Report, incapacitation had emerged as a major justification for the inebriate reformatories:

... we consider it just and right that he [the inebriate] should be detained, not merely for his reformation, but to protect the community against his ill-doing. We are unanimously of the opinion that the detention of the inebriate is justifiable, and necessary, apart from all question of reformation (1908 Report: p 18).

The actual identity and declared purpose of the proposed inebriate institutions was in fact by no means as clear as historical accounts have implied. While the reformers were quite clear that these institutions should treat inebriates, they also regarded them as punitive institutions. Some reformers insisted that the inebriate institution 'should be looked upon as a hospital' (1872 Report: q 621). Others described them as prisons (*ibid*: q 474). To complicate matters further, they often seemed to suggest that punitive measures could contribute to therapeutic objectives – an issue I will return to later. For the moment we can note that this lack of certainty about the precise 'identity' of the inebriate institutions posed considerable problems when it came to the questions of where they would be located, who would control them, and how they would be funded.[8] There was much discussion amongst the reformers about whether inebriate institutions should be attached to prisons, asylums, or workhouses (*ibid*: qq 649–69). And, one major issue in the series of official inquiries which led to the creation of inebriate reformatories was whether they should be under the control of the Board of Lunacy or be

---

8   Determining the primary purpose of the institutions had crucial implications with regard to their funding. The care of lunatics was regarded as the responsibility of local authorities, whereas the punishment of offenders was regarded as the responsibility of central government. The early reformers wanted local authorities to pay for the reformatories, and therefore stressed their affinity with lunatic asylums. Local authorities, on the other hand, insisted that the purpose of inebriate reformatories was punishment and that central government should therefore accept responsibility for their construction and maintenance. This led to later reformers stressing the punitive nature of the institutions: 'The detention of inebriate offenders in reformatories is only in part for their reformation. In part it is a penal measure, and it seems to us improper that punishment should be administered by Local Authorities' (1908 Report: para 95). Lack of funding was one of the main reasons for the collapse of the inebriate reformatory experiment (see Harding and Wilkin 1988: 200).

part of the penal system (1872 Report: q 513). Most reformers, despite their claims that inebriety was a disease with a close affinity to insanity, opted for the latter. We can see an example of this uncertainty in a couple of statements from Alexander Peddie. First, when asked if treatment or punishment was most suitable for the habitual drunkard he gave the following, seemingly confused, reply:

> ... habitual drunkenness ... is a form of insanity, or at least something closely allied to insanity ... the habitual drunkard is more properly a subject for care, as it were, in a hospital, than a person for punishment in a gaol; yet at the same time there must be a certain amount of reformatory treatment entering into every case (1872 Report: q 954).

In this quotation, Peddie seems to be drawing a distinction between *hospital* and *reformatory* treatment; the former being appropriate for the insane, the latter for inebriates. In fact, Peddie seems to see reformatory treatment as lying somewhere between medical treatment and punishment. He seemed unsure of whether the proposed inebriate asylums should be under the control of the Board of Lunacy or be part of the prison system. He finally opted for the former, but then qualified his position as follows:

> I come somewhat unwillingly to this conclusion, and I think it would be very desirable to keep up a clear distinction between such institutions and asylums for the insane. We treat the insane as people labouring under disease; there is nothing disgraceful in their condition ... we avoid as far as we can all signs of incarceration, and shun the very words that indicate the existence of what we are constantly trying to reduce to a minimum. But I think we should be obliged to deal with the drunkard somewhat differently. He is detained against his will, and if supported by the country is forced to work, in spite of the fact that he is still legally sane, and has possession of his civil rights and responsibilities; there is something therefore disgraceful about his position, *and something penal in his treatment* (1872 Report: q 1213, emphasis added).

To explain his position, Peddie pointed out that inebriate offenders would be maintained in institutions at the public expense 'having committed crimes' and that they therefore required 'punitive treatment' (*ibid*: q 954).

This apparent confusion over the identity and purpose of inebriate institutions was a result, I suggest, of the reformers' concern to create an institution which was neither prison nor asylum, but something in between. But how was it possible to conceive of such an institution? How could the fundamentally different *ideas* of punishment and treatment be blended in a single institutional *practice*? We can gain a better understanding of these issues if we turn now to the question of what the reformers actually meant by the word 'treatment'.

The goals and methods of 'treatment'

While the reformers insisted that the inebriate institutions would perform penal as well as therapeutic functions, they tended to present treatment as their primary purpose. The main goal of treatment was not to cure inebriates of their craving for alcohol, but to transform a ne'er-do-well into a responsible and useful individual (see Branthwaite 1907/8: 109). For the reformers, treatment meant more than simply changing the drinking habits of inebriates; it meant effecting a much deeper change in their attitudes and behaviour, making them responsible, hard-working, decent and useful members of the community (1908 Report: 167).[9]

The more specific objective of treatment was to restore the inebriate's moral will or power of *self-control*. As we have seen, the inebriety reformers regarded inebriety as a disorder of the moral will or capacity of self-control. Hence, they conceived of treatment as an activity which would strengthen and restore the inebriate's moral will and powers of self-governance, thereby enabling the inebriate to re-gain mastery over his or her behaviour. This objective was phrased in a variety of ways by the reformers: to 'strengthen and invigorate the will of the patient' (1872 Report: Ackroyd's draft report para 15); 'treatment throughout, when it moves beyond mere detention, seems to take the form of restoring the moral will ... it must restore or install a moral will so that desire can be overcome' (*ibid*: q 1090); 'the most perfect cure is the acquirement of self-control' (*ibid*: 3157); the major objective of reformatory treatment is the 'instalment and cultivation of self-control' (1908 Report: 5–6).

How was this goal to be achieved? Certainly not through medical-somatic treatment, to which the reformers attached little value. For the reformers the functions of specifically medical interventions in the treatment of inebriates were important but limited. The role of medicinal remedies was largely confined to mitigating the physical effects of prolonged drinking and sudden withdrawal, strengthening inebriates so that they could undergo reformatory treatment, and healing any incidental organic diseases. As one manager of a reformatory institution put it:

> Nearly all patients on their admission require medical treatment; stimulant, sedative and narcotic remedies are usually administered at the outset, followed by alternative medicines to improve and correct the secretions, after which tonics, both vegetable and mineral, are given, calculated to add tone and strength to the system. When we have organic diseases, appropriate remedies adapted to each particular case are administered to relieve and assist nature in removing the same. *Outside these functional and organic difficulties very little medical treatment is demanded or required ...'* (1872 Report: 2973, emphasis added).

Throughout their campaign, the reformers maintained a polemical attack against the increasingly popular notion that there were medicinal cures for

---

9   This helps explain the reformers' hostility towards the 'quack cures' for inebriety which were becoming popular at the time. The reformers did not believe that medicinal remedies could cure the habit of drunkenness. Just as importantly, however, they objected to such remedies on the ground that the objective of treatment was not just to make drunkards sober but was to transform an irresponsible and idle profligate into a responsible and hard-working individual. The reformers' attitude towards medical 'cures' will be discussed in more detail later in this chapter.

drunkenness. Those who claimed to be 'in possession of a specific remedy for the cure of drunkenness' were dismissed by the reformers as 'quacks' (*ibid*: q 2974). One witness at the 1872 inquiry stated: 'I think there is a popular impression abroad ... that there is some sort of specific treatment for drunkenness; some radical cure. No such thing within my knowledge exists' (*ibid*: q 2717). By 1908, the reformers' opposition to the notion of medical cures had grown even stronger. One reformer stated: 'I do not think medical treatment is of the faintest use. All these drink cures, I think, are pure frauds' (1908 Report: q 736). That the reformers regarded the purveyors of 'cures' for inebriety as major opponents is clear from the following statement, in which Dr Branthwaite – the Inspector of Inspector Reformatories and Retreats – pitches his medical credentials against the unqualified promoters and proprietors of 'specific remedies':

> A reason for the restricted use of retreats is to be found in the multiplicity of patent remedies for drunkenness, promising cure and future immunity after a few days' treatment. Most of these are commercial frauds, which depend for their patronage upon free and alluring advertisements, and upon the advocacy of philanthropic persons who, being non-medical, are incapable of judging the value of the facts placed before them, and who are blinded by the plausible representations of the proprietors of such 'cures'. As proof of the extent to which these 'cures' are being resorted to, it is sufficient to say that 37 per cent of all persons admitted to retreats during 1903 had previously submitted to secret treatment (Dr R Branthwaite, quoted in Kelynack 1904/5: 128–9).

As can be seen, it is a total mistake to portray the reformers as advocates of medical-somatic treatment – they were actually strongly opposed to the popular notion that inebriety could be cured through drug or 'medicinal' treatments. When the reformers proposed to treat inebriates what they had in mind was not medical-somatic but *moral* treatment (1872 Report: qq 515–6). The methods of moral treatment – along with 'moral suasion' (1908 Report 168), educational treatment (*ibid*: 169), and 'discipline' (*ibid*: 15 and q 736) – were to be used to invigorate the moral will of inebriates and to restore their powers of self-control. What were these methods?

Moral treatment as applied to inebriate offenders

Changing the environment

First, inebriates had to be torn away from their life-style and their companions. This was to be achieved by confining them in institutions, preferably far removed from their usual district. Hence, the institutional confinement of inebriates was not simply a means of holding them so that they could be given treatment, rather it was the start of treatment itself. Through confinement, inebriates were withdrawn from their old life and could start a fresh one. The inebriate was cut off from 'associations that he has been accustomed to, from the temptation with which he has been surrounded in society, and in that respect is able to come to himself' (1872 Report: q 2607). The abrupt removal of inebriates from their familiar environment was the first step in re-making the person. It effected a:

> ... breaking up of former habits and associations, drawing from the mind those old companions of an intemperate life, forming new thoughts, new ideas, and new and better habits, necessitating a new life in every respect; a radical change (1872 Report: q 2974).

Of course, one had to be careful not to 'import' the inebriate's familiar environment into the reformatory by sending inebriates who knew each other to the same institution:

> I think one of the worst features of the present character of reformatories is that the women of the same locality go mainly to the same reformatory ... when you get a woman sober and anxious to lead a better life an old companion who had known her perhaps in the same doss-house in London, and knew all about her former life, came down, and this woman would laugh at the idea of her companion's reformation, and would undo in a few days what we had been trying to build up for many weeks ... I would send the women as far from their own locality as possible, and I would keep as few women as possible from the same districts together (1908 Report: qq 1090–1).

And, of course, the younger the inebriate, the more successful this procedure of uprooting and re-planting was likely to be: 'I think the younger you can get hold of these people the less likelihood you will find of their going back again' (1908 Report: q 569).

We might note that this notion of removing inebriates from their old lives and starting them on a new life embodied a 'social' understanding of the inebriate habit. Whilst the reformers sometimes represented the inebriate habit as an organic disease, this proposal shows that what they actually believed was quite different: that the inebriate's behaviour was strongly influenced, if not determined, by their social environment.

The logic of moral treatment was that by removing inebriates from the corrupting influences of an immoral environment and exposing them to only moral influences one could bring about a gradual change in their habits. Hence, the inebriety reformers were concerned to plan institutions and regimes which would ensure that the inebriate was immersed in a moral environment. This concern to change and improve 'the whole atmosphere surrounding the patient' (1908 Report: q 741) started with the *architecture* of confinement.[10] For example, the architect of a women's inebriate reformatory in Lancashire was told to 'prepare a scheme in which light, air, and pleasant surroundings should be considered as necessary concomitants to the reformatory' (*ibid*: q 1565). The reformers took great pride in those

---

10 On the role of architecture in the 'fabrication of virtue' see Evans (1982). Other studies of the treatment of deviants which have paid attention to the significance of 'moral architecture' include Rothman (1971), Foucault (1977) and Donnelly (1983: chapter 3).

reformatories which were 'extremely well built, light and airy and clean' (*ibid*: q 1677). Such reformatories would provide a contrast to the own homes of inebriates, which were criticised by the reformers as 'unpleasant, ill-kept and squalid'.[11]

The imposition of paid work

Inside the inebriate reformatory, one of the main methods of treatment was the imposition of regular paid work: 'the instilment and cultivation of self-control is necessarily an affair of time. It can only be effected by the imposition of steady work' (1908 Report: 6). Making inebriates work would also help them overcome their 'habit of idleness' (Peddie 1872) which concerned the inebriety reformers as much as their habit of drunkenness – indeed the two habits were seen as deeply connected. The 1872 Report recommended that inebriate institutions be established on 'the industrial system' (rec'n. 8). The inmate was to be made to work, preferably at useful and remunerative labour (1872 report: q 722; letter of Mr Smith to the chairman of the committee). It was recommended that the proceeds of the inebriate's labour 'should be applied to the payment of the entire cost of maintenance while in the reformatory' and that 'if any excess remain, it should be applied to the maintenance of wife and family' (*ibid*: rec'n. 9).

The imposition of work was often justified by reference to its deterrent value. However, this was not the reformers' main concern, since they strongly opposed the imposition of 'useless hard labour' – which would have performed the function of deterrence – and insisted that work be useful and wherever possible remunerative (*ibid*: Smith's letter). Indeed, the reformers put as much stress on the need for remuneration as they did on the need to impose work.[12] One reason for this was their belief that the proceeds of the

---

11 This concern with making buildings light and airy can be understood in the context of the public health movement which regarded such buildings as necessary to prevent the contagion which occurred in the dark, confined spaces of the dwellings of the poor. Just as light and airy spaces were seen as necessary for the prevention of physical contagion, so they were seen as useful for the prevention of moral contagion (see Pearson 1975: chapter 6).

12 Here, my characterisation of moral treatment differs from that of Foucault (1967: 247–8), which is drawn from his reading of the logic of moral treatment in 'The Retreat' (an 'alternative' lunatic asylum started, in the 19th century, by Quakers, and which subsequently became a model of 'enlightened' psychiatric care). Foucault succinctly captures the logic of work in moral treatment: 'Work comes first in "moral treatment" as practiced at the Retreat. In itself, work possesses a constraining power superior to all forms of physical coercion, in that the regularity of the hours, the requirements of attention, the obligation to produce a result detach the sufferer from a liberty of mind that would be fatal and engage him in a system of responsibilities' (*ibid*: 247). However, Foucault goes on to state: In the asylum, work is deprived of any productive value; it is imposed only as a moral rule; a limitation of liberty, a submission to order, an engagement of responsibility' (ibid: 248). The inebriety reformers, on the other hand, were deeply concerned that work should have productive value. The aim was to not just to impose work in order to teach discipline. Rather, it was to give inebriates work which was not only productive but also remunerative, so that they could grasp for themselves the benefits which they might derive from becoming more disciplined and industrious.

inmate's labour could pay for their stay in the reformatory, for the support of their dependants, and for their own support upon release. Many reformers argued, and seemed to genuinely believe, that inebriate reformatories would become self-financing within a short period. Although some doubted whether 'profitable work can be obtained by force' (1872 report: qq 1206–7), many confidently asserted that enough profit could be made from the inmate's labour to make the institutions financially independent (*ibid*: rec'n. 9, Ackroyd's draft report para 17 and rec'n. 6, qq 722, 954, 2946; Peddie 1872: para 3). Idealistic as this hope was, many expressed the even more optimistic belief that inmates could make enough money to not only support their stay in the institution but also to support their dependants on the outside (1872 report: rec'n 9, qq 1524–9) and to have some left over which could be saved up and given to them on release (*ibid*: qq 2948–53). Thus, two evils of the existing penal response could be avoided: the inebriate's family would not be thrown upon the poor rates (*ibid*: qq 1524–9) and the inebriate would not leave the institution penniless and hence with no choice but to resort to crime (*ibid*: Smith's letter). As Peddie put it:

> ... inmates might have an opportunity of earning wages, out of which a deduction should, in the first instance, be made for their own maintenance, then for the support of their families, if such there be, and the remainder go to secure additional comforts while in the institution, and to form a reserve fund for their own use after a trial of liberty is made (Peddie 1872: para 3).

One of the major obstacles to the reformers' scheme was, of course, the opposition of 'ordinary business' and 'free labour'. To overcome this obstacle it was suggested that 'some greater attempt might be made to produce goods now manufactured out of England, and to compete with foreign rather than English free labour' (1908 Report: 26 and 167). In the case of women – who, we can recall, constituted the majority of reformatory inmates – there was less of a problem. The domestic work which was considered appropriate for women, such as laundry work, could be useful and even profitable without being seen as a threat by ordinary business and labour.

For the reformers, forcing inebriates to do *paid* work also had an educational purpose. Paying inmates for doing forced work, and saving some money for them to be used on their release, was a way of teaching them about benefits that the industrious and thrifty person could enjoy. Allowing inmates to use some of the proceeds of their labour to secure additional comforts was also a way of teaching them the value of rational economic behaviour.

There were other reasons, besides these direct economic benefits and lessons, for the reformers' insistence the inebriates undertake labour. Through being made to work, the inebriate would receive training in specific skills and trades which would enable them to 'earn a living when they leave' (1872 Report: Ackroyd's draft report para 17, Smith's letter). So, even those who accepted that prolonged detention of inebriates would entail great expense supported the inebriate reformatory experiment on the ground that it would turn idlers into 'useful industrial people' and produce 'long term gains by making habitual drunkards productive, therefore saving on poor law rates (*ibid*: q 1230). Forced work was also advocated for its moral value – submitting to the routines of work was a way of developing 'moral and regular habits' (*ibid*: q 473). Hence, according to Peddie, 'work itself rehabilitates' (*ibid*: q 954). For Peddie:

> No better counteractive to the tendency to intemperance can be employed, none better fitted to generate feelings of self-esteem, and gradually strengthen the power of self-control, than occupation and the steady cultivation of industrial habits, especially with stimulus of obtaining some immediate as well as ultimate advantages from the same (Peddie 1872 para 4).

The reformers' proposals regarding work were designed mainly for male inebriates. The vocational training of female inebriates was to be slightly different in its character. They were to be taught domestic skills 'so that they will make good wives' and be trained to 'make working class homes comfortable and habitable' (1872 Report: q 831). This training also included instruction in the 'rules of hygiene' (*ibid*: q 2967). The inebriate woman was to be taught to take pride in a clean and orderly – albeit humble – home. As Lady Somerset, who ran an inebriate reformatory at Duxhurst, explained:

> I have taken great pains in the cottages at Duxhurst to see that they have only such surroundings and such things as they would have in their own homes if they were living as self-respecting citizens under conditions such as they ought to have. I think it is a help to them when they go out to have lived in homes conducted in this way and to realise that that is what their own homes must be (1908 Report: q 1902).

Regularity and order

Another feature of reformatory treatment was its emphasis on regularity, which was regarded as the antidote to the irregularity and indiscipline of a drunken and idle life. Moral and regular habits would result, the reformers suggested, from living according to a precise and strictly enforced timetable: 'prompt attendance at meals and upon religious exercises; retirement at ten o'clock in the evening and lights to be extinguished at half past ten' (*ibid*: Ackroyd's draft report para 20). The reformers attached considerable therapeutic importance to living by a set timetable. Hence, their discourse includes numerous descriptions of the daily routines of inebriate reformatories. The following is a typical example:

> The daily routine, which illustrates the policy of the house, may be of some interest: Rise at 6.30 am; morning prayers 7.15; breakfast 7.30 to 8 am; work 8 – 12.30 pm; dinner 12.30 – 1.30 pm; work 1.30 to 5 pm; tea 5 to 5.30; exercise and recreation 5.30 – 8.30; supper 8.35; prayers 8.50; retire 9 pm; all lights out 9.30 (1908 Report: 170).

It is worth emphasising that such timetables were not just a means of maintaining discipline within the reformatory. Rather, they were seen as methods of reformatory treatment. Treatment involved training the inebriates to live their lives according to an established and orderly routine.

Incentive strategies

Another key element in reformatory treatment was the use of incentive strategies. For example, Peddie (1872: para 4) advocated a system of 'rewards and benefits immediately derivable from industry and good behaviour'. The system in American inebriate asylums, whereby patients who obeyed the rules for eight weeks were allowed out twice a week to visit the nearby city, was recommended. However, this temporary liberty was much more than a simple inducement to good behaviour; it was a test of the inebriate's moral will. If patients returned sober after a limited exposure to 'the temptations of freedom' they could be deemed on the road to recovery (1872 Report: Ackroyd's draft report: para 20). In this event, the patient could be given even more privileges and freedom. As the superintendent of an American Inebriate asylum put it:

> When a patient has been with us three or four months, has been obedient to all the rules, and is what we call an excellent model patient, I grant him other privileges, and do not restrict him to going out twice a week (1872 Report: q 2975).

Breaches of the rules were, of course, to be punished by withdrawal of privileges (*ibid*: Ackroyd's draft report, para 20). This was not simply a means of enforcing institutional discipline. Rather, it was conceived as a method of moral education – hence for the reformers *punishment was a method of treatment*. Other methods of punishment included the imposition of fines (which was another reason for having remunerative labour) and 'limiting particular creature comforts, and withholding certain pleasures' (Peddie 1872: para 4).

The logical development of this idea of using rewards and punishments to discipline the inebriate was to call for 'indeterminate sentences' which would give the superintendents of inebriate institutions the power to adjust the period of detention according to the inmate's conduct. In the early part of the campaign, inebriety reformers did indeed argue that the 'superintendent should exercise his own judgment as to the release of the dipsomaniac' (1872 Report: q 481), but for the rather different (and more familiar) reason that 'no definite period can be given of how long a cure will take' (*ibid*: q 709). The medical metaphor came into play here:

> the proposition which is lying at the back of this committee [is] the establishment of institutions in which a person can be ... kept and treated for such a length of time as in the judgment of those in charge of him will be sufficient to effect his cure (1872 Report: q 473).

However, the reformers did not pursue the policy of indeterminate sentencing – a policy that actually was highly unpopular amongst British penal reformers.[13] Instead, they pursued the policy of semi-determinate sentencing. And importantly, they tended to justify semi-determinate sentences, less by drawing analogies between reformatory and medical treatment, more by pointing to the advantages of semi-determinate sentences for operating a broader incentive strategy. Resisting the arguments of some reformers for indeterminate sentences, the 1872 Select Committee recommended that inebriates be given a fixed maximum sentence, but that the superintendents of inebriate institutions be given powers of early release and of recall (1872 Report rec'ns. 4 and 6). The reformers fully intended to use the power of early release. The possibility of early release for good behaviour would, of course, encourage obedience and good behaviour. But just as importantly for the reformers, combined with a power of recall it made it possible to test the inebriate's recovery before granting him or her unconditional liberty. The self-control of inebriates could be tested by seeing how they coped with their conditional freedom. If they relapsed they could be returned to the reformatory; if they remained sober their treatment could be deemed successful: not until the patient 'has regained the power of self-control under temptation, and that self-control has been fairly tested, should the patient be considered cured' (1872 report: Ackroyd's draft Report: para, 11; see also Peddie 1872: para 9).

Moreover, for the reformers this 'parole period' was actually a method of treatment. During the period of licensed freedom, they argued, inebriates would be subject to the temptations of freedom, yet would not be totally exposed to these temptations since they would be aware that giving in to them would lead to their re-incarceration. This was important since treating the inebriate involved teaching them to resist temptation and to exercise their moral will. This lesson could not be fully taught in the reformatory where inebriates had little choice over their behaviour. Rather, as one reformer put it, if the inebriate was to learn how to resist temptation and acquire self-control, 'he should go where the temptation is' (1872 report: q 2761).

---

13 Long before critics of the rehabilitative ideal attacked the idea of indeterminate sentences, the idea was regarded with much suspicion by British penal reformers who were otherwise strongly in favour of rehabilitation. Hence, in 1927 the reviewer (probably George Ives) of L Gillin's *Criminology and Penology* praised his emphasis upon the goal of reformation but added: 'On one point we differ from Professor Gillin entirely. He advocates the absolutely indeterminate sentence, without any maximum (p 711), and this is a power we refuse to give to any official body; the more, as there seems some danger at the hand, led by fanatics, appealing to science to give support to their prejudices and disguised instincts. Thus any unpopular individual, or even any helpless minority, might be put away as abnormal, or dangerous to society. Anti-vaccinators, vegetarians, sunbathers, and especially any group of sex-life reformers, might easily be classed as "degenerates" and shut up where they would cease from troubling. The English people will never allow the building of a Bastille' (*Howard Journal* 1927).

After-care

In proposing this policy of semi-determinate sentences and licensed freedom, the reformers seemed to be trying to address one of the major limitations of their institutional response to the problem of inebriety: that at the end of the 'treatment period' inebriates would be returned to their old environment with all its temptations and corrupting influences. No matter how well they had responded to the moral influences of reformatory treatment, once they were beyond its reach and again surrounded by immoral influences it was likely that they would revert to their old habits. As the campaign progressed, the reformers became increasingly aware of this problem.

> I do not know whether any assistance is given to them to start life afresh in some other neighbourhood and give them an opportunity of that kind, I think it would be very useful, but at present, if they have no means, they must go back to the district in which they formerly lived ... if they come back to their old neighbourhood I think their fate is sealed (1908 Report: qq 1148–9).

As this reformer suggested, without continuous 'after-care' reformatory treatment was often going to be in vain. This was a problem which the inebriety reformers did not solve.

THE TREATMENT OF 'NON-CRIMINAL INEBRIATES'

As I explained in the previous chapter, the reformers proposed to extend compulsory treatment to all those whom they considered to be inebriates, even if they had not broken any specific criminal law. However, to send non-criminal inebriates to the same institutions as criminal inebriates, or to subject them to equally harsh routines, would have been unthinkable. As we saw earlier in this chapter, the reformers perceived an ethical distinction between those who had committed crimes and those who required control but had not broken specific laws, and they insisted that offenders be treated more harshly than non-offenders. Perhaps even more pertinent was the fact that the treatment of non-offender inebriates would be paid for privately, by the inebriates themselves or by their families (see Peddie 1872: paras 2–5).

Non-criminal inebriates were to be sent to 'inebriate retreats'. Unlike reformatories, these could not be attached to prisons or workhouses (1872 Report: q 649, 669) but were to be established as totally separate institutions in rural districts. Instead of the harsh methods of treatment employed in the reformatories, retreats would employ some of the gentler methods of moral treatment:

> ... sanitary and hygienic measures, restraint from business and the busy scenes of everyday life; quiet, reading, writing, pure air, well-ventilated rooms, good-nourishing diet, regular hours for meals, rising and retiring, proper physical exercise (1872 Report: q 2973).

There was a world of difference then between these 'private' inebriate retreats and 'public' inebriate reformatories; Radzinowicz and Hood (1990: 294) describe the former as 'temporary refuges for gentleman alcoholics'. It is important to realise, though, that despite these differences, the *underlying logic* of moral treatment in the inebriate retreat was much the same as that of reformatory treatment. It was simply that in the retreat the principles of moral treatment were to be adjusted to the requirements of fee-paying clients who were to be released to middle and upper class society and to the world of business. In the reformatory, on the other hand, the principles of moral treatment were to be adjusted to the requirements of criminals, treated at the public expense, who were to be released to the world of industrial labour. The principles of moral treatment were flexible enough to be adapted to both tasks (see Digby 1985).

Confinement in both reformatories and retreats was conceived as a means of removing inebriates from their familiar environment and surrounding them with only moral influences. A central theme in the discourse of moral treatment is that idleness must be overcome by activity. In the reformatories, this took the form of imposing industrial work and domestic duties. In the retreat it took the form of encouraging proper physical exercise and rational leisure pursuits. In the reformatory, a strict timetable was imposed. In the retreat, the emphasis was on regular hours for meals, rising and retiring. Finally, the procedure of rewarding good patients with the privilege of being allowed out, and punishing disobedience with the withdrawal of this privilege, was also employed in retreats.

CONCLUSION AND SOME IMPLICATIONS OF THIS ANALYSIS FOR EVALUATION OF THE INEBRIATE REFORMATORY EXPERIMENT

The inebriety reformers, amongst whom medical professionals were particularly prominent, initiated a new policy towards habitual drunkards. They sought to establish a new network of institutions to which habitual drunkards could be sent for reformatory treatment. And they sought legal powers to confine habitual drunkards in these institutions for a period long enough to effect a cure.

Despite considerable resistance to this new policy, and despite the reluctance of the authorities to invest in the proposed institutions, the inebriety reformers had some temporary success in bringing about a policy change. By 1908 there were 11 inebriate reformatories at work, along with approximately 20 inebriate retreats (see Kelynack 1904/5; 1908 Report). The reformers also obtained the legal power to confine habitual drunken offenders, and certain other offenders who were deemed to be inebriates, in reformatories. However, they did not obtain the power to commit non-criminal inebriates to these institutions, although they did obtain the power to detain those who committed themselves.[14] During World War I, however, the inebriate reformatory experiment collapsed – the institutions and the legal powers fell into disuse (see East 1949: chapter 3).

A few decades ago, the historian Roy MacLeod portrayed the inebriety reformers as fairly enlightened reformers who, in their attempts to ameliorate the lives of a previously neglected group of ill people, had to struggle against 'public apathy, parliamentary ignorance, and resistance from self-appointed advocates of "individual liberty"' (MacLeod 1967: 215). No doubt, 'critical' criminologists and socio-legal theorists would view them rather differently – as instruments of the state who employed the ideology and techniques of medical treatment to extend and strengthen expert and official control over a group of social deviants. It is highly unlikely that my account of what the reformers actually meant by 'treatment' will help to resolve this conflict – it probably provides ammunition for both sides. However, my analysis does have implications for those who might wish to undertake a more detailed assessment of the inebriate reformatory experiment. To conclude, I will briefly indicate *some* of these implications.

If we accept, for the sake of analysis, that there was a genuine problem of inebriety in late Victorian Britain, we can begin to assess the inebriety reformers by asking whether their proposed solution to this problem could have worked if properly implemented and, if so, whether its economic and social costs were acceptable. However, in order to address these questions we need to understand the nature of the inebriety reformers' proposed solution. The point I have made in this chapter is that their proposed solution has been misunderstood in fundamental ways.

It has been assumed that the reformers proposed giving confirmed inebriates medical-somatic treatment in an attempt to cure them of their insatiable craving for alcohol. If this assumption were correct, the debate would be much simplified. Those who are professionally concerned today with the prevention and management of alcoholic addiction have themselves developed cogent criticisms of the assumption that the problem can be effectively handled through medical-somatic treatment. For instance, as we saw in the introduction to this case study, Kendell (1979) expresses strong doubts about the efficacy of medical treatment and argues that the concentration of resources upon medical treatment has hampered the development of political and educational policies which, while more difficult to implement, would be much more effective as solutions. It would be fairly simple to extend these criticisms to the inebriate reformatory experiment. However, as I have shown, the inebriety reformers did not propose to solve the problem by medical-somatic treatment. Rather they proposed to solve it

---

14 For details of these legislative developments see MacLeod (1967), Radzinowicz and Hood (1990: chapter 9) and Harding and Wilkin (1988).

through a range of methods which were informed by the notion of moral treatment. These methods avoid many of the problems of medical-somatic treatment, but they were problematic in other ways.

One of the most important limitations of medical-somatic treatment would be that it addresses the biological and psychological factors which contribute to problem behaviour, which are usually of minor significance, and fails to address the environmental factors, which are usually of major significance. Moral treatment, as proposed by the inebriety reformers, did not suffer from this limitation. Although the inebriety reformers often proclaimed a disease concept of inebriety, their treatment proposals were actually informed, as I have shown, by the assumption that 'environment' was a major cause of inebriety and that environmental change could reform the inebriate. However, unable to change the environment, their solution was to isolate inebriates from their familiar environment and to place them in a better one.

One major problem with this solution is that it was based upon a very crude and naive understanding of the relationship between individuals and their environment. The reformers seemed to assume that removing individuals from the corrupting influences of an immoral environment could stop them from being influenced by that environment. This ignores the depth and extent to which individual personality and character is shaped by early social learning. Another problem with the reformers' scheme, which I have already discussed, is that it failed to deal with the problem of what to do with inebriates once their treatment had finished. As they realised, any positive effects of reformatory treatment would soon be reversed if inebriates returned to their old environment, yet they offered no alternative. One reason for this was that the alternative of much longer-term social support, the provision of housing and employment in a new area, and so on, would not have been economically feasible. In a period when many of the industrious and honest poor lacked decent housing and jobs, it would have been unthinkable to provide these for habitual drunken offenders.

A further problem with the reformers' scheme was its economic and social costs. One of the main reasons for the eventual collapse of the scheme was a lack of financial support for inebriate institutions. The reformers' claims that the institutions would soon be self-financed, through the labour of their inmates, clearly failed to convince the authorities. Local authorities simply were not willing to devote considerable resources to the treatment of inebriates, whom they probably regarded as unworthy. The other main option for the reformers was having wings of prisons converted into inebriate reformatories, which would hence be funded by central government. The consequence of this option, however, was that reformatories came to be seen as a part of the prison system and as purely punitive institutions.

The main social costs were those that attach to confinement generally: inebriates were deprived of their liberty for considerable periods and their dependants were deprived of whatever support they received, however meagre this might be. The reformers' vision of inebriates earning enough to support their dependants whilst in confinement was a pipe-dream.

These are just some issues which would need much deeper discussion in a proper assessment of the inebriate reformatory experiment. I have raised these issues in order to demonstrate that criticisms of the medical model would be less than helpful for undertaking the complex task of evaluating the inebriate reformatory experiment. The debate about the medical model diverts attention away from the real problems – as well as the advantages – of the reformers' proposed solution to the problem of inebriety.

CHAPTER 4

TREATING THE VAGRANT ALCOHOLIC OFFENDER, 1960s AND 1970s

INTRODUCTION

The inebriate laws and institutions, discussed in chapters 2 and 3, fell into disuse after World War I. Between the 1920s and 1950s, penal policy makers and professionals showed little concern with inebriates.[1] During the 1960s and 1970s, however, habitual drunken offenders again became the focus of official and professional concern. Those treatment professionals who 'rediscovered' the problem of habitual drunkards in the 1960s had much in common with their forerunners, the inebriety reformers. They were highly critical of the existing methods of dealing with habitual drunken offenders. They proposed to replace the existing penal response to the problem with therapeutic interventions and to divert habitual drunkards from the criminal justice system to a treatment system. And they tended to support these proposals with an argument about the true nature of the problem, ie that habitual drunkenness was not a crime but an illness.

In this chapter, through a close reading of the discourse of those who advocated and attempted to establish a system of treatment for habitual drunken offenders in the 1960s and 1970s, I examine the nature of the proposed treatment programme. I look at its objectives and methods and at the concerns and ideas which informed it. I focus, in particular, on the extent and ways in which the proposed treatment system differed from the existing system of penal interventions into the lives of habitual drunken offenders. I argue that we cannot understand what was distinctive about the proposed treatment system for habitual drunken offenders by looking at the medical model of alcoholism. Not only was the treatment system not informed by the medical model of alcoholism, it was based upon a rejection of many of the assumptions of the medical model. To indicate what is at stake in this argument, it is necessary to start with a brief account of the medical model of alcoholism and of the uses to which it has been put.

---

1   This dramatic decline in concern with a group that had been regarded as a major social problem for about half a century seems to have been due, in part, to a substantial decrease in both the numbers of convictions for drunkenness offences and the numbers committed to prisons for these offences. The 1971 Home Office Working Party on Habitual Drunken Offenders reported that convictions of drunkenness declined dramatically during World War I, from 189,000 in 1913 to 29,000 in 1918. More importantly, although they rose again to 96,000 in 1920, they fell again to 30,000 in 1932 (1971 Report: app D, para 19). A Royal Commission Report of 1932 found 'excessive drinking ... greatly, even spectacularly, diminished' (*ibid*: para 20). Convictions went up to 53,000 in 1939, but declined during World War II to 20,000 in 1946. However, after World War II, the number of convictions started to rise to 48,000 in 1950 and 79,000 in 1968 (*ibid*: para 21).

The medical model of alcoholism

Since the 1940s, certain doctors and medical researchers, along with others concerned with problem drinking, have undertaken a massive campaign to persuade fellow medical professionals, politicians, and the public that alcoholism is an illness which is susceptible to medical treatment (see Conrad and Schneider 1980: chapter 4). This campaign has been quite successful in changing the attitudes of medical professionals and the public about habitual drunkenness. It led, in the early 1950s, to 'alcoholism' being recognised as an illness by the World Health Organisation. It has also led to considerable resources being spent on medical research into the problem of alcoholism and its treatment. And perhaps most significantly, it has led to hospitals and other medical institutions establishing treatment programmes for alcoholics.

The key elements of the medical model of alcoholism, which informed and was used to promote these developments, can be summarised briefly as follows. Its focus is on people who seem to be unable spontaneously to give up drinking.[2] It views these as 'people with a disease that can be defined in medical terms and requires a proper regime of treatment' (Kessel and Walton 1965: 16). More specifically, the inability to give up drinking spontaneously is attributed to biological or psychological disorder. In some versions, this disorder is regarded as inborn, and perhaps hereditary. In other versions, it is regarded as acquired through excessive drinking over long periods.

Those who subscribe to such a model of alcoholism often object, in principle, to the criminal prosecution and punishment of alcoholics on charges of public drunkenness. The logic of this objection is that 'alcoholism is a disease ... and it is immoral to punish people because they are sick' (Goff 1969: 95).[3] In the United States the medical model has been used – with some success during the 1960s – to challenge the constitutionality of public intoxication laws (*ibid*; see also Johnstone 1991: 41–2).

Those who subscribe to the medical model of alcoholism propose that treatment facilities should be available to those who suffer from the illness, and that general practitioners should be trained to recognise and understand the nature of the condition and should know about the treatment facilities which are available. Various methods of treatment are advocated, ranging from the purely physical to the purely psychological. At one end of this spectrum is the drug 'antabuse' which, when taken, changes the effect of

---

2　See the definition of an alcoholic in Kessel and Walton (1965: 16–17). They divide people into teetotallers, social drinkers, excessive drinkers and alcoholics.

3　Goff was quoting or paraphrasing Justice Fortas of the United States Supreme Court.

drinking alcohol from pleasurable to unpleasurable sensations.[4] At the other end, are aversion treatments (see Kessel and Walton 1965: 144–5)[5] and hypnosis (*ibid*: 145–6). The nature of these treatments vary considerably, but they are all targeted at the individual alcoholic.[6]

The treatment system for habitual drunken offenders

In what follows I try to show that it would be a mistake to assume that the nature of the proposed treatment system for habitual drunken offenders can be inferred from the medical model of alcoholism. If we examine the discourse of treatment professionals on habitual drunken offenders we find that their conception of alcoholism was quite different than that found in the medical model and that what they meant by treatment was something quite different from the physical and psychological treatments which the medical profession provides. I discuss five main differences:

1   The main concern of those who promoted the treatment programme was not with all of those who seemed to be unable to give up drinking. Rather, it was with a much smaller group of people: vagrant or 'skid row' alcoholics.

2   What rendered these people ill, in the eyes of treatment professionals, was not their dependence on alcohol as such, but rather their damaged personalities and isolation from society. Proponents of treatment did not use the concept of alcoholism to refer to an illness which rendered the person unable to resist the desire for alcohol. Rather, they used the concept to refer to a condition which rendered those afflicted unable to form

---

4   The nature of this treatment is described by Kessel and Walton as follows: 'Antabuse is the well-known trade-name for the chemical compound disulfiram. It comes in tablet form. By itself it produces no effects. However, it interferes with the way the body deals with alcohol. When alcohol is metabolised in the body it is oxidised to carbon dioxide and water. At an intermediate stage in this chemical process a toxic substance, acetaldehyde, is formed but it is so rapidly broken down that no ill effects are felt. When a person drinks on top of antabuse, this process is blocked, so that the acetaldehyde from alcohol is only slowly broken down and its level in the blood rises. Accumulating acetaldehyde brings about a sequence of physical sensations which each patient learns for himself ...The first symptom to occur in the antabuse-alcohol reaction is flushing and warmth of the face. Then a pounding is felt at the temples as the heart beat accelerates. A headache commonly develops. Another common effect is a catch in the breath, as if there is some sort of obstruction in the windpipe; there may be a coughing or a choking sensation ...' (Kessell and Walton 1965: 130–31).

5   Although these usually work by producing an unpleasant sensation when alcohol is drunk, they differ from antabuse in that with antabuse the unpleasant sensation is produced by chemical means whereas with aversion therapies it is produced by psychological means.

6   Before moving on we should note that, as we saw in the introduction to this case study, the medical model of alcoholism has been much criticised in recent decades. A great deal of this criticism has come from persons within the medical profession who themselves regard alcoholism as a pathology to be prevented by expert interventions, but who prefer a public health perspective to the medical model (see Bunton 1989: especially p 3).

satisfactory social attachments to others. Habitual drunkenness was significant only as an indication of a deeper lack of social attachment. It was regarded as an incidental symptom of a lack of socialisation.

3 The vagrant alcoholic's under-socialisation was usually attributed by proponents of treatment, not to inborn physical or psychological disorder, but to a lack of satisfactory adult models, problems in early learning and damaging experiences during the early formative years.

4 Proponents of treatment did not object in principle and totally to the criminalisation and punishment of habitual drunkards on the ground that, being ill, they were not morally responsible for their behaviour. Rather, their criticisms of existing penal responses to habitual drunkards were more pragmatic and limited. Proponents of treatment objected to existing penal procedures and methods on the ground that they impeded, rather than effected, the objective of rehabilitation or social re-entry of the habitual drunkard. This shortcoming was attributed, less to the punitive character of penal interventions, more to two quite specific problems: (a) penal interventions were sporadic rather than continuous and (b) the social relations in penal institutions were authoritarian. Similar criticisms were directed against the interventions of certain social agencies which sought to ameliorate the lives of habitual drunkards and were also directed, to some extent, against conventional medical interventions. Hence, what treatment professionals sought to establish was a system of intervention which was continuous and less 'directive'.

5 What treatment professionals sought in replace of existing penal methods was not hospital and conventional psychiatric treatment, but a coordinated network of 'treatment' facilities consisting of social support agencies and hostels run as 'therapeutic communities'. This treatment network was intended to provide a more continuous, but less authoritarian, style of social supervision than that provided by existing penal and social agencies. A central feature of the treatment system was that it would re-structure relations between helping professionals and their habitual drunken 'clients' – effecting a shift away from the authoritarianism of traditional penal and medical institutions towards a more democratic structure, in which habitual drunken offenders would participate as social equals in their treatment. The aims of this system were not confined to making habitual drunkards sober or enabling them to stop drinking spontaneously. Rather, they included making them more social and more responsible.

THE PROBLEM: VAGRANT ALCOHOLICS

In order to understand the nature of the treatment programme for habitual drunkards offenders, it is of crucial importance to realise that it was not designed for every person, nor even every offender, who happened to be dependent upon alcohol. Rather it was designed for 'vagrant alcoholics'. Unless this is understood, it is impossible to make sense of central features of the proposed treatment scheme, such as its emphasis upon hostels as the core of the network of treatment facilities or its emphasis upon the objective of social re-entry.

To a large extent, the movement to establish a system of treatment for habitual drunken offenders was initiated by voluntary organisations whose primary concern was with the problem of vagrants rather than with the problem of alcoholics. This statement must be qualified, however, by pointing out that by the 1960s, the problem of vagrancy had become intertwined, in the public mind, with the problem of alcoholism:

> In the 1950s the term uncontrollable alcoholism gained currency and replaced uncontrollable wanderlust and congenital laziness as the primary characteristic of the homeless man (H Bahr, quoted in Cook 1975).

One organisation that played a major role in the 're-discovery' of the problem of habitual drunkards was the Alcoholics Recovery Project (ARP). Despite its title, the primary concern of this organisation was with vagrants (Cook 1975: preface and chapter 2). In his book *Vagrant Alcoholics* (1975), Tim Cook[7] traces the origins of the ARP to concern among the residents of the south London borough of Southwark about the problems caused by 'down-and-outs' sleeping rough in the area. The initial concern was about the problems caused to the local residents (ie the settled residents) by the existence of vagrant alcoholics: 'A local newspaper described Southwark as "one of the worst hit boroughs by 'down-and-out' crude spirit drinkers"' (*ibid*: 7).

This focus on down-and-out vagrant alcoholics can also be seen in the *Report of the Home Office Working Party on Habitual Drunken Offenders, 1971* (hereinafter 'the 1971 Report'). The Working Party stated that, except in two areas of London, the public tended to be indifferent to the existence of habitual drunkards; although there were some complaints from residents of coastal towns (ie holiday resorts) that habitual drunkards, by their appearance alone, detract from the town (1971 Report: para 6.5). The two areas of London referred to were the boroughs of Southwark and Tower Hamlets. Residents of these boroughs saw habitual drunkards as a 'gross nuisance' (*ibid*: para 6.7). The Health Committee of Southwark Borough Council complained:

> These people ... urinate, defecate, and vomit wherever they may be, and their clothing is filthy. Public places, subways and highways are worse for their presence (1971 Report: para 6.7).

---

7   Cook was a major figure in the treatment movement. As well as campaigning for the establishment of treatment facilities, he himself started and became warden of Rathcoole House, a 'model' hostel for ex-alcoholic offenders.

It needs to made quite clear that this was not middle-class snobbery towards 'undesirable persons'. The 'conflict' was between two 'low status' groups: vagrant alcoholics and the residents of the some of the poorest areas of London. There were actually relatively few 'vagrant crude spirit drinkers' in London, but these tended to be concentrated in two relatively deprived areas, where 'public spaces and amenities are small and few in number' (*ibid*: 6.8–6.12). For the Home Office Working Party the most disquieting feature of the problem was:

> ... that local people should feel inhibited from making full use of public amenities in a part of London where objects of natural beauty and colour and recreational facilities are conspicuously lacking (*ibid*: 6.19).

Voluntary care organisations, which sought to ameliorate the lives of these vagrant alcoholics by providing basic shelter and sustenance were seen, by local residents, as exacerbating the problem by attracting habitual drunkards to the area. Local residents' groups began to advocate compulsory detention and treatment as the only solution to the problem (*ibid*: paras 6.8–6.12). In this context, the ARP and other local voluntary groups, such as the 'Action on Skid Row Group', began to plan a hostel for 'crude spirit drinkers' (Cook 1975: chapter 2).[8] That this hostel was designed for a group of down-and-out vagrants, who were defined as alcoholics only because this was a highly conspicuous feature of their behaviour (a paradigm case of labelling), can be seen in the following recollection from Cook:

> ... at no stage in the proceedings did anyone seem to wish to state who was in fact a 'crude spirit drinker' and what criteria were being used to define him. Local newspapers talked of 'methies', 'jake drinkers' and 'surgical spirit drinkers'; the London prisons reported on 'recurrent drunks'; research workers wrote about 'Skid Row alcoholics'. Yet, all were agreed that a hostel for 'crude spirit drinkers' was needed. One document neatly illustrates the confusion: 'the task of this hostel would be strictly defined as that of helping the chronic drunkenness offender – in other words, the vagrant surgical spirit drinker' (Cook 1975: 11).

Cook goes on to state:

> After some months the term 'vagrant alcoholic' gradually came to be accepted and by the time the hostel opened in May 1966 there seemed little dispute that, whatever the social manifestations, the down-and-out drunk was *in the majority of cases* an alcoholic too (Cook 1975: 12, emphasis added).

The un-social life of the habitual drunken offender

This development intersected with the development in penal policy whereby the Home Office became concerned 'to relieve prisons of people who did not

---

8   We should note that treatment *professionals* often played an important part in the running of these 'voluntary' groups.

really warrant the full rigours of imprisonment' (*ibid*: 10; 1971 Report: chapter 1). Drunkenness offenders clearly came within this category – and attempts were made to explore therapeutic alternatives to repeated imprisonment of habitual drunken offenders (*ibid*: 13).[9] This policy development led to a number of research projects exploring the characteristics and treatment needs of habitual drunken offenders (Cook et al 1969). This research revealed, *inter alia*, that those with the worst records were people who were 'cut off from society'. Many of them had no contact with family or friends. Few had regular employment. Habitual drunken offenders typically had few, if any, social affiliations:

> Forty per cent had not attended a cinema, dance, church, or other social function during the preceding five years. Less than ten per cent belonged to a club, union, or formal organisation (Gath 1969: 22).

Many of them had at some time slept in a reception centre (for single homeless people). A large number of them were 'homeless', ie they did not have their own accommodation such as a house, flat, or furnished room, and usually slept rough when they were not in prison.

IN WHAT SENSE WERE THESE PEOPLE REGARDED AS ILL?

Vagrant alcoholics were defined as 'ill' by treatment professionals. But, what rendered them ill was not their dependence upon alcohol, or at least not alcohol dependence in itself. Rather, what rendered them ill was their 'damaged personalities' that left them incapable of entering into and sustaining social contacts, unable to develop fundamental habits of sociality, and incapable of settling or holding a steady job. As Cook put it: 'we are dealing with a complex disorder of which alcohol is a conspicuous but at times minor component' (Cook 1969: 102).

The vagrant alcoholic's inability to hold down a job, form stable social relationships, or settle was often attributed, by the public and policy-makers, to his habitual drunkenness. According to this popular view, it was the alcoholic's dependence of drink which made him lose contact with his family and friends and which caused him to lose and be unable to find regular work.[10] The treatment professionals reversed this assumption, suggesting that *it was the vagrant alcoholic's under-socialisation which led him to become dependent on drink*. For treatment professionals, alcoholism was not the cause of the vagrant alcoholic's social incompetence, rather it was a symptom of it.

---

9   See Stonham (1969) for the official view of the problem – Lord Stonham was Minister of State, Home Office.

10   In the light of these frequent references to regular work it should be remembered that the period under discussion was one of relatively full employment, in which attributing an individual's unemployment to purely personal failings was not manifestly nonsensical, as arguably would be the case today.

Vagrant alcoholics, they suggested, turned to drink in order to find the comfort that they were unable to obtain in less damaging ways – and then became dependent on it:

> ... the pioneers have fought so hard to persuade the public that alcoholism is a disease that we may be in danger of confusing the disease with the symptom. Is not alcohol only too often the substitute-support, the substitute-security, the substitute-love, to which those deprived of the genuine article resort as the most easily available alternative? (Silkin 1969: xiv).

One crucial implication of this idea was that curing vagrant alcoholics of their illness – which many treatment professionals continued to refer to, confusingly, as 'alcoholism' – did not mean making them able to stop drinking spontaneously. Even if such an objective could be achieved through medical treatments such as antabuse, or through psychotherapy, aversion therapy or hypnotism, the vagrant alcoholic would still be ill, ie he would still have a damaged personality. A vagrant alcoholic who was cured of his addiction to alcohol would become a 'sober drunk' (Cook 1969: 103). Conversely, a vagrant alcoholic who managed to settle, obtain a steady job, stay out of prison, make some normal social contacts, join a club, and so on would be considered well on the road to recovery 'even if drinking bouts still occurred two or three times a year' (*ibid*: 102).

Alcoholism, understood as an inability spontaneously to give up drinking, was not regarded as the illness by treatment professionals. This was only a symptom of the real illness, which was the inability to form stable social relationships. But as a symptom of illness, habitual drunkenness was important. It could be a sign of a damaged personality. So, although the treatment professionals sought to shift the focus away from the drinking behaviour of vagrant alcoholics and towards their personality problems, in one respect they attributed an even greater significance to drinking behaviour than did proponents of the medical model of alcoholism. For the treatment professionals, habitual drunkenness was indicative of deeper personality problems. Habitual drunkards were no longer regarded as persons with a mere drinking problem. Rather, they were regarded as damaged personalities.

Skid Row as a state of mind

> Of course not all habitual drunkards belong to Skid Row, but it is significant that many of them say that Skid Row is as much in the mind as it is a place (Cook 1969: 101).

The conception of 'alcoholism' discussed above might be illustrated further by examining the use which researchers into the problem of vagrant alcoholics made of the concept of 'Skid Row'. Habitual drunken offenders were often described, by researchers and treatment professionals, as 'Skid Row alcoholics'. This concept originated in the United States and referred to a *geographical* area:

Skid Row was originally an American term which described a distinct geographical area with its flop-houses, pawnshops, cheap restaurants, taverns and missions (Cook 1975: 32).[11]

The term 'Skid Row alcoholic' referred to the drunkards who lived and slept rough in these areas. Through this term, it became easy to imagine the Skid Row alcoholic as cut off from the rest of society. It also made it possible to imagine solving the problem by removing drunkards from Skid Row and relocating them in more normal areas.[12]

In Britain, there were no distinct geographical areas that would qualify for the label 'Skid Row'. Nevertheless, researchers suggested that Skid Row existed in Britain, but as a state of mind rather than a real place (*ibid*; Edwards et al 1966). The Skid Row alcoholic was psychologically in Skid Row:

> In so far as it is appropriate to talk of a Skid Row in England, it is possibly true to say that the phrase represents an attitude of mind, an outlook on life, a resignation to the worst society can do, a lack of belief in self and a feeling of rootlessness. It is not getting the man off Skid Row that it is the problem, but getting Skid Row out of the man. Skid Row is 'as much a state of mind as it is a place' ... This implies considering Skid Row as perhaps some kind of continuous psychological territory or as an institution without walls (Cook 1975: 32).

BECOMING A VAGRANT ALCOHOLIC

> We must examine the nature of alcoholism even more closely, in a social and cultural setting and not just a medical one (Cook 1969: 107).

The origins of the Skid Row state of mind were usually located, not in biology or inborn psychological disorder, but in 'damaging experiences during the early formative years' (Cook 1969: 101). At birth, it was suggested, most habitual drunken offenders were physically and psychologically normal. It was as a result of harmful experiences during their early years that they began to develop emotional problems. These emotional problems made it difficult for them to relate normally to others, which led to them suffering further damaging experiences, which led to them becoming even more damaged emotionally, and so on in a vicious spiral. Damaging experiences and the resultant personality problems re-enforced each other so that, by adulthood, the person had become wholly incapable of forming or sustaining normal social relationships. If we look in a little more detail at this social-psychological explanation of the habitual drunkard we will see that it would be an overstatement to suggest that treatment professionals were unaware of the social dimensions of the problem.

---

11 For a more detailed account of the origins and evolution of the term 'Skid Row' see Light (1986). On perceptions of Skid Row in the United States see Wiseman (1970: chapter 1).

12 Of course, some imagined they could solve the problem by demolishing Skid Row.

Treatment professionals drew their image of the habitual drunkard from the work of sociological and psychological researchers who undertook investigations into the backgrounds of selected groups of habitual drunkards, such as people appearing in court on drunkenness charges, prisoners with a record of drunkenness convictions, and alcoholic patrons at a soup kitchen (see 1971 Report: chapter 5; Cook *et al* 1969: part A). This research showed that habitual drunken offenders were usually from 'lower class' families and were often born into 'abject poverty' (1971 Report: para 5.13 and app H; Hamilton *et al* 1978: chapter 2).[13] It also showed that many of them had a drunken and often violent father and that, in their early life, they were surrounded with disorder and disturbance (1971 Report: app K). Their parents were often separated, or there were frequent parental rows. Typically, there was 'a history of disturbed parent–child relationships, of broken homes, and of poor home backgrounds' (Glatt 1964; see also 1971 Report: para 5.14 and app K). These damaging experiences led to emotional and behavioural problems. These problems affected the (future) habitual drunkard's education. Habitual drunkards – who usually received minimum schooling in the poorest schools – presented behavioural and disciplinary problems at school. These interfered with their education and got them into trouble with 'authority'. This, in turn, compounded their emotional problems (see Glatt 1964: 282; 1971 Report para's. 5.13, 18.2, app H and K). By the time they were in their mid-teens, most habitual drunkards were involved in delinquencies including burglary and prostitution (1971 report: app K). It was around this time that most started to drink excessively (*ibid*). Heavy drinking, it was stressed, formed part of a general pattern of misbehaviour and was a reaction to a long history of emotional, behavioural and social problems. It was not the cause of these problems.

In adulthood, the habitual drunkard found it difficult to obtain and hold steady employment and had a tendency to drift (1971 report: *passim*; Gath 1969; Cook 1975: para 7.38). Most remained single and any marriages that were entered into were usually unsettled and short-lived (Hamilton *et al* 1978: chapter 11). More generally, the habitual drunkard began to avoid making contact with other people or entering into personal relationships. Most began to lose what contact they did have with their families. With their worsening social isolation, habitual drunkards became increasingly apathetic and irresponsible and began to develop feelings of guilt, anxiety, inadequacy and rejection (Glatt 1964: 276; Hamilton *et al* 1978: chapter 7; 1971 Report: *passim*; d'Orban 1969). In this condition, the habitual drunkard became increasingly dependent upon drink and upon the fleeting, non-committed company of fellow inhabitants of Skid Row.

---

13 Here, it would be possible to list numerous sources for each point, but I will confine myself to just one or two references.

CRITICISMS OF THE PENAL REVOLVING DOOR

Proponents of treatment were highly critical of the existing penal response to habitual drunken offenders. It is important to realise, however, that their criticisms were based on pragmatic rather than moral considerations. Their main point was *not* that it was wrong to punish habitual drunkards (because they were not responsible for their behaviour). Rather, it was that the existing system of criminalisation and punishment was *ineffective* as means of achieving the objective of rehabilitation or re-socialisation of habitual drunken offenders. The following quotations, from Lord Stonham,[14] typify the terms in which the existing penal response was criticised:

> Everyone agrees that the present system of dealing with these unfortunate people by arrest, prosecution, and short sentences of imprisonment, is clumsy, wasteful, and largely ineffectual, both as a means of rehabilitating the individual and as a remedy for society (Stonham 1969: 3).

> The work of drying out and cleaning up these men, well knowing that they will soon be back [in prison], is a stupid waste of our badly-strained resources, particularly at prisons like Pentonville, where drunks account for one in six of all admissions. Neither the excellent clinic there nor the fresh air we provide at Spring Hill open prison is a substitute for the continuous support these people need if they are to be, at least partially, restored to useful citizenship. Prison is not the place (Lord Stonham, quoted in 1971 Report: chapter 3).

The metaphor of a revolving door was used to highlight the ineffectiveness of the existing penal approach to the problem of habitual drunkards (see Pittman and Gordon 1958). Vagrant alcoholics frequently entered the penal revolving door by being arrested, charged and – almost as a matter of routine – convicted. They were then ordered to pay a small fine or to serve a short prison sentence. In either event, they were soon back on Skid Row, ie they were returned to exactly the same situation as they were in before they entered the revolving door. Their short journey through the penal system had changed nothing. It was therefore not long before the next arrest re-started the cycle (1971 Report: para 7.8).

Importantly, the criticisms of the penal approach were not directed at punishment in general. Rather, proponents of treatment identified two quite specific features of the existing penal approach which, in their view, impeded rather than advanced the goal of socialising the vagrant alcoholic. First, they argued that penal interventions were too short and sporadic for rehabilitation purposes. The penal system undertook intensive interventions into the lives of habitual drunkards, but only at sporadic intervals and only for very short periods – too short for the purpose of treatment:

---

14   Minister of the State, Home Office in 1968. The quotation comes from his introductory address to an international symposium on the drunkenness offence held at the Institute of Psychiatry, London, 1968. The proceedings were published as (Cook *et al* 1969).

The shortness of their sentences generally makes it impracticable for the prison service to undertake psychiatric treatment or even to attempt to inspire a wish to have treatment on release, or to make after-care arrangements to counter-act the lack of social support they will, in the ordinary course, experience on discharge (1971 Report: para 7.13).

Also, as the above quotation makes clear, once they were discharged, habitual drunkards were usually neglected. Under the penal approach, the habitual drunkard's life consisted of long periods during which nothing was done to or for them, interrupted by short periods during which they were subject to arrest, prosecution and (often) imprisonment.

Proponents of treatment acknowledged that some habitual drunkards were subject to probation orders, and hence to a more long-term form of penal supervision (*ibid*: para 7.40–7.47). However, the supervision of probation officers was considered too weak to be effective. In practice, it was argued, the probation system had very little influence over habitual drunkards. Although probation officers had once been much involved in the supervision of habitual drunkards, they had become less inclined to work with habitual drunken offenders as other, perhaps more rewarding work became available (such as matrimonial work, after-care of ordinary prisoners and the preparation of social inquiry reports). Even when probation officers were inclined to work with habitual drunken offenders, their capacity to keep track of and to influence persons who usually had no fixed abode, and who often drifted from place to place, was very limited.

The second criticism was aimed, not at the penal approach in general, but at the prison specifically. It was argued that the structure of social relations in the prison hindered rather than furthered the objective of rehabilitating habitual drunken offenders. Prisons, it was pointed out, had highly authoritarian structures. In prison, every aspect of the habitual drunkard's daily life was regulated by detailed and rigidly enforced rules. Whilst many ordinary offenders experienced such an authoritarian structure as burdensome, the habitual drunken offender, it was argued, actually found it quite agreeable. In the prison, habitual drunkards did not have to assume any personal responsibility. They could avoid taking control of their own lives. They could allow others to make even the most basic decisions for him. And, their most basic needs for food and shelter were met by others.[15]

This problem was compounded, it was argued, by the fact that after spending a few weeks in this highly structured, authoritarian regime, in which their lives were totally controlled by others, habitual drunkards were then released to the total 'freedom' of the community, in which they were subject only to very loose forms of control. From a situation where no personal responsibility was required, habitual drunkards were returned

15 1971 report: chapter 10. Similar criticisms were made of 'staff-directed' hostels for homeless alcoholics; the paternalism of these hostels was seen as an obstacle to recovery.

suddenly to a situation which demanded total personal responsibility. This was a situation for which habitual drunkards were unprepared. It was not surprising, then, that they frequently ended-up back in prison within a short time of their release. Indeed, some proponents of treatment argued that habitual drunkards often deliberately got themselves arrested so that they could return to prison. There was a popular theory, born out by ethnographic studies of Skid Row alcoholics, that habitual drunkards saw a prison sentence, especially during winter, as a means of obtaining a few weeks shelter without which they could not survive (see Archard 1979). What was being argued by proponents of treatment was that prison also met the *emotional* needs of habitual drunkards; ie that the prison functioned as an emotional, as well as a physical, shelter. As one researcher put it, referring to habitual drunkenness offenders in Holloway prison:

> ... their frequent return to prison suggests that they have become quite dependent on the institution. They gain a sense of security and emotional support in the firmly structured and familiar community of Holloway. Their institutionalisation in prison is underlined by their uneasiness about changes in prison routine ... Their relationship with the staff and with each other is emotionally undemanding. Prison life is able to meet their physical and emotional needs better than any available alternative (d'Orban 1969: 59–60).

According to proponents of treatment, habitual drunkards required something other than occasional, short periods of 'secure' imprisonment, followed by a sudden transition to the insecurity and temptations of freedom (1971 Report: para 7.11). They required a more continuous, long-term, system of supervision and a different style of supervision from that found in prisons. This alternative response was described as 'treatment'. I will now look at the nature of the proposed treatment system in little detail. It should become quite clear that, in this context, the term 'treatment' was used to refer to something quite different from medical treatment.

THE REHABILITATION HOSTEL

The creation of rehabilitation hostels for habitual drunken offenders was regarded as a first and crucial step in the establishment of a treatment system. This emphasis on hostels was due, in part, to a totally pragmatic concern:

> It is worth asking ... why a hostel was established as opposed to some other form of 'treatment'. Other methods of treatment were in fact not debated by the working party. The crucial element of homelessness led to the position that, unless a decent roof was provided, talk of recovery or sobriety held little or no meaning for the habitual drunkard (Cook 1975: 14–15).

However, the hostel was to be much more than a 'decent roof'. It was to be a method of treatment: an environment in which vagrant alcoholics could learn to be social. The hostel was to be organised as a 'therapeutic community', ie a problem-solving community in which – as against the hierarchical structure typical of prisons and other 'shelters' – there would be a horizontal association of mutually responsible human beings (see Rotman 1990: 66). In the hostel, a changed pattern of communication would allow habitual drunkards to develop a sense of mature responsibility.

The hostel compared with the prison and 'liberty'

The hostel was conceived as an institution that would have a social structure half-way between the restricted and highly authoritarian structure of control found in prisons, and the permissive, loosely regulated structure of normal social living. Indeed, the American term for the rehabilitation hostel was 'the half-way house' (Rubington 1967), a term which was gaining some popularity in Britain.

Hostels would differ from prisons in a number of ways:[16] they would be much smaller than prisons; unlike prisons they would always be located in the community in which the 'client' ordinarily lives; their internal regimes would be more permissive than those of prisons; and, unlike the prison inmate, the resident of a hostel would be allowed, or rather encouraged, to leave the hostel and to mingle and interact with ordinary people. On the other hand, whilst residing in a hostel, the habitual drunkard's behaviour would be subject to detailed observation and scrutiny. The residents of a hostel could not, as they might do in a prison, become 'invisible' by keeping to themselves and staying out of trouble. The habitual drunkard's movements and activities would be much less restricted than in prison discipline. But, these movements and activities would be observed and examined much more closely.

Whilst life in the hostel would be quite different from life in the prison, it would also be quite different from total independence and 'liberty', with which the habitual drunkard could not cope. The habitual drunkard would be sheltered from the full pressures of independence by the supportive environment of the hostel. The resident of a hostel would receive a variety of 'services' such as personal counselling, education, training, advice and assistance in finding employment and housing, and crisis intervention. Through this, the habitual drunkard could gradually acquire the social and practical skills necessary in order to function independently in the community and to adjust to normal community life (Johnstone 1991: 38; Miller 1975: 1–2).

Admission and duration of stay

In the scheme proposed by treatment professionals, habitual drunkards

---

16 On the following see Johnstone (1991: 37–8), in which I discuss the place of hostels in the wider scheme of community treatment for offenders.

would be able to be admitted to hostels in two ways. First, those who had just completed a prison sentence could enter a hostel, rather than return directly to the 'freedom and temptation of the community'. The return from the almost total control of the prison to the almost total permissiveness of normal social life could then be made gradual rather than sharp. Secondly, habitual drunkards who were not in prison could enter the hostel by being referred to it by other 'treatment agencies', such as reception centres or hospitals.[17] Admission to the hostel was to be, in all cases, voluntary, and hostels were to be non-custodial. It was acknowledged that offenders might be pressured into entering a hostel by being offered probation instead of a custodial sentence on the condition that they underwent hostel treatment. But, for reasons which will become clear, such a path into the hostel was not favoured because it was felt that treatment was incompatible with any degree of coercion. The duration of the habitual drunkard's stay in the hostel was not to be determined in advance. Rather, the habitual drunkard was to be allowed and encouraged to remain a resident of the hostel until the objectives of treatment had been achieved.

The goals of hostel treatment

The attainment of sobriety was just one, and not necessarily the most important, objective of hostel treatment. As Cook put it: 'Something more than sobriety is needed' (Cook 1969: 102):

> ... let us remember that whilst sobriety is to be valued at all times, nonetheless we must not be content to produce 'sober drunks'. A man may well need a more demanding criterion of success, paradoxical though it may seem, than just staying sober (Cook 1969: 103).

The other, and more important, objectives of hostel treatment comprised helping the habitual drunkard 'to achieve social rehabilitation, including steady employment, reintegration into the community, and, if appropriate, reconciliation with the family' (Ingram-Smith 1969: 162). The ideal was that the habitual drunkard would reach a level of competence at which he could function normally without expert, professional support and supervision (1971 Report: chapter 10). However, it was acknowledged that with many habitual drunkards, this was an unrealistic goal. Some habitual drunkards would require life long support. For these, adjusting to life in a hostel could be an end in itself. Some proponents of treatment suggested that, in so far as living in a hostel was the closest some habitual drunkards would ever get to normal domestic living, it was desirable that they should stay in a hostel as long-term residents rather than return to Skid Row (Cook 1971: 236).

---

17 I will discuss the other parts of the proposed 'network of treatment facilities' in the next section of this chapter.

Treatment methods rejected as inappropriate

Given the nature of the goals of treatment, it is not surprising to find that medical-somatic treatment was regarded as of very limited value. As we saw earlier, drugs for the treatment of alcohol dependency were available. However, even if these could help habitual drunkards to achieve 'sobriety', this was not the sole nor even the main goal of treatment. Moreover, some treatment professionals suggested that these drugs often failed to achieve the limited effect of assisting the alcoholic to become 'sober':

> Most residents had used Antabuse and Abstem in the past, without success; the majority of them had little confidence that these drugs could keep them sober, and had often drunk whilst taking them (Pollak 1969: 111).

Most proponents of treatment also regarded conventional methods of psychiatric treatment as being of little value for the task of socialising the habitual drunkard. Conventional in-patient treatment was rejected on the ground that institutional forms of treatment could make no contribution to the objective of instilling the social skills required for a fully independent life in the community. Hospital treatment shared some of the defects of imprisonment; it sheltered the Skid Row alcoholic from the pressures of independent life instead of teaching them how to cope with such pressures:

> Nor is it likely that conventional hospital treatment on a larger scale would be effective. At the end of the period of in-patient treatment, the man has to return to a society in which manifestly he lacks the social skills to survive, having lost or never possessed such skills (Gath 1969: 25).

> Conventional psychiatric therapies, such as one-to-one psychotherapy and psychoanalytic group psychotherapy, were also rejected as being of little value by proponents of hostel treatment (Cook 1975: 20).

Treatment methods advocated

The objective of getting alcoholics off Skid Row and into normal society was to be achieved by developing a unique 'social structure' within the hostel, a regime quite different to that found in prisons and other institutions occupied by habitual drunkards. As the Home Office Working Party on Habitual Drunken Offenders put it, the 'social structure probably holds the key to the success or failure of a hostel' (quoted in Cook 1975: at p 26).

One of the key distinctive features of the social structure of the hostel was its emphasis upon the *participation* of the residents in its day to day running. The hostel was to be run as a participatory democracy, subject to obvious limitations such as the power of the staff to set limits, veto decisions, and so on. In contrast to both the hierarchical, disciplinary regimes of prisons and the paternalistic, staff-directed regimes of 'lodging houses' in which vagrant alcoholics occasionally stayed, the hostel would be run by the residents, in cooperation with the staff. Residents would participate in all aspects of hostel life, from carrying out mundane house-keeping tasks such as keeping the place clean and paying bills, to making major policy decisions such as selection of potential residents (Cook 1975: 23):

> We felt it was important to involve the residents more and more in policy decisions, both to relieve the strain on the staff and, above all, to make the man's stay at Rathcoole House more positive and demanding (Cook 1971: 230).[18]

Treatment professionals thought that it was crucial to get the right mix between staff and resident direction. Too much staff direction created a paternalistic structure that prevented habitual drunkards from acquiring confidence and a sense of responsibility. Too little staff direction, on the other hand, would lead to no therapy taking place:

> It is evident that neither an under- nor an over-supportive or directive approach can be wholly satisfactory ... and that the group approach is more likely to foster the self-confidence that a man needs if he is to function independently (1971 Report: para 11.26).

A second key feature of the hostel's social structure was its balance between permissiveness and control. In contrast to prisons and lodging houses, formal rules were avoided as far as possible. The one fundamental rule in established hostels was the no-drinking rule. This rule and its sanction, ie expulsion from the hostel, was decided upon the by residents themselves.[19] Apart from the no-drinking rule, formal rules were regarded as an impediment to rehabilitation because they demanded nothing of the resident other than passive obedience: 'staff direction which is expressed in terms of a list of rules does not ... seem to be as efficacious as an approach which demands more from the residents' (1971 Report: para: 11.27). The hostel regimes required self-motivation and willed commitment, not just avoidance of sanctions, again simulating normal social life and its looser controls. Moreover, it was argued, the imposition of formal regulations by staff 'produces in some residents resentment against rules which in a freer setting would be accepted in a more positive fashion' (*ibid*: chapter 8).

This, however, did not imply total permissiveness. Permissive regimes, which had no rules at all and so made no demands upon the habitual drunkard, were viewed with disfavour. 'Permissive shelters', run by voluntary organisations, in which drinking was allowed, were criticised by treatment professionals on the ground that they colluded 'with the men's idea of themselves as "hopeless drunks"' (1971 Report: chapter 12). By refusing to set expectations for the habitual drunkard, one was confirming their self-

---

18 Rathcoole House, established in May 1966, was the first of a number of experimental hostels to be established. For accounts of its regime, by professionals involved in establishing and running it, see Pollak (1969), Cook (1971) and Cook (1975: 15–28). Hostels for habitual drunkards are described and discussed in the 1971 Report, chapters 10 and 11.

19 The reasons for the adoption of this rule are explained by Cook (1971) and (1975: 17–20).

image, which was characterised by Cook as: 'I'm just an alcoholic dosser so don't ask anything of me' (Cook 1975: 19). So, according to proponents of treatment, some regulation was required, but this had to take a form other than the imposition of formal rules 'from above'. A more informal code of conduct, one which required active involvement rather than docile obedience, was preferred. And, in order for it to be effective, the residents would have to play a major part in the creation of the code.

These features of the social structure of the hostel can be illustrated further by looking at the concept of the 'culture carrier'. These were residents who were settled for a considerable period. Their task was to inform new residents of the code and, more generally, to ensure continuity of the culture and ethic of the house. These culture carriers were important for a number of reasons. First, they were symbols of successful self-help; they were tangible proof that recovery through personal effort was possible (Cook 1975: 102). Secondly, since culture carriers were not external figures of authority, but fellow habitual drunkards, they helped reduce the 'them and us' division which was a characteristic feature of other institutions such as prisons and shelters. The hostel code was more likely to be taken seriously when it was clear that it was created by the residents, for themselves, rather than created by 'authority' and imposed upon them: 'Too often men can reject what staff say about the House but they are much less easily able to do this with fellow alcoholics' (Cook 1971: 231).

Another feature of the social structure of the hostel was its emphasis on creating a group spirit. Some ways in which this was achieved were through weekly group meetings and the establishment of an Alcoholics Anonymous (AA) group in the hostel. Officially, the AA meeting was a forum in which residents could gain insight into their drinking problem. But, for proponents of hostel treatment it was also useful as a way of promoting a sense of solidarity. It was a setting in which the habitual drunkard could learn to interact socially with other people. And, crucially, this social interaction was based on the new rehabilitative culture, not on the old Skid Row culture:

> Early in 1968 the Rathcoole AA group began meeting on Monday evenings. Its effect on the House was remarkable. Talk about drinking became positive instead of humourous nostalgia about bomb-site adventures ... above all it increased beyond measure the group spirit and wish to be involved in the House (Cook 1971: 230).

By residing in a hostel for a period of time, the habitual drunkard could be gradually integrated into the normal community. The emphasis on democratic participation would enable the habitual drunkard to learn how to become an active and responsible citizen. The rejection of 'external control', through formal rules governing every aspect of the habitual drunkard's daily routine, in favour of a looser system of control, would enable habitual drunkards to develop a capacity to control their own behaviour. And the emphasis on solidarity amongst the residents would ease the habitual drunkard into normal habits of sociality. Eventually, it was hoped, the habitual drunkard would be confident enough to dispense with the support offered by the hostel and to re-enter normal society as an independent, active, social and useful citizen. However, for treatment professionals, the move from the hostel to the normal community, even though more gradual than the sudden move from imprisonment to the normal community, was still too sharp. A move from the relatively sheltered environment of the hostel, to the 'freedom and temptations of the community' could be too much for many habitual drunkards, who might then revert to Skid Row. Treatment professionals therefore advocated, in addition to the hostel, a network of treatment facilities in the community, which would provide social support for the recovering Skid Row alcoholic.

A COORDINATED TREATMENT SERVICE

The hostel was the central institution in the proposed network of treatment facilities for habitual drunken offenders. But, according to proponents of treatment, its successful operation depended upon it being part of a broader spectrum of treatment services. Treatment, it was argued, could not take place within a single institution. Rather it required the establishment of a 'coordinated treatment service' for habitual drunkards. In this section, I will describe some aspects of the proposed 'treatment continuum', which consisted of new services and a new role for 'existing services'.

New services

Along with hostels, the treatment system for habitual drunkards was to include detoxification units. These were places to which the habitual drunkard could be taken if arrested, instead of being put through the penal revolving door (1971 report: chapter 15; Cook 1975: chapter 6; Hamilton *et al* 1978). Detoxification units were to be established, preferably, in psychiatric hospitals. They would undertake functions which were currently performed in police stations and prisons – such as 'drying out' the habitual drunkard under medical supervision and cleaning him up – but without resort to criminal procedures. They would also attempt to educate habitual drunkards about alcoholism, help them to find accommodation, and try to motivate them to enter the treatment system. One basic difference between this approach and the existing penal approach to the problem was that whereas the penal system had no official interest in habitual drunken offenders once they had paid their fine or served their prison sentence, the detoxification unit would attempt to direct habitual drunkards into a treatment system. Whilst the penal system returned habitual drunken offenders to Skid Row, the detoxification unit would attempt to place them on the path to recovery and social re-entry. It was also envisaged that detoxification units would 'catch' those habitual drunkards who had lost their place in hostels by breaking the no-drinking rule (Hamilton *et al* 1978). Such units could, therefore, ensure that once vagrant alcoholics had entered the treatment system, they would leave it only through the door to normal society.

It was also proposed that services such as 'shop-fronts' be established (Cook 1975: chapter 4). These would be set up in areas where Skid Row alcoholics tended to congregate. Staffed by social workers and recovered alcoholics, their function would be to provide a place where habitual drunkards could 'drop in' for a few hours of warmth and companionship. This would help establish initial contacts with Skid Row alcoholics, without frightening them off with pressure to change their life-styles. Once habitual drunkards had become used to such surroundings, efforts could then be made to motivate them to undergo treatment. Those who appeared to be good treatment prospects could then be referred to the appropriate agency.

Proponents of treatment also proposed that habitual drunkards might be provided with 'sheltered employment' under the Disabled Persons (Employment) Acts 1944 and 1958 (1971 report: para 10.23). This was an important proposal since, according to proponents of treatment, if habitual drunkards were to be restored to full personhood and citizenship it was essential that they found *gainful* employment. As well as keeping habitual drunkards occupied, gainful employment would help them to become independent. Through this, they could gain self-respect:

> An important aspect of social rehabilitation is performance at work. Once he is gainfully employed a man is able to pay his way, spend or save money of his own, and thus be another step towards becoming a useful member of society and being able to command a degree of respect (1971 Report: para 8.21).

Until habitual drunkards were able to find and hold ordinary employment, they could learn both the technical skills and attitudes required in sheltered employment schemes.

A new role for existing services

Along with the establishment of new services, the advocates of treatment proposed that all existing agencies and services, both professional and voluntary, that came into contact with habitual drunkards be integrated into a treatment network. These included penal, medical and welfare agencies and services: the probation and after-care service, the prison service, the courts, the police, psychiatric clinics, hospitals, the Supplementary Benefits Commission, 'crypts',[20] shelters and lodging houses (1971 Report: chapters 7–9, 12–13). If these services were to contribute to the goal of rehabilitation, certain aspects of

20 Crypts were similar to hostels, but were usually run by religious bodies.

their operations would have to be changed. It was important, for instance, that voluntary bodies which had established shelters for vagrant alcoholics made efforts to alter the social structure in these shelters. If they continued to run them as staff-directed, paternalistic institutions, which demanded nothing of vagrant alcoholics except passive obedience to rules, they would provide a place where vagrant alcoholics could retreat from the responsibility demanded by other treatment agencies such as hostels. Similar considerations applied to prisons to which vagrant alcoholics were sent.

Proponents of treatment contended, in particular, that if these various agencies and services were to contribute to the goal of socialising the habitual drunkard, it was essential that they be *coordinated*. Such coordination would ensure that the habitual drunkard's needs were met as fully and as efficiently as possible. It would prevent duplication of some services and the non-provision for some needs. It would also mean that each agency understood the functions of the others. A particular agency would therefore know where appropriate help for a particular habitual drunkard was available and would be less likely to make inappropriate referrals, such as directing an alcoholic in need of detoxification to a rehabilitation hostel. Above all, coordination of services would prevent the problem of habitual drunkards slipping through the treatment net. In a coordinated network of treatment services, the habitual drunkard would not leave one agency or service without first being referred to another. Sometimes this would be an advance along the rehabilitation path, eg a move from a detoxification unit to a hostel. In other cases, it would prevent the habitual drunkard from leaving the rehabilitation path altogether, eg the shop-front was a means of enabling a 'relapser' to remain in contact with the treatment system.

In general, this coordinated range of treatment services was intended to provide a path from Skid Row to the normal community. According to treatment professionals, the journey along this path would be an arduous one, but it was much preferable to the penal revolving door which took alcoholics off of Skid Row temporarily, but quickly returned them to it. Moreover, those who failed to complete the journey would not be condemned to Skid Row. They could occupy permanently a space, such as a hostel, somewhere between Skid Row and the normal community. Those who were simply not capable of fully independent social functioning could receive continuous professional support and supervision so that they would be able to take on some degree of personal responsibility and independence.

CONCLUSION

If the policy of replacing the punishment of habitual drunken offenders with a system of treatment is to be assessed adequately, it is crucial that its logic is understood. It would be a mistake to assume that what was proposed was a medical model of alcoholism. As I have shown, treatment professionals were concerned, less with alcoholism as conventionally understood, more with a complex personality disorder of which alcoholism was a symptom. Also, what was proposed was a system of social therapy based upon a social-psychological understanding of this disorder, not a system of medical treatment based upon a disease concept of alcoholism.

One assumption which the proponents of treatment *did* share with proponents of the disease concept of alcoholism was that the behaviour with which they were dealing was pathological. For treatment professionals, vagrant alcoholics were not devotees of total liberty whose alternative life-style should be a celebrated as a protest against the straight-jacket of settled society (cf O'Connor 1963). Rather, they were damaged, miserable people who required help. Critics such as Archard (1973 and 1979) would no doubt both distrust and object to such a 'pathologising' attitude towards the phenomenon of vagrant alcoholism. My research cannot resolve *this* argument. What it can do, however, is provide us with an understanding of the precise sense in which proponents of treatment regarded the life of the vagrant alcoholic as pathological and of precisely what they proposed to do to ameliorate it.

At the start of the campaign to establish a system of treatment for habitual drunken offenders there were two ways of dealing with habitual vagrant alcoholics: penal intervention or non-intervention. It is important to realise that proponents of treatment did not usually object in principle to penal intervention. Rather, they regarded penal intervention as better than non-intervention. According to treatment professionals, penal intervention provided a setting in which some of the vagrant alcoholic's basic needs could be met and in which some social contact could be established. The problem with penal intervention was that it was not designed for dealing with the type of problem presented by vagrant alcoholics and was ill-equipped for the task of re-socialising them. For proponents of treatment an alternative was required: a system of treatment.

What was proposed was not a system of medical treatment but a system of social therapy based upon a complex social-psychological interpretation of the Skid Row alcoholic. Its goal was to provide a system of therapy which would provide social support for the vagrant alcoholic, whilst gently pushing them towards becoming more independent and responsible. The ideal outcome of this intervention would be the re-entry of the Skid Row alcoholic to society. However, it was argued persuasively that even if this ideal outcome was not achieved, the type of intervention proposed would be better than either penal intervention or non-intervention.

INTRODUCTION TO STUDY B

In my second case study I examine the attitudes and policies of treatment professionals towards 'psychopathic offenders' since around the middle of the 19th century. Today, the label 'psychopath' tends to be applied to offenders who manifest a persistent inability to adapt to social requirements of them, especially if their anti-social behaviour seems incomprehensible and is indulged in for obscure reasons and if they also display other peculiarities of character (see Clare 1980: 19; Prins 1995: 130). Such persons were once regarded and handled as grossly depraved characters. If they broke the criminal law, they were dealt with as ordinary criminal justice cases. However, since around the middle of the 19th century, treatment professionals have developed a new way of seeing and dealing with such offenders. They have argued that, although 'psychopaths' are not mad or mentally ill as those terms are conventionally understood, their extreme and apparently inexplicable anti-social behaviour results from illness or mental abnormality. Accordingly, they argue, 'psychopathic' offenders should be processed and handled differently to ordinary offenders.

The story of this change in attitudes and policies towards 'psychopathic' offenders was once conventionally recounted as one of scientific progress with beneficial consequences for 'psychopaths' (eg Henderson 1939; McCord and McCord 1956: chapter 2). According to this conventional story, those who deal with offenders and those who deal with the mentally ill have always encountered persons whom we would now classify as 'psychopaths'. However, although they were puzzled by such cases they assumed that, since these persons were not insane, they must be mentally normal people who were simply very wicked. Hence, they dealt with such persons as ordinary criminal justice cases, which meant holding them fully responsible for their depraved behaviour and punishing them. But, in the 19th century, so the story goes, some psychiatrists *discovered* a previously *unrecognised* type of mental abnormality which explained why such people behaved as they did. Not fully understanding the nature of this condition they misleadingly named it 'moral insanity' or 'moral imbecility'. Then, towards the end of the 19th century, there was an advance in understanding of this condition which led to its being renamed, 'psychopathic disorder'. More recently, the story goes, some experts on the condition have questioned the appropriateness of this designation and have again changed its name, to 'personality disorder'.[1] The discovery of this condition has led to attempts to divert 'psychopathic offenders' – however they are designated – away from the normal processes of law and punishment, into a system of treatment. It was once widely assumed that such diversion would benefit 'psychopaths'.

---

1   Herschel Prins traces the historical development of definitions of the condition in more detail: 'Manie sans délire; moral insanity; moral imbecility (defectiveness); (constitutional) psychopathic inferiority; "neurotic character"; psychopathy and sociopathy; anti-social personality disorder; dissocial personality' (Prins 1995: 122).

Today, those who adhere to the view that 'psychopathic offenders' should be regarded and treated as mentally abnormal persons are compelled to acknowledge that the psychiatric-therapeutic approach to such persons has so far failed to advance significantly our capacity to explain or to improve their behaviour. Although there has been a vast amount of research into the aetiology of psychopathic disorder, its causes remain obscure (Prins 1995: 124–28). And, although psychopaths have been subjected to almost every type of therapy imaginable, they have been unresponsive to treatment, so much so that many regard them as untreatable (*ibid*: 134–6).[2] Nevertheless, many of those who deal professionally with 'psychopathic offenders' remain convinced that a psychiatric-therapeutic framework is most appropriate for understanding and dealing with the problem of 'psychopathic behaviour'. They assume that, although psychopathic disorder is less tractable than other psychiatric disorders, the causes and more successful forms of treatment can and will eventually be found as research in this area becomes more sophisticated.

However, amongst psychiatrists, there have always been many who have not accepted that those who are defined as 'moral imbeciles' or 'psychopaths' are really ill or mentally disordered (Clare 1980: 20). Some of these sceptics insist that treatment is inappropriate for so-called 'psychopaths', and would divert such persons back to the criminal justice system or perhaps to social workers (*ibid*). As psychiatrists and their allies have discovered that psychopaths are not only untreatable, but are also very difficult to manage, this sceptical attitude has become more prevalent.

Whilst many within psychiatry are uncertain about whether psychopathic disorder really exists, or at least about whether it exists as an illness appropriate for medical or psychiatric attention, there are those outside of psychiatry who are even more critical of the concept, regarding it as an unfounded medical invention. 'Psychopathic disorder' is frequently dismissed by criminal prosecutors and by 'conservative' politicians and members of the public as a *pseudo-illness*, invented by 'liberal' psychiatrists in order to help wicked people to avoid responsibility and punishment for their misdeeds. They would perhaps be surprised to find that many philosophers and social scientists seem to concur (even though their motives for criticising the concept are often rather different). One of the best known critics of the concept is the social scientist, Barbara Wootton, who – writing around the time that the category of 'psychopathic disorder' was given legal recognition by the Mental Health Act 1959 – criticised the concept as the product of illogical and confused thinking. She pointed out that the concept of psychopathy was used in attempts to excuse certain 'offenders' from moral and legal responsibility

---

2   For a view to the contrary see the letter to the *Guardian* (9 November 1994) by C Heginbotham, Chairman, Michael Buchanan Inquiry Panel.

for their crimes.[3] But, she argued, usually the only evidence that alleged psychopaths were mentally abnormal was that they had a history of wrongdoing or that the very crimes with which they were charged were so extreme that only mentally abnormal persons could have committed them. Hence, she contended, through a circular and logically defective argument, wrongdoing was used to excuse wrongdoing:

> The volume of literature on the subject of psychopaths is rivalled only by the depth of confusion in which this literature is steeped ... the psychopath makes nonsense of every attempt to distinguish the sick from the healthy delinquent by the presence or absence of a psychiatric syndrome, or by symptoms of mental disorder which are independent of his objectionable behaviour. In his case no such symptoms can be diagnosed because it is just the absence of them which causes him to be classified as psychopathic. He is, in fact, *par excellence*, and without shame or qualification, the model of the circular process by which mental abnormality is inferred from anti-social behaviour while anti-social behaviour is explained by mental abnormality (Wootton 1959: 250).[4]

Wootton suggested that the confused reasoning, which led psychiatrists to posit the existence of mental abnormality solely on the basis of anti-social conduct, was the result of a desire to help certain offenders avoid responsibility and punishment, but at the same time to cling to the notion that some offenders may be responsible and may deserve punishment. However, the legal philosopher, Jeffrie Murphy (1979b), maintains that the arguments which are used to help so-called psychopaths evade responsibility and punishment can also be used to deny them the rights and dignity to which *persons* are entitled. For Murphy, the individual who is diagnosed as a psychopath loses as well as gains – something often not seen by proponents of the concept. Murphy's main concern is with some fairly abstract philosophical questions concerning rights, responsibilities and what it is to be a 'person', rather than with practical questions of penal policy or legal reform. However, he does imply that, in practice, those offenders who are labelled as psychopaths might – by being subjected to coercive therapy designed to restructure their personalities – be treated as non-persons and as not entitled to 'human dignity' *(ibid*: 134–5).

This line of criticism is taken a step further by Ramon (1986). She concurs, at least implicitly, with the views that the 'psychopathic disorder' is a medical 'fiction', that the idea is logically defective, and that there are detrimental as well as beneficial consequences of being labelled as a psychopath. However, she maintains that the concept continues to be employed, despite its *obvious* shortcomings, because it performs useful social functions: 'despite the

---

3   For a classic example of a criminal case in which a diagnosis of psychopathy formed the basis for a (unsuccessful) plea of insanity, see the trial of Neville Heath (Critchley 1955). For a discussion of 'psychopathy in court' see Walker and McCabe (1973: 215–18).

4   Walker and McCabe (1973: chapter 10) argue, however, that Wootton exaggerated the circularity of the diagnostic process.

contradictions in the concept of psychopathy and the repetitive failures of social and therapeutic interventions, the category persists because of what it makes possible' (Ramon 1986: 239). What, in Ramon's view, does the concept make possible? First, she argues that the interpretation of undesirable and aggressive behaviour as symptoms of psychopathic disorder shifts attention away from the social sources of such behaviour and focuses it solely upon individual psychological factors (*ibid*: 220). The concept implies that, whilst the individual is not morally responsible for 'psychopathic' behaviour, such behaviour nevertheless arises from defects within the individual, and not from defects in the wider society. The concept therefore performs the ideological function of 'shifting guilt for such behaviour as far as possible from the arena of collective responsibility' (*ibid*).[5] Secondly, Ramon argues that the labelling as psychopaths of persons who are not insane, and for some reason may not be sent to prison, facilitates and 'legitimises' their confinement – confinement which would otherwise be difficult to justify. The concept thereby facilitates the social control of 'persons who would otherwise fall outside the ambit of both the criminal justice system and the psychiatric system itself' (*ibid*: 227). She suggests that the legal category of psychopathic disorder has not been abolished, *despite widespread doubts about its usefulness for medical purposes*, because it is useful for social control purposes. It:

> ... enables the state to accomplish the social management of a troublesome group of individuals, and it enables psychiatry to maintain its mandate over those whose conduct is socially undesirable yet who do not fall within the ambit of our system of criminal justice (Ramon 1986: 240).

The debate which I have briefly outlined is conducted at a very high level of generality. Most participants in the debate agree that there are individuals whose behaviour is extremely anti-social, and who differ from other offenders in that the motives for their behaviour are obscure and in that they exhibit some very peculiar personality features. What is disputed is whether such offenders are ill (or mentally abnormal) and hence whether they should be dealt with as medical (or psychiatric) cases. This dispute seems unresolvable. Participants in the debate usually attempt to resolve it by putting forward an arbitrary definition of illness (or psychiatric disorder) and then arguing that 'psychopaths' fall within or outside this definition. Such arguments are usually contested by putting forward a different, but equally arbitrary, definition of illness/psychiatric disorder.

One problem with conducting the debate at this highly general level is that 'therapeutic' interventions into the lives of those classified as psychopathic offenders tend to be either supported as appropriate or criticised as

---

5   This point was made with reference to the use of the concept to explain high levels of aggression and cruelty during World War II. However, the point is clearly intended to apply more generally. Ramon's views on mental illness and psychiatry are set out in more detail in her book, *Psychiatry in Britain* (1985).

inappropriate and non-legitimate prior to any investigation of the nature of those interventions or of the ideas about 'psychopathic offenders' which inform them. It is often implied that if psychopathic offenders are ill, therapeutic interventions are appropriate, whereas if they are not ill, therapeutic interventions are inappropriate or are really no more than disguised forms of social control.

In this case study, I propose to examine, in a rather different manner, therapeutic interventions into the lives of those defined as psychopathic offenders. I will by-pass the questions of whether there is such a thing as psychopathic disorder, whether it is a real illness, and whether so-called psychopaths are psychiatrically disordered. I will look instead at the *concrete* proposals of treatment professionals concerning how 'psychopathic offenders' should be classified, understood, and handled. I will ask: Who has been included within the category of 'psychopathic offenders'? Precisely in what sense are they understood to be ill or mentally abnormal? How is the process of becoming a psychopath explained? How are those who are classified as psychopathic offenders processed and treated? What is the position of treatment professionals on the question of the moral and legal responsibility of psychopathic offenders for their misdeeds? What are the 'operational objectives' of therapeutic interventions into the lives of 'psychopathic offenders'? What methods are advocated and employed to achieve these objectives? Through addressing these questions I aim to provide a detailed descriptive analysis of the nature of therapeutic interventions into the lives of psychopaths and, especially, of the ideas which inform and which are embodied in these interventions. On the basis of this descriptive analysis we should be able to reach a better informed assessment of the appropriateness and legitimacy of these interventions.

In chapter 5, I focus upon two concepts which preceded the concept of psychopathic disorder: moral insanity and moral imbecility. I look at the meaning of these concepts, at the types of offender who were included within the category of 'moral imbeciles', and at proposals for diverting moral imbecile offenders away from the ordinary processes of law and punishment, into a new system of therapeutic social control. In conventional accounts of the historical development of the concept of psychopathic disorder, the concepts of moral insanity and moral imbecility are usually treated as mere precursors of the concept of psychopathy, with little intrinsic interest. I show in this chapter that the historical development of these concepts and of policies towards moral imbecile offenders was far more complex than is suggested by conventional accounts. I also show that a study of the debates that took place about the status of these concepts and about the processing and treatment of moral imbecile offenders can advance significantly our understanding of the nature of the changing relationship between psychiatry and criminal justice and of some of the concerns which led to the emergence of therapeutic responses to offenders.

In chapter 6, I study developments in attitudes and policies of penal treatment professionals towards moral imbeciles or, as they were re-named, 'psychopathic offenders', between the mid-1870s and mid-1950s. I show that far from there being a gradual psychiatrisation of the problem, the historical development of attitudes and policies towards this group of offenders was characterised by numerous abrupt shifts of direction. What seems to have been agreed upon, by most participants in the debate about how to make sense of and respond to psychopathic offenders, was that there was a group of offenders who did not fall into any of the existing sub-categories of mental abnormality, but who were not mentally normal. Virtually everything else was the subject of dispute. Treatment professionals disagreed about the size of this group, about the criteria for membership, about how people developed psychopathic disorder, about whether such offenders should be held legally responsible for their misdeeds, about whether such offenders were treatable, and about how they should be managed. In describing in some detail the various shifts in attitudes and policies towards psychopathic offenders I attempt, in this chapter, to impart some of the internal complexity of the ideas which informed therapeutic interventions.

In chapter 7 I focus upon developments since the mid-1950s, looking at how treatment professionals have defined, made sense of, and tried to deal with, those whom they designate as psychopathic offenders. I start by describing the legal developments which must be understood in order to make sense of the discourse of treatment professionals on psychopathic offenders. I describe how 'psychopathic disorder' came to be legally recognised as a distinct category of mental disorder, ie distinct from both mental illness and mental defectiveness, and I outline the legal provisions for the compulsory detention of certain types of psychopathic patient. These legal provisions have been regarded as a threat to the liberty of those labelled as psychopaths. I do not challenge this view directly. But I do show that the Royal Commission which recommended these provisions was, in fact, concerned to liberalise mental health laws and that, in practice, these powers did not lead to a significant increase in the confinement of deviants on the ground that they suffered from psychopathic disorder. In the second section of chapter 7, I move beyond these 'civil liberties issues' which have been at the centre of debate, to describe developments which have received much less attention. I look, in particular, at developments in methods of managing and treating psychopathic offenders and at the assumptions about the nature of psychopathic disorder which are embodied in these methods. Through this investigation, I show that far from being medicalised, the problem of psychopathic offenders has been 'sociologised'. The final section of chapter 7 look at developments since the 1970s. It shows that there has been a move away from diverting psychopathic offenders from penal to medical institutions and that many treatment professionals – regarding medical treatment as a failure – recommend that psychopaths should be sent to prison.

I argue, however, that this does *not* constitute a regression from a therapeutic approach to a punitive approach to the problem. To the contrary, I argue, those who advocate sending psychopaths to prison do so on therapeutic grounds: prisons are better equipped than hospitals for the task of re-socialising the psychopath.

CHAPTER 5

THE PRE-HISTORY OF THE CONCEPT OF PSYCHOPATHY
MORAL INSANITY, MORAL IMBECILITY AND PENAL POLICY, 1835–1874

INTRODUCTION

In the middle decades of the 19th century, some psychiatrists began to describe certain kinds of offender as 'morally insane' and as 'moral imbeciles' and to propose that such offenders be processed, not as normal lawbreakers, but along the same lines as lunatics and mental defectives. In this chapter, I look in detail at the meanings of the concepts of moral insanity and moral imbecility, at what types of offender were classified as morally insane and as moral imbeciles, and at the proposals of psychiatrists for dealing with such offenders.[1] The period covered is from around 1837, when James Cowles Prichard first proposed the concept of moral insanity, to 1874, when Henry Maudsley proposed in his book, *Responsibility in Mental Disease*, that virtually all habitual criminals were moral imbeciles or persons born without moral sense.

One of my aims in this chapter is to show that the 'invention' of the concept of moral insanity *cannot* be understood as a crude attempt to attribute immoral behaviour and crime to mental disease, thereby defining 'vice' as a problem for medicine rather than as a problem for the law and for other 'official' protectors of morality, such as the clergy. Rather, the concept of moral insanity resulted from the attempts of psychiatrists to make sense of some puzzling cases, encountered in clinical practice, of extreme and inexplicable behaviour which did not fit into the existing categories of insanity but which otherwise seemed clearly to indicate abnormality of mind. The formation of the concept was made possible by a long term trend in medical thought and by developments in other areas such as philosophy and ethnology. Moreover, those who initiated the concept were concerned mainly with its implications for psychiatric theory and practice. It was only later that its relevance to immorality and crime were emphasised.

---

1   The concepts of moral insanity and moral imbecility are often regarded as interesting because they are precursors of the modern concept of 'psychopathic disorder' (see McCord and McCord 1956: chapter 2; Walker and McCabe 1973: chapter 9; Pichot 1978; Smith 1978: chapter 1; Prins 1995: chapter 5). However, the impact of *these* concepts upon penal policy and practice has seldom been regarded as a topic of interest in its own right. As a result, the importance of these concepts – as opposed to the modern concept of psychopathic disorder – for the development of penal policy, and for the development of relations between psychiatry and criminal justice, has been poorly understood.

A second aim in this chapter is to show that, amongst those psychiatrists who accepted the concept of moral insanity, there was considerable divergence of opinion about what types of case should be classified as morally insane and about how morally insane offenders should be handled. Some psychiatrists included in the category only a few individuals who exhibited a fairly well-defined pattern of problem behaviour. Others included all persistent delinquents within the category. And, at the level of policy, some were mainly concerned to argue that the law should excuse morally insane offenders from responsibility and punishment. Others were more concerned about the social danger represented by moral imbeciles. They argued that new laws and institutions were required so that moral imbecile offenders could be subject to preventive detention and treatment. So, in order to understand the impact of the concept of moral insanity upon penal policy it is necessary to realise that what is under discussion is a highly flexible concept and a range of quite different policy concerns and proposals. This complexity must be acknowledged and understood if we are properly to assess the concept. It would be wrong to focus discussion on one particular use of the concept and to assume that all of those who used it did so in the same way. It would also be mistaken to focus on one set of policy proposals on the assumption that these were the only ones informed by the concept.

This chapter also presents two more specific arguments which are crucial to our understanding of the development of therapeutic interventions into the lives of psychopathic offenders. First, it argues that during the 1860s there was a fundamental change in the nature of psychiatry's concerns in the area of crime and punishment. Until the 1860s, its primary concern was to obtain compassion for a small number of offenders whom the law regarded as sane and responsible but whom psychiatry viewed as insane and non-responsible. During and after the 1860s, psychiatrists became less concerned with these issues of justice and more concerned to develop the implications of new psychiatric categories for thinking about social danger and social defence. This shift in psychiatry's concerns was articulated, in complex ways, with a change in the way psychiatrists employed the concepts of moral insanity and moral imbecility.[2] The significance of this argument here is that, apart from highlighting an often missed but crucially important shift in the nature of psychiatry's concerns, it shows that a single psychiatric concept can have quite contradictory impacts upon penal policy and practice. The concept which is employed in one context to save offenders from the gallows can be used in another to justify the establishment of a new apparatus of therapeutic social control.

The second specific argument is about what happened after this transition in psychiatry's concerns took place. I argue that what emerged after the 1860s was not a single psychiatric discourse on moral imbecility but rather two over-lapping, yet distinguishable, discourses. First, the concept was used in

2 I discuss this transition in more detail in Johnstone (1996). For a similar transition in French psychiatry see Castel (1975).

discourses on the problem of the 'criminal class'. In this discourse, psychiatrists such as James Bruce Thomson and Henry Maudsley contended that persistent delinquency was, in itself, a sign of moral insanity or moral imbecility. They concluded from this that habitual criminals should be subject to the sorts of intervention to which dangerous lunatics and mental defectives were subject. In the second discourse, the concept of moral imbecility was applied to a narrower group of offenders: those who exhibited a reasonably well-defined pattern of violent and criminal behaviour: a tendency, from an early age, towards troublesome conduct; a tendency towards wrongdoing for pleasure rather than profit; a persistence in these tendencies despite being frequently punished; and an apparent lack of moral feeling. Much attention has been given to the first of these discourses, especially by those critical of therapeutic approaches to crime. I suggest, however, that it was the second of these discourses which had the deeper impact upon penal policy and practice and that it was in this discourse that the modern notion of the psychopathic offender crystallised.

'INSANE IN CONDUCT AND NOT IN IDEAS': THE CONCEPT OF MORAL INSANITY

The term 'moral insanity' was coined in the 1830s by the physician James Cowles Prichard.[3] Prichard criticised what was then the dominant conception of madness on the ground that it was too narrow: it restricted the concept to disturbances of reason and failed to include cases in which only the feelings, affections or habits were disordered. Within the dominant conception of madness, persons who were emotionally unstable, appeared to lack moral feeling, or had a propensity to violent paroxysms of rage, would be regarded as sane if their capacity of understanding was not seriously impaired. This 'intellectualistic' outlook towards insanity was most dominant in the 18th century when, as Carlson and Dain put it:

> ... to lose one's reason was to become insane, and, conversely, to be insane was to have lost one's reason. A madman might also suffer from disturbed

---

3 See Prichard (1837). Carlson and Dain (1962) provide a useful brief guide to the meaning and history of the concept. Leigh (1961: chapter 3) is a useful guide to Prichard's life and works, and shows how the concept of moral insanity fitted into his more general approach to mental disorder. Skultans (1975: 180–86) reproduces the most relevant excerpts from Prichard's work. Alongside his contributions to psychiatry, Prichard was an ethnologist – and it is in this field that he is actually better known. His main contribution to knowledge was his *Researches into the Physical History of Man* (1973, 1st edition originally published in 1813). Stocking's introductory essay to the 1973 publication is an excellent guide to Prichard's ideas in this area and to his place in British anthropology. Prichard seems to have maintained a firm distinction between his psychiatric and ethnological interests (Stocking 1973: xxv). His writings on moral insanity make no reference to his ethnological work (and *vice versa*), even though his ethnology contains ideas about the evolution of mental faculties and psychological characteristics which would seem relevant to the understanding of moral insanity (see Leigh 1961: 198–9). As we shall see, later writers on moral insanity did use evolutionary theories in their discussions of moral sense.

emotions but it was impaired intellect rather than any eccentric or anti-social behaviour which led others to deem him insane (Carlson and Dain 1962: 130).

This rationalistic definition of insanity had, in fact, been under attack for at least half a century before Prichard announced his critique of it. At the very beginning of the 19th century, the French psychiatrist, Philippe Pinel, developed the concept of *manie sans délire* to classify cases in which patients displayed no lack of understanding, but were insanely violent in their actions (*ibid*: 132). In the early decades of the 19th century such persons were routinely dealt with in French hospitals as cases of insanity under the label of *folie raisonnante*. Prichard was well aware of these developments but, until the 1830s, he rejected explicitly the idea of *manie sans délire* in terms which would later be used by critics of his own concept of moral insanity – ie he did not deny that persons diagnosed as suffering from the disease were insane, but he contended that they actually suffered from a lesion of the understanding which had not been detected (see Leigh 1961: 163–6). In his first book he stated:

> I may observe, that in all these instances of madness, which have been represented to me as examples of disorder affecting the active principles, without lesion of understanding, I have discovered, on adequate inquiry, that the case was in reality otherwise. After minutely interrogating such patients, I have traced some latent impression, which has sufficiently accounted for the change observed in the feelings and affections (Prichard, from *A Treatise on Diseases of the Nervous System*, 1822; excerpt reproduced in Leigh 1961: 165).

By the mid-1830s, Prichard had reversed his position completely.[4] In his *Treatise on Insanity* (1837), he criticised the conventional wisdom that 'the intellect or the reasoning faculty is principally disordered in persons labouring under mental derangement'. He insisted that there were other types of insanity, such as moral insanity, in which the intellectual powers were wholly intact, but the feelings and moral will were deranged (Prichard 1837: 20–30). There were forms:

> ... of mental derangement in which the intellectual faculties appear to have sustained little or no injury, while the disorder is manifested principally or alone, in the state of the feelings, temper or habits. In cases of this description the moral and active principles of the mind are strangely perverted and depraved; the power of self-government is lost or greatly impaired; and the individual is found to be incapable, not of talking or reasoning upon any

---

4   Carlson and Dain attribute this change of mind to his clinical experience: 'Esquirol and Prichard both initially rejected Pinel's concept of *manie sans délire*, and only after years of contact with mental patients did they reverse their stand' (1962: 133). This is how Prichard himself represented his change of mind (see Skultans 1975: 181). However, Stocking (1973: xxxi) suggests that the change might also have been due to broader developments in Prichard's psychological thought: 'one may question whether it was simply an accumulation of data which led Prichard to change his mind on this issue. Certainly there is a coherence between the new concept and the development of Prichard's views on other issues' (*ibid*).

subject proposed to him, for this he will often do with great shrewdness and volubility, but of conducting himself with decency and propriety in the business of life (Prichard 1837: 15).

It is important to be precise about the significance of this new concept for psychiatric thought and practice. Although its long-term implications for psychiatry were profound, its immediate impact upon psychiatric practice was probably slight. The kinds of behaviour which Prichard described as indicating moral insanity were, to a large extent, already being interpreted as signs of insanity in practice. Indeed, Prichard supported the concept by an appeal to his clinical experience; he claimed that he had encountered such persons in his experience as a physician. However, the established theory dictated that such persons *must* be suffering from damaged reason, even if this damage was not easy to detect. What was at stake, then, was less the practical question of whether or not to classify such persons as insane, more the theoretical question of whether such persons suffered from some latent impairment of the understanding.

However, the concept of moral insanity had crucial implications for the social meaning of insanity and of eccentric, immoral and criminal behaviour – implications which would be highlighted only from the late 1840s. First, the concept played an important role in disturbing the sharp boundary which had previously been perceived to exist between sanity and madness. The concept of moral insanity implied that, not only was there a massive borderland between full sanity and absolute madness, but that certain individuals were sane in some respects and insane in others.[5] Such persons might be perfectly capable of thinking and conversing reasonably, but lack the capacity to experience normal moral emotions, such as repugnance towards evil. According to the concept, such persons were by no means absolutely mad, since they were capable of rational thought and conversation, but they were insane in certain respects. The existence of such persons, if it were acknowledged, posed a number of perplexing questions: How could such persons be recognised? How should society handle them? What were their rights and obligations?

Secondly, the concept of moral insanity disturbed the boundary perceived to exist between madness, on the one hand, and eccentricity and wickedness on the other. The most prominent symptoms of moral insanity were eccentric and disgraceful conduct. For instance, one case presented by Prichard to illustrate the condition concerned a county magistrate who often became:

... boisterous, irascible, extravagant, and given to intoxication; he would wander about the country in the dress of a horse-jockey, frequented fairs and markets ... and made the most extravagant purchases of horses and dogs, and

---

5   This notion was informed by, *inter alia*, phrenology, which represented the mind, not as a unity, but as an entity composed of a number of independent powers (see Carlson and Dain 1962: 134). The power of reason, for instance, was conceived as independent of the moral feelings.

associated with people of the lowest class. During these times he was overbearing and impetuous; has been known to horse-whip his female domestics ... This person displayed in conversation no trace of a cloud on the understanding; he was under no illusion or hallucination (Prichard 1847; excerpt in Skultans 1975: 185).[6]

Few, apart from the magistrate himself, would have disputed that such behaviour was eccentric and immoral. The concept of moral insanity implied, however, that such behaviour might arise, not from 'natural' eccentricity or wickedness, but from mental disease. Moreover, it seemed as if there was no easy way of determining whether it was caused by insanity or by mere peculiarity of character. As Prichard acknowledged:

> It is often very difficult to pronounce, with certainty, as to the presence or absence of moral insanity, or to determine whether the appearances which are supposed to indicate its existence do not proceed from natural peculiarity or eccentricity of character (Prichard 1847; excerpt in Skultans 1975: 184).

This issue was raised, most acutely, in the debate between medicine and the law about the legal responsibility of morally insane offenders, which I will examine in a moment. First, however, it is important to point out that Prichard himself tended to define the scope of the concept quite narrowly and usually avoided inferring moral insanity from eccentric or immoral behaviour in itself. Rather, as defined by Prichard, the concept of moral insanity was applicable mainly to cases in which there was evidence of a *sudden change* in moral sensibility or character (see Donnelly 1983: 138). Hence, in discussing moral insanity, Prichard repeatedly referred to cases in which there had been 'an alteration in temper and habits' (Prichard 1837: 21). The concept was typically applied to cases in which a person's 'temper and dispositions are found on inquiry to have undergone a change; to be not what they were previously' (*ibid*). Most of the cases which Prichard used to illustrate the condition contained some reference to a sudden deterioration of behaviour. For example, one case concerned a farmer who was:

> ... a man of sober and domestic habits, and frugal and steady in conduct, until about his forty-fifth year, when his disposition appeared to have become suddenly changed ... He became wild, excitable, thoughtless, full of schemes and absurd projects ... (Prichard 1837: 41).

The crucial point is that although moral insanity was diagnosed upon the basis of gross disparity between the individual's behaviour and the prevailing social norms, the norms departed from were not simply social norms, they were also established by persons themselves in their own past conduct. The person who had always behaved in an eccentric or wicked manner would not, according to this narrow usage, be diagnosed as morally insane. Hence, whilst

---

6   For numerous cases exemplifying the description of moral insanity see Prichard (1837: 36–61).

the concept muddled the distinction between madness and deviance it did not – at least as used by Prichard – demolish this distinction.

ANTAGONISM BETWEEN MEDICINE AND LAW: MORAL INSANITY AND CRIMINAL RESPONSIBILITY

One crucial issue raised by the concept of moral insanity was that of the status before the criminal law of defendants who were diagnosed as morally insane. In the criminal law, insanity had long been regarded as an incapacitating condition. Insane persons were held to be not responsible for criminal acts committed under their incapacity.[7] Hence, a crucial issue for the criminal law was where to draw the line between sanity and insanity. Until the late 18th century, the law tended to employ fairly crude tests such as the 'right-wrong' test and the 'wild beast' test. An insane person was one who could not distinguish between right and wrong and was like a brute. In the late 18th century, following Blackstone's *Commentaries on the Law of England* (1765–9), insanity came to be more precisely and explicitly defined (Donnelly 1983: 71). During this period, doctors had relatively little influence upon the legal practices for defining insanity. As Porter (1987b: 116) points out, 'it was most unusual for doctors to testify in court. In establishing insanity, the testimony of friends, neighbours and relatives counted most'. This would change in the 19th century when 'members of the emergent profession of alienists ... increasingly thrust themselves forward in trials as "expert witnesses"' (*ibid*: 115).[8]

During the first half of the 19th century, the re-evaluation of the accepted criteria of insanity that was taking place within psychiatry created the potential for conflict between judges and doctors. Judges identified insanity with disordered reason, whereas psychiatrists were beginning to classify disorders of emotion and conduct as cases of insanity. Accordingly, doctors sought a broadening of the legal definition of insanity to take account of newly discovered mental diseases such as moral insanity and monomania. The courts, on the other hand, were reluctant to excuse lawbreakers whose powers of understanding were not seriously impaired. This was not, as is

---

7   See Porter (1987b: 114–17). On the history of the insanity defence see Walker (1968). For a riveting study of the insanity defence in Victorian trials, in its cultural, intellectual and political contexts see Smith (1981). Those acquitted on grounds of insanity at the time of their offence were kept in custody 'at crown pleasure'. Legal provision for such confinement was made, following the acquittal of James Hadfield who fired at and wounded George III, by an *Act for the Safe Keeping of Insane Persons charged with Offences* (1800).

8   'Alienists' was the name given, prior to the 19th century, to experts who studied and treated mental pathologies. The origin of the term is explained by Caleb Carr in a frontnote to his novel *The Alienist* (1994): 'Prior to the 20th century, persons suffering from mental illness were thought to be "alienated" not only from the rest of society but from their own true natures'.

often assumed, due simply to stubborn conservatism on the part of the judiciary. Rather, legal recognition of moral insanity as an incapacitating condition would have had serious legal and social ramifications, of which judges were well aware. The proponents of the concept of moral insanity *seemed* to be implying that immoral behaviour was in itself an indication of insanity. To recognise such a notion would lead to more than a broadening of the insanity defence – it threatened the very possibility of distinguishing between sane and insane offenders by criteria external to their criminal behaviour (cf Wootton 1959: 231). Moreover, in inferring insanity from bad behaviour, the concept threatened to destroy the very notion of moral responsibility for crime. Ultimately, it was feared, it would be impossible to convict and punish any offender:

> ... opponents of the concept feared that a person charged with a crime would automatically plead moral insanity and thereby escape punishment; some alarmists even contended that immoral behaviour would rage uncontrolled if, by pleading moral insanity, defendants were absolved of responsibility and crime was allowed to go unpunished (Carlson and Dain 1962: 135).

The issue was complicated further by the fact that, as we have seen, psychiatrists thought it was 'difficult to pronounce, with certainty, as to the presence or absence of moral insanity' (Prichard 1847). If Prichard, with all his clinical experience, found it so difficult to distinguish morally insane people from sane persons who simply behaved badly, how could the ordinary juror distinguish the two? To accept moral insanity as an excusing condition would therefore, it seemed, 'take the ultimate responsibility for judicial decision away from the laymen on the jury and confer it upon psychiatrists' (Carlson and Dain 1962: 135).

For doctors, on the other hand, the law's refusal to excuse those whom they diagnosed as morally insane meant that persons who were not intentionally wicked, but who committed criminal acts as a result of their mental disease, were being punished as if they were deliberate wrongdoers. In effect, sick people were being hanged for displaying the symptoms of their disease. Hence, from the 1840s on, psychiatrists became increasingly critical of the criminal law's practices for defining insanity and responsibility. Prichard himself criticised the legal definition of insanity in a book, first published in 1842, called *On the Different Forms of Insanity in Relation to Jurisprudence*.[9] In this book, Prichard suggested that the courts adhered to the 'rationalistic' conception of insanity.

> It seems on the whole to be the settled doctrine of English courts at present, that there cannot be insanity without delusion ... that is, without some

---

9 I have been unable to gain access to this book. What follows is based on the lengthy excerpts provided by Leigh (1961: 181–5) and Skultans (1975: 184–6) and upon my reading of Prichard's earlier treatment of these issues in chapter 11 of his *Treatise on Insanity* (1837). See also Winslow (1843) who was the leading medical agitator in this debate.

particular erroneous conviction impressed upon the understanding (Prichard 1847, cited in Leigh 1961: 182–3).

Hence, according to Prichard, those who were morally insane but not suffering from delusion would be deemed sane by the criminal courts and held responsible for their crimes. The result, according to Prichard, was that many defendants who ought to have been pronounced insane and exonerated were convicted of crimes (*ibid*: 183).

In this book, Prichard probably exaggerated the extent to which the legal test of responsibility was 'intellectualistic'. For a few decades before 1842, the scope of the insanity defence had in fact been gradually widened. Indeed, it was in response to a series of decisions which seemed to be expanding the scope of the insanity defence that the judges, in 1843, formulated the famous M'Naghten rules which *re-affirmed* the narrow 'loss of understanding' definition of insanity. These rules arose out of the case of Daniel M'Naghten who attempted to kill the Prime Minister but, not knowing what he looked like, instead killed his private secretary. M'Naghten was acquitted on grounds of insanity, even though he did not seem to be suffering from disordered reason – according to Prins (1980: 17) he 'suffered from what we would describe today as paranoid delusions'. The decision created considerable controversy and, in contradiction of the established procedure for making criminal law, the question of the correct ambit of the insanity defence was referred to the judges of the House of Lords. They proposed what has subsequently become known as the M'Naghten Rules, which re-stated the intellectualistic 'right-wrong' test:

> To establish a defence on the ground of insanity, it must be clearly proved that, at the time of committing the act, the party accused was labouring under such a *defect of reason*, from disease of mind, as not to know the nature and quality of the act he was doing; or, if he did know it, that he did not know he was doing what was wrong (*per* Tindal CJ, emphasis added).[10]

Following the formulation of the M'Naghten Rules, the potential discord between the judges and doctors developed into full-blown antagonism. During the 1840s and 1850s, psychiatrists sustained a polemical attack upon the law. By 1862, the psychiatrist Thomas Laycock was summarising the deep disagreements that existed between law and medicine over the definition of insanity and the proper response to the insane offender in very bitter terms:

> Medicine maintains that a theoretical and practical study of mental diseases and defects is necessary to a proper understanding and detection of defect; law denies this, and says it is a fact to be determined by any dozen of ordinary men in consultation on the case. Medicine says a man may be insane and irresponsible, and yet know right and wrong; law says a knowledge of right and wrong is the test of both soundness of mind and responsibility to the law. Medicine says restrain and cure the insane offender against the law; law says

---

10 *M'Naghten's Case* (1843) 10 Cl and F 200.

hang, imprison, whip, hunger him, and treats medical art with contempt (Laycock 1862: 593–7).

A shift in medical concern: from the insanity defence to the restraint and cure of the criminal class

Discussions of the relationship between psychiatry and criminal justice tend to be drawn towards the issue of the relation between insanity and criminal responsibility. What is often not realised is that, since the 1860s, this issue has become a secondary – albeit still very important – concern for many psychiatrists with an interest in criminal policy. The antagonism between law and medicine, summarised by Thomas Laycock, had reached its climax by the early 1860s. However, Laycock did mention an aspect of the disagreement between law and medicine which, if not entirely new, was only beginning to emerge as a major issue in the 1860s: 'Medicine says restrain and cure the insane and imbecile offender against the law; law says hang, imprison, whip, hunger him'. Laycock was hinting here that medical intervention could achieve something else, besides rescuing insane offenders from the hangman. It could also provide a means of controlling them and could even manage and cure the diseases which caused them to break the law. Hitherto, doctors had sought only to wrest criminals from the gallows by demonstrating that they were insane; now, they sought to prevent crime by using 'medical art' to manage and cure criminals.

Some few years after his paper on 'the antagonism of law and medicine in insanity', Laycock's passionate concern about the criminal law's definition of responsibility had mellowed. In an article titled 'Medico-Mental Science and the Prevention of Crime', he found it sufficient, despite the fact that the judges were showing no signs of recognising medical claims, to state: 'That medico-mental science is often at variance with the doctrines and decisions of the courts of law is a fact too well known and too generally admitted to need formal proof (Laycock 1869: 334). Laycock's interest had by then shifted to a rather different and, in terms of the numbers of offenders involved, much larger problem:

> There is a large number of criminals termed in France the 'classes dangereuses' and in English phrase 'known to the police' and another still more numerous body, not exactly of this class, but incorrigible vagabonds, drunkards, mendicants. All these, numbering tens of thousands, are really so constituted corporeally that they possess no self-control beyond that of an ordinary brute animal ... They are, for the most part, *immoral imbeciles*, so that however frequently they may have been subjected to prison or other discipline, the moment they are set free, they resume their vicious and criminal course (Laycock 1869: 342, emphasis added).

Laycock was not alone in shifting his interest from the insanity defence to the dangerous classes. In the 1850s, the *Journal of Mental Science* – the major outlet for psychiatric writing on crime in this period – published numerous articles concerned specifically with the scope of the insanity defence. From the mid-1860s fewer articles on this subject appeared, while a new concern emerged and began to dominate: a concern with the psychology of the criminal class and the problem of their control. For a brief period, these concerns were inter-twined and articles would give equal attention to both matters (eg Symonds 1864/5; Haynes 1864/5). But, within a few years, articles on the new subject – the psychology and control of habitual criminals – began to make at most only passing reference to the issue of the insanity defence (eg Thomson 1870 and 1871). Within the space of a few years, the insanity defence had become a secondary issue for medico-legal science. It had been pushed aside by a new concern with the criminal class.

Of course, medical criticisms of the legal definition of the insanity defence did not stop. To the contrary, the dispute was given fresh impetus by the acceleration of the campaign for the abolition of the death penalty during the 1860s (see Radzinowicz and Hood 1990: chapter 20). Because of its importance for the debate about the death penalty, the *Royal Commission on Capital Punishment*, 1864–66 explored the issue of the insanity defence with considerable thoroughness and so became the forum for yet another heated debate between lawyers and doctors, with doctors now arguing that the law should recognise degrees of responsibility, instead of insisting that a person be deemed either responsible or non-responsible (Haynes 1864/5: 548–9). And, of course, cases in which the sanity of the defendant was in question continued to occur and to become the occasion for a medical attack upon the M'Naghten Rules.

However, as I have indicated, in the 1860s the insanity defence became a less central concern within psychiatry. Although psychiatrists continued to criticise the legal practices for determining a defendant's sanity, the intensity of this criticism diminished. Eventually, as I will show later, many psychiatrists even came to accept the legal definition of insanity. But, this partial withdrawal by psychiatrists from their battle with the law over the insanity defence did not mean an end to hostilities. To the contrary, a new, and in many respects larger, conflict emerged – a dispute over how to understand and respond to the growing problem of people 'known to the police'. Psychiatrists continued to criticise penal policy and practice, but the nature of their criticism changed profoundly.

First, there was a shift in the scope of the conflict. Previously, the dispute was over whether defendants who possessed reason but were diagnosed as suffering from mental diseases such as moral insanity should be able to avail themselves of the insanity defence. Whilst there was a great deal at stake in this dispute, the number of offenders affected by it was relatively small. Since a successful plea of insanity led not to straightforward acquittal but to confinement as a criminal lunatic, the defence was attractive only to those charged with capital offences. Relatively few offenders were directly affected by the outcome of this debate. In the 1860s, psychiatrists became interested in a much larger group of offenders – the so-called 'criminal class'. As we have seen, Laycock estimated their number as 'tens of thousands'.

Secondly, this expansion of psychiatry's interest went hand in hand with a shift in the nature of its concerns. Previously, its central concern was to obtain compassion for those offenders whom it considered to be insane. It argued for a relaxation of the criminal law, not just for those who lacked reason, but also for those suffering from disordered feelings and affections. Now, its concern was to ensure that the *criminal classes* were restrained and cured. Psychiatrists criticised the existing response to such offenders, not on the ground that it was unsympathetic or unjust, but on the ground that it failed to regard such offenders as mentally abnormal and so failed to take proper steps to effect their control. The emphasis now was not upon obtaining fairness for insane offenders, but upon ensuring that they were subject to effective constraint. Hence, an article by Symonds (1864/5) starts out in what was by then familiar territory, discussing the various positions taken up in the debate about criminal responsibility in relation to insanity. However, he soon moves on to pose some relatively novel questions about the insane offender:

> Why was the criminal at large? Why was he in the enjoyment of the privileges of society, if he were not answerable to the law which protects those privileges? (Symonds 1864/5: 273).

By the conclusion of this article, the question of 'what constitutes a man irresponsible for a criminal act' has been long forgotten (*ibid*). Symonds advice to policy makers relates, not to this issue, but to the more general issue of how best to respond to the dangerously insane person:

> I think it would eventually appear that it is better, nay, that it is fiscally and economically preferable to deposit a brain-sick man in a hospital for the insane, where he may be CURED as well as kept out of the way of harm to himself or others, than to allow him to remain at large till he has committed some crime which will cause him ... to be maintained at the public expense as a convict ... or executed (Symonds 1864/5: 275, emphasis in original).

THE CONCEPT OF MORAL IMBECILITY APPLIED TO THE PROBLEM OF THE CRIMINAL CLASS

The concept of a criminal class occupied a central position in the discourse of penal policy during the 19th century.[11] By the 1850s, policy makers were beginning to believe in 'the existence of a class of persons who pursue crime as a calling, and are not led astray by casual temptation, or by temporary indulgence of the passions' (M D Hill, quoted in Radzinowicz and Hood 1990:

---

11 See Radzinowicz and Hood (1990: 73–84). In Johnstone (1996) I describe some of the social and legal conditions for the emergence of this concept.

74). In their history of penal policy in the 19th century, Radzinowicz and Hood state:

> From 1858 onwards the official count of 'known thieves and depredators', 'receivers' and 'suspected persons' led many contemporaries to conclude that 'there exists an enormous class of professional criminals – a class to be numbered by tens of thousands; that their trade is most lucrative and that they ply it with complete impunity.' *The Times* insisted that 'a good deal more than 100,000 persons live by crime'. Matthew Davenport Hill claimed that the 'predatory class' in London was, at the lowest estimate, 5,000 persons, committing 5,000 crimes a day or 1,825,000 a year. T R W Pearson went so far as to estimate that the criminal class comprised 15.4 per cent of the entire population. In 1860 the computation went up to a total of 135,000 ... (Radzinowicz and Hood 1990: 77).

This was the group with which psychiatrists became increasingly concerned during the 1860s. The concept of moral insanity, and the closely related concept of moral imbecility, occupied a key position in their discourse on this problem. In what follows I will look at how these concepts were applied to the criminal class and with what consequences.

According to psychiatrists, those who made up the criminal class – ie 'habitual criminals' – differed in their mental structure from 'other civilised and criminal men' (Thomson 1870: 485). Members of the criminal class suffered from an inherited, or at least inborn, mental disease which somehow explained their life of crime and depravity. It was not that they were devoid of reason or intelligence, although some doctors suggested that criminals were 'weakminded' (see Thomson 1867). Rather, they suffered from moral insanity or moral imbecility. Watson (1988) points out that these two terms were used interchangeably in this period. However, as I will now suggest, there were important differences between the notion of moral insanity and that of moral imbecility.

In order to understand the significance of this shift in terminology, from moral *insanity* to moral *imbecility*, it is necessary to look, briefly and very simply, at the basic classifications of mental disorder that were emerging around this time (see diagram over page). As we have seen, psychiatrists drew a fundamental distinction between 'intellectual' disorder and 'moral' disorder. Within, the area of intellectual disorder, there was another fundamental distinction between the insane and mental *defectives*: the insane had lost their capacity of understanding, mental defectives had never *developed* it. Loss of mind was distinguished from lack of mind (see Jones 1972: chapter 8). During the 19th century the category of mental defectives was extended to include *imbeciles*, imbecility being defined as a mental defect which was not quite so severe as the long-recognised condition of idiocy (*ibid*).[12]

---

12 As we shall see later, the category was further extended to include the even milder disorder of feeble-mindedness (see Rose 1985: chapter 4).

	Disorders of Understanding	Moral Disorders
Loss of Mind	Insanity	Moral Insanity
Lack of Mind	Mental Defectiveness (idiocy, imbecility, feeblemindedness)	Moral Defectiveness (moral idiocy or moral imbecility)

Diagram: Classification of Mental Disorder, emerging c 1870

In the area of 'moral' disorders, psychiatrists were beginning, in a similar manner, to draw a distinction between the morally insane and moral defectives. The former had lost their moral feeling whereas the latter had never developed it in the first place. This condition presumably was regarded as analogous to idiocy or imbecility and hence became known as 'moral idiocy' or 'moral imbecility' (Maudsley 1874: 179). It was the latter term which became most popular. It was this label which was applied, by psychiatrists such as James Bruce Thomson and Henry Maudsley, to the 'criminal class':

... violent and habitual criminals are, as a class, moral imbeciles (Thomson 1871: 321).

... If there be a class of persons who are without the moral sense, who are the true moral imbeciles, it is the class of habitual criminals (Maudsley, quoted in Skultans 1975).

One important effect of this shift in terminology is that it assimilated this group of offenders, not with the insane, but with *mental defectives*. As we shall see in the next chapter, when legal provision was eventually made for the control of this group of offenders, it was along with mental defectives, rather than with the mentally ill, that they were classified. This had important implications for the way this group were perceived and handled.

Before proceeding, we should note that there was a circularity in this use of the concept of moral imbecility to describe habitual criminals, a circularity that was avoided in the concept of moral insanity. In the case of moral insanity, although the symptoms of the condition included anti-social behaviour, the disorder was not inferred from immoral conduct alone. Rather, as we have seen, it was the sudden change in character and conduct which rendered persons morally insane. So, in arguing for the existence of moral insanity, Henry Maudsley was well aware of the need to avoid inferring disease from crime alone. He realised that, for most people, the description of the morally inane person was:

> ... simply the description of a very wicked person, and that to accept it as a description of insanity would be to confound all distinction between vice or crime and madness (Maudsley 1874: 173).

He headed off such criticism by pointing out, as Prichard had previously done, that a diagnosis of moral insanity was not based upon simple criminal behaviour, but was based upon a study of the *case history*:

> The vicious act or crime is not itself proof of insanity; it must, in order to establish moral insanity, be traced from disease through a proper train of symptoms ... the evidence of disease will be found in the entire history of the case. What we shall often observe is this – that after some great moral shock, or some severe physical disturbance ... there has been a marked change of character; he becomes 'much different from the man he was' in feelings, temper, habits, and conduct. We observe, in fact, that ... a person exhibits symptoms which are strangely inconsistent with his previous character, but which are consistent with moral insanity (Maudsley 1874: 173–4).

The term 'moral imbecility' referred, however, to a *congenital* deficiency (*ibid*: 179). It was used to describe people who supposedly were born with an 'absence of moral sense' (*ibid*). This deficiency was evident from the fact that, from early childhood, they had a tendency towards extremely bad behaviour:

> ... when we find young children, long before they can possibly know what vice or crime means, addicted to extreme vice, or committing great crimes ... when we ascertain that they are the victims of an insane inheritance; and when experience proves that punishment has no reformatory effect upon them – that they cannot reform – it is made evident that moral imbecility is a fact (Maudsley 1874: 179).

There is a crucial difference between the way one diagnoses moral insanity and moral imbecility. In diagnosing moral insanity, one is looking at the person's life history in order to determine whether there has been a sudden change in conduct or sentiments. In diagnosing moral imbecility, however, what one is looking for is the precise opposite – not a 'strange inconsistency' but a consistent pattern of bad behaviour from an early age. The existence of moral imbecility was inferred, not from a deviation from the individual's past normal behaviour, but from a gross disparity between the individual's behaviour and prevailing social norms. Hence, the process of diagnosing moral imbecility is much more circular than the process of diagnosing moral insanity. The existence of moral imbecility is inferred from persistent vicious or criminal behaviour, there are no other grounds for assuming its existence. At the same time, persistent vicious of criminal behaviour purportedly is explained by moral imbecility. From this position, it was a very short step to arguing that all habitual criminals were moral imbeciles. As Maudsley himself stated: 'cases of this kind obviously bring us very near the class of criminals' (*ibid*: 180–1).

Given the near circularity of the concept it would be tempting to join with many of Maudsley's contemporaries and dismiss 'moral imbecility' as 'an unfounded medical invention' (*ibid*: 171). However, my concern here is not to assess the scientific validity of the concept but to examine its impact upon penal policy and practice. Hence, I will now turn to the question of how the concept of moral imbecility affected the way persistent delinquents were perceived and handled.

Critics of the medical model of crime will probably observe that the concept deflected attention away from the immediate socio-economic determinants of the behaviour of the 'criminal class'. They might also notice that the concept confirmed the comfortable belief that the conduct of members of the criminal class was irrational – that it arose from a moral disease of the mind rather than from choices which, in the circumstances, were perfectly rational and perhaps even justifiable. Such observations may be correct. However, the concept had other important implications for penal policy and practice. In order to trace these, we need to look a little closer at the meaning of the concept of moral imbecility.

Moral sense

By applying the concept of moral imbecility to members of the criminal class, psychiatrists implied that these people behaved as they did because they were born without moral sense (Maudsley 1874: 31–5). I will now ask: What, according to these psychiatrists, was moral sense? How was it possible to be born without it? What were the consequences for the individual of being born without it? I will focus on the writings of Henry Maudsley who did most, at this stage, to promote the concept of moral imbecility.

The concept of moral sense was developed by 18th century philosophers, such as Francis Hutcheson, for whom the moral sense was 'the capacity to experience feelings of approval and disapproval' (Raphael 1973: 230). Hutcheson used the concept in a philosophical attack against proponents of 'rationalist ethics' for whom moral distinctions were perceived by reason (*ibid*; see also MacIntyre 1985: chapter 2). However, the psychiatrists who used the term in the 19th century did so without the moral relativism of 'intuitionists' like Hutcheson. For them, the moral sense was the part of the mind which we use to perceive the (objective) moral quality of conduct, ie whether it is right or wrong, good or evil (see Burt 1944: chapter 2).

According to Maudsley, moral sense was *acquired* by our ancestors, but once acquired was transmitted, like other mental attributes, through education and hereditary action (Maudsley 1874: 60–2). At the beginning, human beings were 'bare of all true moral feeling'. However, in primitive families and tribes the habitual reprobation of injurious acts generated a sentiment of right and wrong. Such sentiment was in the course of generations 'transmitted by hereditary action'. The acquisition and development of moral sense facilitated, but was in turn promoted by, the rise from a nomadic state to national existence. It was a 'concomitant effect' of evolution.

For Maudsley, the moral sense was clearly a special attribute, the condition of civilised co-existence. It was the possession of a highly developed moral sense which distinguished civilised mankind from more primitive peoples (Maudsley 1874: 61–2). However, since moral sense was 'the last acquired faculty in the progress of human evolution' it was the easiest lost – 'the first to suffer when diseases invade the mental organisation' (*ibid*: 62). Hence, moral insanity was likely to precede intellectual derangement and end in destruction of mind (*ibid*: 62–3). But how, precisely, could one lose or be born without moral sense?

For Maudsley, the moral sense – like other mental attributes – had a material base.[13] Hence, it could be perverted or destroyed by injury to, or disease of, the brain – or more precisely by disorder of the supreme nerve centres of the brain (*ibid*: 15, 63–4). Less obviously, Maudsley suggested occasionally that the moral sense could decay from disuse (Maudsley 1873, quoted in Skultans 1975: 189).[14] And crucially, for Maudsley, mental derangement – of any kind and however contracted – could be transmitted through hereditary action to offspring, where it could take the form of moral imbecility. One could inherit an '*immoral* in place of a *moral* sense' (Maudsley 1874: 29).

Persons who were born without moral sense – ie moral imbeciles – would, from birth, be in the same state as morally insane persons – they would lack moral feeling. Such persons would therefore have a greater tendency than others towards vicious and criminal acts. For Maudsley, the concept of moral imbecility could therefore help to explain habitual criminality. The concept was pertinent to an understanding of 'the way in which criminals are produced' (*ibid*: 28). Occasionally, indeed, Maudsley implied that all moral imbeciles were habitual criminals. Moreover, he often suggested the converse (ever though it did not strictly follow) – ie that all habitual criminals were

---

13 'No one now-a-days who is engaged in the treatment of mental disease doubts that he has to do with the disordered function of a bodily organ – of the brain' (Maudsley 1874: 15).

14 Although a materialist, Maudsley allowed for psychological causes of mental disorder. He argued, however, that these operated *through* physiological processes. For a brief account of Maudsley's thought, particularly as it bore upon the debate about 'degeneration', see Pick (1989: 203–16).

moral imbeciles. Hence, he agreed with the prison doctor, James Bruce Thomson,[15] whose years spent closely observing criminals had led him to realise that:

> Habitual criminals are ... without moral sense – are true moral imbeciles; their moral insensibility is such that in the presence of temptation they have no self-control against crime (Maudsley 1874: 31).

Implications of applying the concept of moral imbecility to habitual criminals

In suggesting that the members of the criminal class were congenital moral imbeciles, psychiatrists implied a number of things. First, they implied that habitual criminals could not be reformed – although their behaviour might be slightly improved by proper upbringing. Habitual criminals had inborn criminal instincts, which were often strengthened by faulty upbringing so that they acquired 'a power which no subsequent efforts to produce reformation will ever counteract' (Maudsley 1874: 29). The habitual criminal, Maudsley contended, had a criminal nature, which could not be altered by personal or social influences:

> A true reformation would be the re-forming of the individual nature; and how can that which has been forming through generations be re-formed within the term of a single life? Can the Ethiopian change his skin or the leopard his spots? (Maudsley 1874: 33, emphasis in original).[16]

Secondly, the link between moral imbecility and persistent delinquency also had implications for the status of habitual criminals. The evolutionary theory of moral sense used by Maudsley implied that those without it were closer, in their moral nature, to primitive people rather than to civilised people. Thirdly, it was implied that the offspring of habitual criminals would also suffer from insanity or moral imbecility. Hence, if crime was to be prevented in the next generation, it was necessary to prevent habitual criminals, as well as other insane people, from breeding mental defectives. For Maudsley, this could be achieved 'by abstention from marriage or by prudent intermarriage' (*ibid*: 283). Fourth, it implied that in assessing offenders – in determining their capacity for reform, or their potential dangerousness – one should look not just at their own past behaviour, but also at their ancestry. If there was a tendency towards insanity, intemperance, or criminality in the offenders ancestry, there was a greater likelihood that they lacked moral sense.

---

15 For a brief account of Thomson's career as a prison doctor and his views on crime, see Jayewardene (1963/4: 164–7).

16 Once again, there was a circularity in this claim that habitual criminals, being moral imbeciles, were irreformable: the notion that habitual criminals possessed criminal instincts was inferred from the fact that attempts to reform them had failed – the claim that criminals were irreformable was then inferred from the 'fact' that they had criminal instincts.

These notions – that some criminals were irreformable, that habitual criminals were like primitive people in a civilised environment, that a tendency towards criminality could be transmitted by hereditary action to the next generation, and that there was much to be learned from study of the ancestry of offenders – all occupied a central position in official discourses on the problem of habitual criminals throughout the last quarter of the 19th century. These ideas were already in circulation before they were popularised, from the 1870s on, by 'criminal anthropologists' (see Jayewardene 1963/4).[17]

Proposals for the treatment of moral imbeciles/habitual criminals

To conclude this section, I will look at some of the policy proposals which were informed by the idea that habitual criminals were moral imbeciles. For Maudsley, the discovery of moral imbeciles had profound implications for the criminal law, in that it put in question the fundamental assumption upon which the law was enforced – ie that all adult, sane persons had the capacity to obey the law. This supposition enabled the courts to by-pass questions about the actual moral responsibility of individual offenders:

> Laws are made and enforced on the supposition that all persons who have reached a certain age ... and are not deprived of their reason, have the capacity to know and obey them; so that when the laws are broken, the punishment inflicted is in proportion to the nature of the offence and not to the actual moral responsibility of individuals. The legislator can know nothing of individuals; he must necessarily assume a uniform standard of mental capacity so far as a knowledge of right and wrong, and of moral power so far as resistance to unlawful impulses, are concerned (Maudsley 1874: 24).

This assumption, Maudsley contended, was quite wrong. There were many persons who were not insane but who lacked moral sense. Such persons might have an intellectual understanding of right and wrong, but possess no real feeling for the distinction. Such persons were:

> ... of lower moral responsibility than the average of mankind; they have been taught the same lessons as the rest of mankind, and have a full theoretical knowledge of them, but they have not really assimilated them; the principles inculcated never gain that hold of their minds which they gain in a sound and well-constituted nature (Maudsley 1874: 24–5).

The obvious conclusion to draw from this is that the law should not be enforced against such persons – 'it would be wrong to punish an offender at all; he ought rather to be pitied and kindly cared for' (*ibid*: 26). However, Maudsley's actual conclusion is somewhat different and quite strange. He points out, quite conventionally, that although moral imbeciles/habitual

---

17   On criminal anthropology see Ellis (1891). For a critique see Gould (1981: 122–45). For an account of Lombroso's criminal science in its socio-historical context, see Pick (1989: chapter 5).

criminals deserved compassion rather than anger, it was still necessary to deprive them of liberty in order to prevent them from committing further crimes: 'though the criminal might be compassionated, it would still be necessary to deprive him of the power of doing further mischief' (*ibid*: 27). What one expects to follow is an argument that such persons should not be punished by law but should be detained in an institution like a lunatic asylum, where they would receive care and treatment. In fact, Maudsley suggests that it is appropriate to send such persons to prison:

> If we are satisfied that our prison-system is the best that can be devised for the prevention of crime and the reformation of the criminal, we may rest satisfied that it is the best treatment for the sort of insanity from which criminals suffer (Maudsley 1874: 27).

This, seemingly anomalous recommendation can be partly explained by reference to Maudsley's views on the treatment of the insane. Maudsley thought it made little difference whether offenders were sent to prisons or asylums, since both were forms of punishment: 'The measures which are necessarily adopted for the proper care of the insane and for the protection of others are a punishment' (*ibid*: 26). For Maudsley, the appropriate response to the insane was to deprive them of their liberty, make them work, and subject them to discipline. Hence, in reality, the insane were punished. Therefore, to regard offenders as being in the same category as the insane did not mean treating them leniently. And this was Maudsley's main concern. He wanted to assuage the fears of those who felt that to uphold the doctrine of moral imbecility was perilous to society (*ibid*): 'No fear therefore of the practical ill consequences to society need deter us from looking on criminals as the unfortunate victims of a vicious organisation' (*ibid*: 27). Maudsley made it clear that his ideas advanced, rather than hindered, the goal of social defence. His point was that to declare a person to be a moral imbecile did not mean giving up the right to control them, rather it meant the precise opposite.

THE DISCOVERY OF THE PSYCHOPATHIC OFFENDER: A NARROWER CONCEPTION OF MORAL IMBECILITY

As I have indicated, the idea that habitual criminals were moral imbeciles occupied a key position in penal policy discourse during the last quarter of the 19th century. Such a radical and controversial notion inevitably became the focus of a fierce debate. One consequence of this is that, looking back at this period, it is this usage of the concept of moral imbecility which is most visible. However, in this final section I suggest that, as early as the mid-1860s, some psychiatrists were already beginning to use the concept of moral imbecility in a narrower and rather different sense.

An important example of this narrower use comes from an article by the psychiatrist, Stanley Haynes, called 'Clinical Cases Illustrative of Moral

Imbecility and Insanity' (1864/5). In this article, Haynes presents a selection of 15 clinical cases which 'show the general family features of ... moral imbecility' (*ibid*: 533) and discusses briefly the legal implications of these cases. These cases make it quite clear that he does not include simple cases of persistent delinquency within the category of moral imbeciles. Rather, the concept is used to distinguish moral imbeciles from 'normal' persistent delinquents.

Haynes introduces these cases with a very brief explanation of the term 'moral imbecility'. He uses the term to classify all clinical cases in which there appears to be a 'congenital deficiency of one or more of the moral powers' – ie the feelings, emotions, sentiments and passions (*ibid*: 533). He uses the word 'congenital' in a fairly loose way. Hence, included in the category were 'cases in which the disease is obviously strictly congenital', but also ones in which there was an arrest in the development of the brain in early years (*ibid*). Apart from this, Haynes does not state the criteria by which he distinguishes the moral imbecile from the ordinary delinquent. However, a close reading of the clinical cases reveals a number of implicit criteria: moral imbeciles start behaving badly at puberty or earlier; they persist in behaving badly despite the fact they are frequently punished for it – they failed to learn by experience; their behaviour is not only bad but also absurd and extreme; the bad behaviour tends to be episodic – there are often intervals during which their behaviour is fairly normal; they seldom express the slightest regret or shame for their conduct – they do not seem to feel that it is wrong; they are, in other respects, quite intelligent – they have an intellectual grasp of the distinction between right and wrong, they do not suffer from delusions, and are not 'fatuous or furious'; and there is often some family history of insanity or other disorders affecting the mind.

Apart from these clinical cases, Haynes had nothing original to contribute to the understanding of moral imbecility or to the debate about how society should respond to such people. His article concludes with a short discussion in which he argues that the law should recognise 'mental gradations between perfect sanity and absolute insanity' (*ibid*: 548) – but he concedes that this point has already been admirably elucidated by others. What is important about the article is that through its presentation of 15 fairly detailed clinical cases, it identifies a distinct type of delinquent who does not fall into any of the existing categories of insanity or mental deficiency, yet is clearly distinguishable (at least to the clinical observer) from the 'normal' persistent delinquent. I suggest that it is in these clinical cases, rather than in the better known contributions of Maudsley, that one finds – for the first time – a clear concern with the specific types of offenders who would later be labelled 'psychopathic offenders'. Long after the link between mental deficiency and habitual criminality had been discredited, this type of offender would still be regarded as mentally abnormal and be a target of official concern and therapeutic interventions.

CHAPTER 6

ATTITUDES AND POLICIES OF TREATMENT PROFESSIONALS TOWARDS MORAL IMBECILES OR PSYCHOPATHIC OFFENDERS, c 1875–c 1953

INTRODUCTION

I described in chapter 5 how, by the 1870s, a handful of psychiatrists were trying to establish that certain kinds of offender, who seemed to be intellectually sound, suffered from a mental disease called 'moral imbecility' which was the cause of their persistent misconduct. They argued that moral imbeciles should not be held responsible for their criminal acts, but that they were a danger to society and therefore required institutional control. In this chapter, I look at the development of attitudes and policies towards this group of offenders from the 1870s until the middle of the 1950s (ie until just before the official recognition of 'psychopathic disorder' by the Mental Health Act 1959). Throughout much of this period, moral imbeciles – or 'moral defectives' as they were sometimes known – were officially classified along with the 'mentally deficient'. Some familiarity with the category of mental deficiency and with social and penal policies towards the mentally deficient is therefore necessary in order to understand official attitudes and policies towards 'moral defectives'. I start, therefore, with a brief examination of the category of mental deficiency, in which I argue that the inclusion of moral defectiveness in the broader category of mental deficiency was not as anomalous as it might at first appear.

In the following section I look at how moral imbecility was dealt with in the *Report of the Royal Commission on the Care and Control of the Feeble-Minded, 1908*[1] which led to official recognition of the category. I show that, in order to obtain legislative provision for the control of moral imbeciles, those who promoted the category conceded that such persons should be held responsible for their criminal conduct.

The 1908 Report led to the Mental Deficiency Act 1913 which provided that, under certain circumstances, moral imbeciles could be placed in an institution or under statutory guardianship (see Jones 1960: 68).[2] In the following section, I look at the use made of these legal powers. I show that there were considerable differences of opinion within psychiatry about who was included within the legal category of 'moral imbeciles'. Some argued that the category included people who were defective only in morals – ie people who were intellectually normal. In practice, however, most psychiatrists

---

1   Also known as the Radnor Commission.

2   Jones (1972: part 2) is a revised and abridged version of this earlier book.

interpreted the concept more narrowly, diagnosing moral imbecility only in cases where moral disorder was accompanied by some measurable intellectual deficiency. Since such persons could already be subjected to control as 'feeble-minded persons', the power to confine moral imbeciles was of little practical significance. Hence, the passage of the 1913 law did not lead to the construction of an effective apparatus for the control of moral imbeciles. The attempts to establish a system of control were frustrated, not by lawyers, but by more conservative members of the psychiatric profession who refused to classify people as mentally deficient if they showed no signs, other than irresponsible behaviour, of intellectual defect.

In the following section of the chapter I describe how penal administrators and professionals responded to this development by introducing a new term, 'psychopathic' offenders, to describe those whom they had previously classified as moral imbeciles. I argue, contrary to the conventional belief, that the adoption of this term owed little to theoretical commitment to the concept of 'constitutional psychopathy' which had been developed since the 1880s by continental psychiatrists such as Koch. Rather, those who introduced the concept of the 'psychopathic offender' did so for the purely pragmatic purpose of devising a new psychiatric term which could be used to classify a group of offenders for whom special procedures were required, even though they were not insane or lacking in intelligence. I go on to examine policies towards those designated as psychopaths between the early 1920s and the mid-1950s. I show that there was no single policy towards psychopathic offenders in this period. Rather, a range of quite different and often contradictory policies were advocated and implemented. Some regarded psychopaths as improvable and advocated the establishment of special institutions for their care and treatment. Others, regarded untreatability as a defining characteristic of the condition and used the concept to justify the exclusion of 'disruptive psychopaths' from treatment programmes designed for more hopeful cases. Another group of professionals were interested in psychopathic offenders primarily as an object of study. They thought that if they could identify the forces which produced full-blown psychopathic personalities, they could find ways of preventing the disorder from occurring in others. Through this project, discourses on psychopathic offenders merged with wider discourses on child-rearing and socialisation. Also, cutting across these different policies towards psychopathic offenders, there were continuations of older disputes about the scope of the concept. Some treatment professionals continued to use it as a descriptive term for all habitual offenders. Others used it to demarcate a narrower group of 'non-sane non-insane aberrant individuals' (East 1949: 125).

THE MENTALLY DEFICIENT

In the 19th century, social reformers became concerned with the problem of people who, due to severe inborn mental deficiency, were incapable of functioning in society without an unusual level of external assistance and supervision. In the 18th century, the care and control of such people was deemed to be the responsibility of the person's family and immediate community (see Jones 1960: 1). However, industrialisation and urbanisation had the twin effects of making such care and control less feasible and making mental deficiency even more of a social handicap. One result of this was that the mentally deficient often found themselves confined in institutions meant for other types of problem person, such as lunatic asylums, workhouses and jails. In the middle of the 19th century, some reformers began to argue that this response was neither adequate nor appropriate. Hence, a campaign emerged for the establishment of asylums, funded by charity and government, dedicated to the care and control of 'idiots' (Jones 1960: chapter 2; Simmons 1978).

It is of crucial importance to realise that the category of mental deficiency was defined as much in terms of *social* incompetence or maladjustment as in terms of *intellectual* slowness.[3] Those whose mentality was such as to render them incapable of independent and efficient performance of their duties in social situations were regarded as mentally defective (see Report of the Mental Deficiency Committee 1929: 7 – hereinafter the '1929 Report'). Although, with the move to universal elementary education, 'educational failure' came to be regarded as an important indication of mental deficiency, it was the 'general response to school life' rather than academic under-achievement that was considered important (1929 Report: 13). It was not until the 20th century that intelligence tests were considered to have any diagnostic significance, and even then these tests played a secondary role in determinations of mental deficiency (see Rose 1985: chapters 4 and 5). As the authors of the 1929 Report put it:

> ... the only really satisfactory criterion of mental deficiency is the social one, and if a person is suffering from a degree of incomplete mental development which renders him incapable of independent social adaptation and which necessitates external care, supervision and control, then such person is a mental defective (1929 Report: 13).

The expansion of the category of mental deficiency

Initially, the concern of these reformers was with people whom they classified

---

3   But see Burt (1937: chapter 2) who shows that the term mental deficiency had different meanings in Mental Deficiency Acts and Education Acts.

as 'idiots'. Idiots were so deeply defective that they required constant close supervision – they were like very young children. Idiocy was generally accompanied by physical stigmata. The mental development of idiots was so incomplete that:

> ... they are unable to appreciate and protect themselves from the common physical dangers which threaten life ... They are incapable of any scholastic education ... they cannot perform any kind of work, and they have to be washed, dressed and looked after all their lives (1929 Report: 11).

During the second half of the 19th century, however, reformers began to expand the category of mental deficiency to include two milder grades: 'imbecility' and 'feeble-mindedness' (Burt 1937: 61; 1929 Report: 11). Imbeciles were more competent than idiots in that they could be taught to protect themselves from common physical dangers and could be 'trained to perform simple routine tasks under supervision' (1929 Report: 11). However, they were incapable of earning their living and could not look after themselves without supervision.[4]

The feeble-minded were more competent than imbeciles. They could be trained to perform work which might pay for their keep (*ibid*: 11–12). They also lacked physical stigmata. Their main problems were that they were:

> lacking in certain features of intelligence, such as the capacity to look ahead and to make sensible plans for their future, and also in the control and common sense needed to achieve such plans (*ibid*: 12).

And crucially, in some cases feeble-minded people manifested:

> ... such a marked lack of sense of right and wrong, of responsibility and social obligation, together with strongly marked antisocial propensities as to cause the individual to be a grave danger (1929 Report: 12).

This extension of the category of mental deficiency to include feeble-mindedness had an important impact upon the nature of the category of mental deficiency. When the category was confined to idiocy and imbecility, the defining features of mental deficiency were a near total inability to function independently due to severe intellectual retardation. When the category was extended to include feeble-mindedness it began to encompass people who had some capacity to function independently, but who were 'social failures' – ie people who due to mental under-development ended up committing crime, having illegitimate children, becoming habitual drunkards and paupers, and so on (see Simmons 1978: 400). Moreover, such social failure was attributed less to gross intellectual deficiency, more to an apparent lack of common sense and self-control.

So, although the difference between feeble-mindedness and other types of mental deficiency was represented as a quantitative one – ie feeble-

---

4   On the relation of crime to imbecility see Sullivan (1924: chapter 12). Sullivan's view was that idiots were incapable of crime: 'the idiot, from the poverty of his aptitudes, is obviously as incapable of anti-social as of social conduct' (*ibid*: 184).

mindedness was presented as a *milder* grade of mental deficiency – the actual descriptions of the condition suggest that it also differed *qualitatively* from idiocy and imbecility, in at least two ways. First, whereas idiots and imbeciles were grossly incompetent, the feeble-minded seemed to be simply *feckless and irresponsible*. Idiots and imbeciles could not look after themselves – without assistance and supervision they simply could not survive. The feeble-minded, on the other hand, might just survive without social support. What they lacked was less fundamental competence, more a sense of *social responsibility and obligation*. They had no foresight and lacked self-control. They had anti-social tendencies which rendered them dangerous, less to themselves, more to others. Secondly, whereas the incompetence of idiots and imbeciles was due to *severe intellectual deficiency*, the social maladjustment of the feeble-minded appeared to be due to a *lack of 'common sense'*.

The inclusion of feeble-mindedness within the general category of mental deficiency therefore brought about a change in the nature of the broader category. It made it possible to conceive of those who were socially irresponsible, and who appeared to lack common sense, as mentally deficient people, even if they were intelligent enough to look after themselves. Hence, the concept of feeble-mindedness paved the way for the further extension of the category of mental deficiency to include 'moral imbecility' – defined as a condition in which the person does not lack intelligence, but is so lacking in responsibility, common sense and self-control that he or she is unable to function in society without becoming a nuisance and a danger to others.

THE OFFICIAL RECOGNITION OF 'MORAL IMBECILITY'

Towards the end of the 19th century, reformers and organisations concerned with mental deficiency began to campaign for the appointment of a Royal Commission to investigate the extent of the problem of feeble-mindedness, its social implications, and its solutions (see Simmons 1978). The Royal Commission they sought was appointed in 1904 and reported in 1908 (*ibid*: 391). A central feature of the Report of the Royal Commission on the Care and Control of the Feeble-Minded, 1908 (hereinafter the 1908b Report) was the extent to which feeble-mindedness was defined in terms of wayward and anti-social behaviour. In the report, the terms 'feeble-minded' and 'morally incapable' are used almost interchangeably. This confirms the suggestion of Harvey Simmons (1978) that the real concern of reformers was, less with low intelligence, more with crime, pauperism, illegitimacy and alcoholism. As he states, 'policymakers were really trying to solve other social problems such as poverty, crime and illegitimacy by reducing the numbers of feeble-minded people' (*ibid*: 400).

The Royal Commission was concerned quite explicitly with reckless and irresponsible individuals. It stated its concern as being with the large numbers of mentally defective persons:

> whose wayward and irresponsible lives are productive of crime and misery, of much injury and mischief to themselves and to others, and of much continuous expenditure wasteful to the community and to individual families (1908b Report: para 9).

Elsewhere in its Report, the Royal Commission virtually conflated the weak-minded and the morally incapable, and it revealed its main concern as being with social danger:

> There are undoubtedly numbers of person who are not idiots or lunatics, or at least are not regarded as either – persons of weak mind who are socially dangerous. In the affluent classes there are numbers of weak-minded lads. I have known murders perpetrated by lads of that character, who are not thought to be certifiable, but allowed to go about uncertified though obviously weak-minded. Among the poorer classes, there are, no doubt, great numbers of morally incapables who are not certified, and who are moving about and are socially dangerous (1908b Report: chapter 23).

The Royal Commission contended that, although such persons were not mentally deficient enough to be certified as idiots or lunatics, they were not wholly responsible due to weakness of mind. It argued that if such persons committed crimes they should not be released upon serving their sentence but should be detained for so long as they remained dangerous:

> There are cases where weak-minded persons commit crimes, and they are not certifiably insane. They cannot, strictly speaking, be found insane as laid down in *MacNaghten's* case, or under the law as ordinarily administered, and yet they are from weakness of mind not wholly responsible. You cannot say that they are insane, and yet the state of their minds is such that they ought not to be set at liberty and allowed to commit further crimes of the same sort ... (1908b Report: para 436).

The Royal Commission proposed to extend the legal status of the insane and idiots to these weak-minded moral defectives so that they could be subject to control, even though they were not strictly speaking suffering from insanity or idiocy. The psychiatrisation of wayward and irresponsible persons did not mean treating them more leniently. Rather, it was considered necessary from the point of view of social defence. Indeed, the main critics of the Royal Commission's recommendations were those who opposed them on the ground that they were a threat to the liberty of the subject (see Jones 1972: 191ff) On the other hand, it is worth noting that the Royal Commission did not endorse the radical demands of the Eugenics Movement, which wanted to sterilise the feeble-minded in the interests of purification of the race. As Jones puts it in her summary of its conclusions: 'Their final report steered a sane and sensible course between the Scylla of "liberty-of-the-subject" agitation, and the Charybdis of eugenic theory' (Jones 1972: 191).

The legal responsibility of the feeble-minded

To be consistent, the Royal Commission might have argued that if such persons were not responsible enough to be allowed freedom, they should not be held legally responsible for their crimes. As we saw in chapter 5, this was the position of psychiatrists during the 1860s and 1870s. The Royal Commission departed from this consistent position, however, and argued that the feeble-minded would remain legally responsible for any crimes which they committed. They were to be categorised along with the insane and idiots for the purpose of control, but along with the mentally normal for the purpose of criminal liability. The insanity defence was to remain available only to those judged to be insane according to the 'intellectualistic' definition contained in the M'Naghten Rules. A diagnosis of moral imbecility was not to be treated as evidence of non-responsibility for purposes of criminal liability. Such a diagnosis would become relevant only after the issue of the person's criminal liability had been decided by the court. It was only once the verdict had been announced that the question of feeble-mindedness would be raised, as relevant to the question of disposal:

> ... in the case of persons who are charged with offences and are alleged to be mentally defective the principle should be adopted of keeping the question of the committal of the alleged offence separate from questions of alleged mental defect (1908b Report: para 26).

> It is not ... necessary or desirable that the precedents under the Trial of Lunatics Act 1883 ... should be pushed further ... The question of fact may go to the jury, and when that is settled, the question of mental defect may be settled by the court in modification of the sentence (1908b Report: para 460).

Critics might comment that the Royal Commission wanted to have its cake and eat it, ie it wanted to regard the same person as completely sane and fully responsible for the purpose of criminal liability, but as not sane and not responsible for the purpose of compulsory hospitalisation. The Royal Commission actually acknowledged this contradiction but accepted that it would be 'inexpedient' for the courts to create a verdict of 'guilty but feeble-minded' and that feeble-minded persons must, therefore, be held fully responsible for their criminal acts (*ibid*: para: 458). The conciliatory tone towards the law evident in the following statement from the Royal Commission is in marked contrast to that of Thomas Laycock and other psychiatrists, half a century earlier (see chapter 5):

> It is of course true ... that a person must be either responsible or irresponsible; that in the matter of criminal procedure these two terms cover the whole ground, and that where the question is 'guilty or not guilty' it would be impossible for the law to admit the existence of any doubtful territory between the two (1908b Report: para 458).

This problem was represented by the Royal Commission as a practical one. It stated that juries were not competent to determine whether or not a person was feeble-minded. Whereas the lunatic or the idiot could easily be recognised by the layperson, the differences between the feeble-minded and the simply backward or dull could be detected only by experts (*ibid*: para 459). Here, the Royal Commission implicitly was conceding that, in cases involving feeble-minded persons, the question of criminal responsibility must be determined by a jury, and not by experts. Experts' opinions would be introduced only when the verdict had been reached, in order to modify the sentence (*ibid*). A diagnosis of feeble-mindedness would not affect criminal liability, but would be relevant to the questions of whether the person was to be punished as a normal offender or subject to preventive detention, supervision and control as a mental defective and whether they were to be sent to prisons or to special institutions.

MORAL IMBECILITY UNDER THE MENTAL DEFICIENCY ACT 1913

The Mental Deficiency Act, incorporating the recommendations of the Royal Commission, was passed in 1913 (see Jones 1960: chapter 4).[5] The 1913 Act provided for the certification and control of mental defectives. The provisions of the Act covered four grades of mental defective: idiots, imbeciles, feeble-minded persons and moral imbeciles. Moral imbeciles were defined as:

> persons who from birth or from an early age display some permanent mental defect, coupled with strong vicious or criminal propensities, on which punishment has had little or no deterrent effect (Mental Deficiency Act 1913, s 1 (d)).[6]

Dr Charles Mercier claimed that he formulated this definition and insisted on the inclusion of 'moral imbecility', in the Act, as a distinct grade of mental disorder (Mercier 1917; see also Burt 1944: 30–2). Like Cyril Burt, Mercier was of the view that the term 'mental' included what was 'moral' or 'temperamental', as well as what was 'intellectual' (Burt 1944: 31). For Mercier, there should have been no need for a separate clause in the Act providing for moral imbeciles; the term 'mental defect' should have been read as including moral and temperamental, as well as intellectual disorders. The so-called 'moral imbecile' should have been certifiable as a

---

5　This was five years after the Royal Commission produced its report and nine years after its appointment. On the reasons for this delay and developments between 1908 and 1913 see Jones (1960: chapter 4, or 1972: 194ff).

6　For a brief account of how this definition was arrived at and what its implications were, see Burt (1944: 30–1, n.1). For a discussion of some of the problems in interpreting this definition, see Tredgold (1917). Note that the term 'moral imbeciles' was replaced by 'moral defectives' in an amending statute, the Mental Deficiency Act 1927.

feeble-minded person.[7] However, Mercier pressed for a separate clause providing for the certification and control of moral imbeciles because he feared that, without such a clause, the Act would be applied to moral defectives *only if they were also intellectually defective*. Mercier's fear was that, 'magistrates and certifying officers would have been prone to think only of "intellectual" defect, unless explicit sanction had been given' (*ibid*: 32).

However, the definition of moral imbecility contained in the 1913 Act failed to resolve this issue. As it stood, it could be interpreted in two different ways. The inclusion of the words 'permanent mental defect' in the definition of moral imbecility created the very ambiguity which Mercier had been keen to avoid. As it stood, the definition of moral imbeciles could refer to those who were defective in intelligence and also had strong violent or criminal propensities, or it could refer to those who were defective only in morals. As Burt put it:

> The words may mean, first of all, one who is primarily defective in intelligence, but happens, in addition, to possess an incorrigible propensity to crime, a propensity itself independent of, and superimposed upon, the essential defect of intelligence. But secondly, the clause may bear, almost equally well, a totally different sense: it may denote a person whose incorrigible criminality is of itself enough to constitute, or is of itself the necessary result of, an inborn mental defect. With the former meaning, by a curious paradox of legal grammar, a moral imbecile would be an imbecile whose behaviour is not moral; with the latter, he would be an intelligent person whose morals are imbecile. The difference is plain. The one is an immoral defective; the other is defective morally (Burt 1944: 31).[8]

As I have indicated, the proponents of the concept of moral imbecility intended to refer to individuals who were of normal intelligence but lacked moral sense, ie individuals who were 'defective morally'. However, in practice, the label was usually applied to amoral persons *only if they presented some degree of intellectual deficiency*, in addition to moral insensibility (*ibid*; see also Sullivan 1924: 31). But, such persons could probably have been dealt with as feeble-minded persons. Therefore, in practical terms, the legal provision for moral imbeciles was redundant. It would therefore be mistaken to assume that, just because the Mental Deficiency Act made provision for the certification and institutional control of 'moral imbeciles', that such persons were in fact subjected to special forms of control. Those who wanted to subject those who were morally insensible to control as mental defectives failed to achieve their goal at this stage. Even though they managed to persuade the authorities to create legal powers for the control of 'moral imbeciles', they

---

7   The Act's definition of feeble-minded persons encompassed those: 'in whose case there exists from birth or from an early age mental defectiveness not amounting to imbecility, yet so pronounced that they require care, supervision, and control for their own protection or for the protection of others' (s 1(c)).

8   The ambiguity in the legal definition of moral imbecility is discussed also by Sullivan (1924: 200–202).

failed to persuade magistrates, certifying officers, and other medical professionals to use these powers. As Gunn *et al* put it, in their history of the prison psychiatric service:

> 'Moral imbeciles' had been brought within the compass of the 1913 Act in response to evidence given to the Royal Commission by prison (and other) doctors. The former must have rejoiced that these particularly difficult offenders were now to be channelled into the new asylums. But this first attempt to deal with one group of psychopaths was ahead of its time and was rarely used. Doctors came to believe that in order to come within the terms of the Mental Deficiency Acts, the moral defective had also to display defective intelligence. The Act was therefore mainly used for those cases where moral defectiveness was coupled with subnormal intelligence (Gunn et al 1978: 14).

Crime in relation to moral imbecility

I have indicated that there was no consensus about the meaning of moral imbecility in this period. However, before moving on we might consider W C Sullivan's use of the concept as an example of the sense in which the concept was used by many doctors who dealt professionally with offenders (Sullivan was medical superintendent of Broadmoor Criminal Lunatic Asylum). Sullivan was opposed to attempts to 'reduce' crime, even habitual crime, to an inborn anti-social tendency (1924: chapter 1). For him, the question of what role psychopathological conditions played in producing crime was best addressed as an empirical one, to be answered through clinical examinations of individual offenders (*ibid*: 15). Hence, his discussion of 'crime in relation to moral imbecility' avoided sweeping generalisations to the effect that habitual criminals were moral imbeciles. Instead, one of his concerns was to distinguish the moral imbecile from the 'normal' persistent delinquent.

Sullivan's chapter on moral imbecility opened with a selection of cases which illustrate the clinical character of the condition and give a clear idea of the types of offender who would be described as moral imbeciles. It is clear from reading these cases that Sullivan applied the concept, not to ordinary habitual offenders, but to those whose behaviour was in some way extreme and inexplicable. One character, during housebreaking expeditions, was in the habit of 'doing all the mischief he could, turning on water-taps, for instance, and cutting gas-pipes' (*ibid*: 192). Another, cut the throat of an 11-year-old child and 'outraged her after death' (*ibid*: 193). Another, who eventually committed murder, had 'served a term of imprisonment for cruelty to cats – hanging them on a rope, pole-axing them, and cutting them up', acts from which he derived sexual gratification (*ibid*: 194). Another, for no apparent reason, 'took her niece out for a walk, sat the child on a wall by the river-side, told her to look at the water, and pushed her in' (*ibid*: 196). On investigation, it was discovered that all of these characters were troublesome and vicious from early childhood – ie from before puberty. They persisted in troublesome behaviour despite being repeatedly punished for it and despite the knowledge that they would almost certainly be punished again. The most striking feature of these characters, however, was that they showed little remorse or shame in relation to their crimes (*ibid*: 195). A 17-year-old who murdered an old woman and mutilated her sexual parts after death, then 'took some oranges which he found in the house, and rejoined his comrades in the street, sharing the oranges with them and playing at peg-top till he was arrested' (*ibid*: 194–5). 'Later, he seemed to take pleasure in discussing his crime and describing its details' (*ibid*). From these cases, Sullivan summarises the general characteristics of moral imbecility as:

> the early appearance of vicious and mischievous tendencies, their persistence in spite of the repeated experience of the unpleasant results to the moral imbecile himself which follow their indulgence, and the absence of any sort of moral feeling in relation to them (Sullivan 1924: 198).

There was no doubt that these characters were not just bad but also morally insensible. They had little or no capacity for moral emotion; they *felt* no repugnance towards the misconduct of others and showed no remorse for their own misconduct. According to Sullivan, however, moral insensibility was not, on its own, sufficient to bring the person within the definition of a moral imbecile. It had to be combined with some degree of intellectual deficiency:

> The moral imbecile, then, is not simply an amoral person; he is an amoral person who presents some degree of intellectual deficiency; he is a defective whose congenital debility is predominant, indeed, in the sphere of the emotions and the will, but affects also, to however slight an extent, the sphere of intelligence (Sullivan 1924: 200–201).

This sounds straightforward: the concept of moral imbecility is applicable to persons who, from an early age, display strong vicious or criminal propensities, do not respond favourably to punishment, and show no shame or remorse for their gross misconduct, provided they also display definite intellectual deficiency. However, if we look at what could render a person intellectually deficient, in Sullivan's eyes, we will see that his views are not quite as simple as they appear. In some of the cases which Sullivan presented, he suggested that the person's intelligence level, as measured on the Binet-Simon scale, was abnormally low.[9] But, if this was so, such cases could have been classified as feeble-minded; there was no need for a separate category of moral imbecility for such cases.[10] In another case presented by Sullivan as an instance of moral imbecility, the person was described as 'a man of considerable natural ability and acute intelligence' (*ibid*: 198). And in another case he stated that the patient 'refused to cooperate in mental tests, but it was evident that her intellectual level was fairly high' (*ibid*: 196). How did Sullivan

---

9   On the measure of intelligence see Rose (1985: chapter 5).

10 For example, in one of his cases illustrative of moral imbecility, Sullivan claimed that the person's intelligence level was a little under 10 years (Sullivan 1924: 193). Earlier in his book, he stated that feeble-minded persons had an intelligence level of seven to 12 years (*ibid*: 182).

square these statements with his contentions that such persons were moral imbeciles and that the concept of moral imbecility was applicable only to those who were in some way intellectually deficient? Sullivan's answer was that intellectual debility could be inferred from the general character of their conduct and their incapacity to profit by experience (ie to respond to punishment) (*ibid*: 199):

> Even when, as is frequently the case, the moral imbecile makes quite a good showing with the ordinary mental tests, and displays in his conversation some quickness of wit and some capacity for acute, if superficial, reasoning, his real lack of intelligence is revealed clearly enough by his history. Viewed as a whole, his conduct is patently absurd; his life is not only evil, it is foolish (Sullivan 1924: 199).

It appears, from the above, that Sullivan had fallen into the very circularity he wanted to avoid. He insisted that: 'It is only when absence or deficiency of moral feeling is combined with ... intellectual deficiency that we can speak of moral imbecility'. Yet, he inferred intellectual deficiency, not from independent tests of intellectual ability, but from the bad behaviour itself. Moreover, when independent tests of intellectual ability seemed to indicate that the person was not intellectually deficient, he ignored the results. He insisted that their absurd and foolish conduct was itself evidence of intellectual debility. For Sullivan, the *conduct* of these persons exposed the fact that they lacked 'that essential quality of the normal intelligence, common sense' (*ibid*). So, whilst Sullivan insisted that the concept of moral imbecility was applicable to persons only if they were intellectually deficient, he rejected what had become the usual way of defining and assessing intelligence, and replaced it with his own conception in which lack of intelligence could be inferred from foolish behaviour. Sullivan, it turns out, is much closer than he himself believed, to those who argued that moral imbecility was a form of mental defect in which the person displayed no intellectual disorder but only a defective moral sense.

It seems to me that Sullivan's attempt to distinguish the moral imbecile from the 'relatively normal habitual delinquent' in terms of intellectual debility failed. If this distinction were to work he would have to have accepted the results of some 'external' test of intelligence – ie the existence of defective intelligence would have to be established without reference to the persons aberrant conduct.[11] He could not do what he actually proposed, which was to infer intellectual deficiency from 'the record of persistently irrational and unprofitable anti-social acts' (*ibid*: 201). However, things are more complicated still. Towards the end of his chapter on crime and moral imbecility, Sullivan suggested that there was a clear contrast between the *pattern of criminality* of the moral imbecile and that of the normal persistent offender: the criminality

---

11 Sullivan also discussed attempts which had been made to ascertain moral imbecility through ethical discrimination tests. On the limitations of these tests, see Watson (1988).

of the moral imbecile was distinguished 'by the precocity of its appearance, by the variety of its direction, and by its frequently gratuitous character' (*ibid*: 202). The relatively normal habitual criminal usually started his criminal career not in childhood but in youth, tended to be a specialist in his criminal activities, and committed crime for profitable ends. The moral imbecile, on the other hand, started crime in childhood, engaged in a much wider range of misconduct, and seemed to do evil for its own sake – simply to gratify his perverse impulses (*ibid*: 202–3). It is from such a pattern of criminal behaviour that Sullivan inferred moral imbecility.

As I have suggested, Sullivan's attempt to limit the scope of the category of moral imbecility, by insisting that it was applicable only to those with some degree of intellectual deficiency, failed because of his willingness to infer intellectual deficiency from a particular pattern of aberrant conduct. However, this does not mean that he placed no limits upon the scope of the concept; it does not mean that he applied it to all habitual offenders. As we have just seen, he applied the concept only to offenders who manifested a particular *pattern of delinquency*: those who repeatedly thieved and lied as soon as they were capable of doing so, who engaged in a variety of different types of delinquency (such as malicious destructiveness, sexual vice, cruelty to others, thieving and lying); and who did wrong not for profit but for pleasure and whose wrongdoing was often accompanied by superfluous malignancy (*ibid*). Sullivan did, therefore, present reasonably clear criteria for distinguishing the moral imbecile from the 'normal persistent delinquent'. However, these criteria are behavioural rather than psychological.

THE INTRODUCTION OF THE CONCEPT OF PSYCHOPATHY INTO PENAL DISCOURSE

As we saw earlier, those who wanted the types of offender whom Sullivan described as moral imbeciles to be subject to certification and institutional control as mental defectives had, by 1913, secured legislative provision for such certification and control. However, when these legal powers were put into use (which, due to the disruptions of war, was not until the early 1920s), they saw the term being interpreted in a narrow way, to exclude those who did not show any intellectual debility. It was at this stage that the term 'psychopath' began to appear frequently in the discourse of penal treatment professionals. The term 'psychopath' was applied to the 'true' moral imbecile, in an effort to distinguish him from those whose moral defects were accompanied by defective intelligence.

It is important to realise that the adoption of the term 'psychopaths' by those who dealt professionally with offenders owed little to theoretical commitment to theories of psychopathic personality which were being developed by some continental psychiatrists. To the contrary, those penal administrators and treatment professionals who adopted the term 'psychopath' usually had serious reservations about its suitability for designating moral imbeciles. They suggested that the term 'psychopathic personality' referred to a distinct type of psychological disorder, whereas the category of moral imbeciles embraced a variety of psychological types. Nevertheless, they adopted the term as a convenient one for classifying those offenders who displayed no obvious intellectual defect but who, due to an apparent lack of either moral sense or inhibitory control seemed to be unable to behave properly. For these penal treatment professionals, the term 'psychopaths' had the advantage of avoiding words such as imbecility which were widely understood as referring to intellectual debility. The lack of theoretical commitment to the concept of psychopathic personality on the part of those who adopted the term to classify those who were previously categorised as moral imbeciles can be seen in the following statement from the prison doctor, M Hamblin Smith:

> There is a large group of cases which have been described under the unsatisfactory title of 'psychopathic personality' as well as under equally objectionable titles. But the nomenclature is comparatively unimportant; for the group is well-recognised, although ill-defined (Hamblin Smith 1926).

ATTITUDES AND POLICIES TOWARDS PSYCHOPATHIC OFFENDERS, 1920s–1950s

In this section, I look at how psychopathic offenders were regarded and treated by penal treatment professionals from about the middle of the 1920s until the middle of the 1950s. The most striking thing about professional discourse on 'psychopathic offenders' during this period is its diversity; there were numerous quite different approaches to the problem and these different approaches were themselves often inter-woven into a complex melange. It is therefore precarious to attempt to find a pattern in the development of official attitudes and policies towards psychopaths between the 1920s and the 1950s. In seeking to find a pattern, we run the risk of *imposing* one upon developments which are almost patternless. Nevertheless, in what follows I will suggest that it is possible to identify some important general trends.

First, during the 1920s, proponents of the psychological-therapeutic approach to crime began to question the assumption that moral imbeciles were a distinct group within the more general category of mental defectives. There were some attempts to dissolve the category of moral imbecility altogether, by distributing so-called moral imbeciles into other general categories such as intellectual defectives, the insane, and psycho-neurotics. However, these attempts always left a residual number of 'moral imbeciles'. These 'unclassifiable' cases were often placed in the new category of psychopathic personalities, which seemed to be nothing other than a residual category. This residual status of 'psychopathic offenders' has been an important feature of attitudes and policies towards psychopathic offenders ever since.

Secondly, the 1930s saw the emergence of a social-psychological perspective on crime – consisting of a heavily sociologised and somewhat bowdlerised version of psychoanalytic psychology. The emergence of this social-psychological perspective on crime had an important impact upon attitudes and policies towards psychopathic offenders. However, it is difficult to be precise about the nature of that impact. First proponents of the social-psychological approach tended to suggest a new relationship between criminality and mental illness by suggesting that both conditions were alternative manifestations of the same underlying problem: social maladjustment. This gave psychopaths, who seemed to occupy a grey area between the mentally ill and criminals, a new theoretical significance. Secondly, the emergence of the social-psychological perspective was articulated with an important shift in the objectives of psychiatry: from cure to prevention. I will suggest that this new emphasis on prevention led to a re-direction of psychiatric attention towards children who displayed psychopathic tendencies, and to neglect of the plight of 'confirmed psychopaths'.

Third, from the middle of the 1940s on, it is possible to detect a move in the direction of a more pessimistic attitude towards the treatment of psychopathic offenders. This was accompanied by renewed interest in biological explanations of psychopathic behaviour. An ironic outcome of this more pessimistic attitude, I will suggest, was that it led to greater attention to the plight of actual psychopaths and to renewed attempts to find special institutions for them.

Finally, one debate which continued throughout this period was the debate about the scope of the concept. During the period under discussion some treatment professionals regarded all habitual offenders as psychologically abnormal and used the concept of psychopathy to indicate this. Others insisted that the scope of the concept – and more generally the scope of the psychiatric approach to crime – should be more limited.

A residual group

During the 1920s, the psychological assessment of offenders was becoming more widespread and systematic in the penal system (see Garland 1994: 46ff). One of the leading figures involved in such assessments was M Hamblin Smith. Like others involved in the psychological assessment of offenders he was particularly interested in 'moral imbeciles'. However, he rejected the notion of an independent moral sense and therefore regarded the concept of moral imbecility as misleading (Hamblin Smith 1922: 152–5). He suggested that those who were described as moral imbeciles were, upon investigation, found to be intellectually defective (and hence properly to be classified as feeble-minded), insane, or the subject of some mental conflict which might respond to psycho-analysis (*ibid*: 154). In effect, this suggestion dissolves the category of moral imbecility and distributes those who were previously so classified into three broad categories of mental abnormality: intellectual deficiency, insanity, and mental conflict.

However, elsewhere in his work, Hamblin Smith introduces a category of 'psychopaths', which appears to be a residual category, consisting of socially maladjusted people who were not mentally normal but who did not fall into any of the other categories of mental abnormality:

> There exists a class of persons who are not 'insane' and not mentally defective in the sense of being certifiable as such. Further, they cannot be grouped among the epileptics or the psycho-neurotics. But their mental condition is such that they are unable to make proper adjustments to the demands of society ... The group is of a very mixed character, and it is not easy to settle on any satisfactory classification (Hamblin Smith 1922: 146–7).

Hamblin Smith classified such persons as psychopaths – a term with which, as we have seen, he was not entirely happy. For him, the category of psychopaths was clearly a residual one in which were placed a variety of disorders which had little in common other than the fact that they did not belong neatly in any of the other major categories. Hamblin Smith's sub-divisions of psychopathy were: inadequate personality, paranoid personality, emotional instability, criminalism, pathological lying, sexual psychopathy, and nomadism. Those so-called moral imbeciles who were not intellectually defective, insane, or suffering from mental conflicts usually belonged, he suggested, to the sub-category 'inadequate personality'.

With regard to the treatment of such persons, Hamblin Smith had little to offer. There were special institutions for mental defectives and for the insane, and he believed that mental conflicts could be removed through psycho-analysis. However, none of these methods were suitable for psychopaths. For 'psychopaths', 'inadequate personalities' or 'moral imbeciles', all Hamblin Smith could suggest was permanent detention:

> And as regards those who, without discoverable mental defect, cannot, by other means, be made to fit in with Society, there is a growing feeling that, in justice both to the offender and to itself, Society must arrange for their permanent detention in some suitable environment (Hamblin Smith 1922: 155).

The social-psychologisation of psychopathic disorder

In the early 1920s a series of brutal, apparently motiveless, murders were committed by youths. Psychological investigations of these youths revealed that many of them were not afflicted by any recognisable mental disorder. Their horrific behaviour was attributed to 'obscure obliquity's, moral and mental, of which science tells us little' (Anon: 1922). Nevertheless, penal reformers and professionals did put forward more specific explanations. One of the most popular was that the murderers were victims of involuntary childhood neglect (perhaps combined with constitutional weakness of mind) which occurred as a result of the Great War. The murders could not therefore be blamed solely on the youths who committed them. Rather, the whole of society was implicated:

> The only thing we do know is that in each of these cases we have a weakling who has been subjected to stresses greater than he could withstand ... These youths, with all their darkness of mind, are the final product of a world at war; their crimes are our crimes, for they are the result of involuntary neglect during the formative years of their childhood; and we slay them for our sins (Anon 1922: 79).

This marks the beginning of a relatively new focus upon the links between faulty upbringing and adult pathological crime – a focus which was to have important implications for discourse about psychopathic conduct.

By the early 1930s, the notion that psychopathic personality was an hereditary, or at least inborn, condition had lost its dominance. The notion of the congenital psychopath gave way, in the discourse of treatment professionals, to the idea that psychopathic personalities were not born but made. Psychopaths, according to this view, were biologically normal people whose personalities had been damaged by faulty upbringing and poor parental management. One implication of this was that improvements in methods of child rearing could prevent such damage and therefore stop the creation of psychopathic personalities. However, the implication that was most frequently drawn was that children and youths who were beginning to manifest psychopathic *traits* could be corrected, by treatment, before they developed into full-blown psychopathic personalities.

As an example of this approach to the problem of psychopathic disorder, we can consider an article by R Gillespie (1930) called: 'The Service of Psychiatry in the Prevention and Treatment of Crime'. Gillespie described psychopathic personalities as persons who were:

> ... unstable, very easily elated and as readily depressed, vain and selfish, often sentimental and childish, or resentful, irritable, grudge-bearing and suspicious. They bear responsibility badly, and resort readily to alcohol and to delinquencies such as forging cheques (Gillespie 1930: 26).

According to Gillespie, such persons constituted about 45 per cent of the prison population (*ibid*). Some cases of psychopathic personality, he suggested, were the result of congenital causes or head injuries. But, he argued, the majority of cases were the result, at least partly, of flaws in the early environment: 'the majority of psychopathic personalities acquire important parts of their unstable disposition as the consequence of faulty training and environment' (*ibid*). Gillespie's assumption was that, since psychopathic behaviour was in a sense learned rather than instinctive, it could be unlearned. Psychopathic personalities, he suggested, could be re-educated and reformed (*ibid*).

Gillespie contended that it was possible and desirable to identify persons with psychopathic traits 'before anti-social acts appear' (*ibid*: 27). If these persons were treated, it would be possible 'to prevent the creation of psychopathic personalities' (*ibid*). Moreover, Gillespie insinuated that it if one waited until such persons did commit an offence it would be too late to treat them:

> Too often ... they cannot readily be placed under the necessary supervision till they commit a punishable offence, when it is already too late for prevention. Yet, the potentialities can readily be recognised beforehand, and treatment instituted which might well be preventive of further trouble (Gillespie 1930: 26).

The underlying point, of course, is that it is necessary to undertake psychological examinations of children and juveniles whose behaviour is troublesome and that legal powers are needed to enable the treatment of non-offenders who are showing signs of developing psychopathic personality. Gillespie had no patience for the rule which stated that one had to wait until a person, who was obviously heading for a life in crime, actually committed an offence before control could be obtained. He went so far as to advise anxious parents that, under the existing system, 'the best thing that could happen to a delinquent adolescent is that he should commit some legal offence which will compel the authorities to provide institutional care' (*ibid*). It is also important to note, however, that Gillespie's optimism, about the possibility of turning children and adolescents with psychopathic traits away from crime, appears to be accompanied by pessimism about the possibility of doing anything for the full-blown psychopath. He repeatedly implies that, for the adult psychopath, it is too late for treatment. Nor is this simply a ploy to obtain powers to treat troublesome children. Rather, Gillespie seemed quite happy with the policy, adopted in some prisons, of simply segregating adult psychopaths (*ibid*: 27–8).

The nature of the link between faulty upbringing and psychopathic personality was discussed in an article by J Rees (1933). Rees, we might note, applied the concept of psychopathy to practically all habitual delinquents. Indeed, for Rees, it was the professional criminal, rather than the person whose behaviour was motiveless and self-defeating, who was the true psychopath:

> It is true that there are criminals who make crime their profession, who enjoy it and glory in it and do not want cure. But that in itself is an abnormality of outlook which we may rightly call disease ... So, I venture to regard practically all delinquency as a symptom of illness, though I do not mean that every delinquent is necessarily sick in the ordinary sense of the word (Rees 1933: 29).

For Rees, it was not so much that faulty upbringing could turn an otherwise social person into an anti-social psychopath or criminal. Rather, he suggested that, at birth, we all have anti-social or psychopathic tendencies. Rees maintained that all babies have anti-social traits, but as they grew up they usually became socialised. However, a combination of innate temperamental abnormalities and faulty upbringing could impede the process of socialisation:

> The comparison of the baby with the criminal, which has been made, is illuminating and contains a great deal of truth. The infant in its earliest days is completely ego-centric, self-loving and indulgent. Its main object is the attainment of the things that give it pleasure, and it has not arrived at any social values or sense of its place in the family or community. Granted a so-called normal environment, the infant begins to grow up and is so doing becomes increasingly socialised as time goes on. Abnormalities in temperamental make-up and difficulties in environment render this process of social adjustment more difficult (Rees 1930: 30).

This statement echoes the earlier ideas of Maudsley about the evolution of moral sense in the human species (see chapter 5). It portrays the criminal or the psychopath (for Rees they were virtually the same thing) as an immature character. Perhaps its most important implication, however, is that the psychopath is a relatively normal being who has not been properly socialised – that in many cases psychopathic personality results from the effects of bad training or environment upon a relatively normal mind. This focuses attention upon the correctness of the socialisation processes employed in society. Incorrect methods of socialisation will produce psychopathic personalities, whereas the adoption of correct methods of socialisation will prevent, to a large extent, the creation of psychopaths. Hence, around this time, penal treatment professionals were showing increasing interest in parent-child relationships and especially in methods of dealing with problem children.[12] The discourse of treatment professionals about psychopathic personality blended with a wider discourse about the effects of upbringing upon the development of personality. Mothers who spoilt or neglected their children, or those who used parental authority in an unreasonable way, were implicated in the production of criminal psychopaths. The proper upbringing of the child therefore became a public concern.

Limiting the scope of the concept of psychopathy

During the 1930s, as we have just seen, many psychiatrists tended to regard all crime as symptomatic of illness and tended to use the concept of psychopathy to indicate this. However, it would be mistaken to assume that

---

12 Around this period, the *Howard Journal*, which was concerned with penal policy and practice, began to review books of advice on how to deal with problem children such as that by Mary Sayles called, *The Problem Child at Home: A Study of Parent–Child Relationships* (1928), reviewed in the *Howard Journal*, 2 (4), 1929.

all psychiatrists with an interest in crime and punishment subscribed to this view. The notion that all delinquency is a symptom of illness was contested explicitly by many psychiatrists, and most importantly by W Norwood East who, during the 1930s, was Medical Director on the Prison Commission. In his deeply researched account of the development of British criminology, Garland (1994: 49) suggests that Norwood East's views dominated official penal policy making during the 1930s. Norwood East, Garland points out, 'was himself a proponent of a psychological approach to crime, but he considered its scope to be sharply delimited, and consistently warned against the dangers and absurdities of exaggerating its claims' (*ibid*). This is born out by Norwood East's views on the scope of the concept of psychopathy.

In the early 1930s, Norwood East was already insisting that it was a travesty to suggest that crime is a disease and was warning against the tendency to assume that anti-social conduct was in itself evidence of mental defect (East: 1933: 63; 1934: 52). However, his most explicit statement about the relationship between psychopathic personality and crime was in an article published in the *Journal of Mental Science* in 1945.[13] In this article, Norwood East described the criminal psychopathic personality as a non-sane, non-insane aberrant individual (East 1949: 125). His view was that psychopathic personality could not be inferred from repeated misconduct alone since there were many other causes, beside mental abnormality, of misconduct (*ibid*: 127). He therefore disagreed with those who argued that the habitual criminal was a socially sick person. To the contrary, he argued, the habitual criminal was often a person who had deliberately chosen crime as a career, and usually showed none of the criteria necessary for a diagnosis of psychopathic personality or other mental abnormality (*ibid*: 127–8). Habitual offenders should be diagnosed as psychopaths, according to Norwood East, only if they showed other signs of a psychopathic disposition. These 'other signs' included a tendency to violent loss of temper, impulsive conduct, fits of depression and uncontrolled weeping, suicidal attempts and fugues (*ibid*: 129).

Norwood East clearly held a much narrower conception of psychopathic personality than any we have discussed so far. He estimated that the number of true psychopaths amongst juvenile delinquents and adult offenders was quite low. He cites the study of juvenile delinquents carried out by Healy and Bronner in the United States, in which they found that 2.8 per cent were psychopathic personalities, as a useful indication of the proportion of offenders who were psychopaths (*ibid*: 127; see Healy and Bronner 1936). This contrasts markedly with the estimates of Gillespie, Rees and others who, as we have seen, often estimated that the proportion of psychopathic personalities amongst offenders was about 45 per cent.

---

13 This was subsequently re-published in 1949 as chapter 8 of his book, *Society and the Criminal*. Page references are to the 1949 edition.

Towards pessimism about the treatability of psychopaths

> Psychopaths are an eternal source of trouble to all who have to deal with them and psychiatrically are neither fish, flesh nor fowl and certainly not good red herring! (Neustatter 1953).

D K Henderson's book, *Psychopathic States* (1939), urged psychiatrists to devote more effort to the socialisation of the 'group of struggling humanity' which he referred to as psychopaths (see, in particular, the foreword). Henderson was convinced that with psychiatric-therapeutic intervention, many psychopaths could be turned into useful members of society (see, for example, pp 27–8). This was psychiatry at its most optimistic. For Henderson, psychopaths were, by definition, people who had failed to respond to any other type of intervention – penal, medical or social (*ibid*: 16–17; see also Henderson 1944). Moreover, they suffered from an illness for which psychiatrists had no specific explanation. Yet, Henderson believed that with research the causes of the condition could be better identified and effective treatments found.[14] From the middle of the 1940s, however, it is possible to detect the beginnings of a more pessimistic attitude towards the treatment of psychopathic offenders, which was to some extent combined with a re-assertion of biological explanations of the phenomenon. Here I will discuss a number of articles which appeared in the Howard Journal,[15] in which this pessimistic attitude was expressed.

In 1946–47, the *Howard Journal* published an article by J C Penton in which it was argued that the principles developed in the army to select personnel for particular jobs could be applied to the classification of delinquents.[16] Here I will discuss just one part of this interesting article: its account of a classification scheme developed for deserters and its applicability to civilian delinquents. During the war, Penton was asked to undertake a psychiatric examination of deserters who were being held, pending legal and disciplinary action. The purpose of this exercise, from the army's point of view, was to make the most effective use of all available manpower: to find out whether it was possible to make any further use of the services of these deserters during the war. Penton recognised five main groups amongst the deserters: (i)

---

14 One of Henderson's most influential contributions to thinking about psychopathy was his typology in which psychopaths were classified as predominantly 'aggressive' 'inadequate', or 'creative'. The last of these classifications is interesting since it appears to include cases in which a psychopathic personality renders the person more useful to society rather than a danger or a nuisance to it. However, most psychopathic offenders were subsequently classified as either predominantly aggressive or predominantly inadequate.

15 From its beginnings in October 1921, until around the late 1960s (when it became more of an academic journal) the *Howard Journal* was a major outlet for the discourse of penal administrators, penal treatment professionals and penal reformers.

16 See Rose (1989: pt 1) on how the experience of war shaped the development of psychiatry and psychology.

'normal men', who broke down for tangible reasons; (ii) 'immatures', who ran because they were scared; (iii) 'dullards', who didn't understand their responsibilities; (iv) 'emotionally inadequate and unstable men', whose desertions were precipitated by the failure of their personalities to stand up to the strain of war; and (v) 'anti-social people', who were simply following the pattern of their anti-social reaction towards society. Penton argued that all but the fifth group could, after appropriate treatment/re-training, be re-employed as soldiers in tasks suitable to their capacities.

For Penton, one of the points of this study was that it showed that a great deal of delinquency was due to psychiatric breakdown and that, with psychiatric treatment, delinquents could be rehabilitated – ie turned into useful, productive members of society. The tone of the article is optimistic, then, rather than pessimistic. However, it is pertinent that Penton identified one group whose delinquency was not due to breakdown but was quite consistent with their anti-social attitudes. According to Penton, this group could not be rehabilitated. They had deeply ingrained anti-social tendencies which rendered them beyond treatment and rehabilitation. Penton did not use the term psychopaths to describe this group. I suggest, however, that – in penal discourse – the term 'psychopathic offenders' became used to describe offenders who fitted Penton's fifth category: offenders who offended simply because they had anti-social personalities and who were beyond treatment and rehabilitation.

In an article on 'Biology and Juvenile Delinquency', Erwin Frey (1948–49) employed the term 'psychopaths' to classify various groups who suffered from 'constitutional and probably hereditary abnormalities of character'. Psychopathy, Frey argued, should be viewed as a 'biological, not a social problem' (ibid: 230). Nearly all psychopaths 'came from extremely tainted families' (ibid). Psychopaths were therefore not reformable, nor could the condition be prevented by social means (ibid: 232). Frey's tone is explicitly pessimistic. The article is openly opposed to 'utopian notions' of preventing psychopathic disorder through environmental improvements and of reforming psychopathic personalities, converting them into normal persons. However, a somewhat ironic result of this pessimistic attitude towards prevention and reform is that Frey, unlike say Gillespie or Rees, addresses the question of what should be done with *actual* psychopaths. Also, although Frey was pessimistic about the possibility of totally reforming psychopaths, he believed that modest improvements could be made in them. Frey therefore set out some modest, and perhaps more realistic, goals with regard to psychopaths:

> If these psychopathic young delinquents cannot be re-educated entirely, they may still be able to earn their living more or less honestly later on. We may consider it a definite educational success if later on they commit only casual offences instead of becoming incorrigible habitual criminals (Frey 1948–9: 232–3).

The next article I will consider is by W Neustatter (1953), and concerns the power, provided by s 4 of the Criminal Justice Act 1948, to require an offender to reside at a mental hospital for a period of up to one year as a 'voluntary' patient, as a condition of receiving probation. A large part of the article is devoted to a discussion of the usefulness of this power for dealing with psychopaths. Neustatter's verdict is that the power is of little use because mental hospitals can do little to influence psychopaths. Disciplinary treatment had virtually no effect on them (*ibid*: 252). The opinion of most psychiatrists was that the mental hospital was not a suitable place for psychopaths (*ibid*).

Neustatter, following Henderson (1939), distinguished between two main types of psychopaths: aggressive and inadequate. Neustatter preferred aggressive psychopaths, but not because they were more treatable or reformable. Rather, for most of the time they were more *manageable* than inadequate psychopaths:

> ... they are in many ways the best of the psychopaths, as they are cooperative and well-behaved between their outbursts, and often genuinely concerned and contrite at their lack of control. In appropriate surroundings with mild discipline, and no stimuli to arouse the impulsiveness, they behave well ... (Neustatter 1953: 252).

The problem was that, because of the relative seriousness of their offences, aggressive psychopaths rarely came to mental hospitals via the powers provided in the 1948 Act (*ibid*). These powers were much more likely to lead to the hospitalisation of 'inadequate psychopaths': drifters and incorrigible law-breakers (*ibid*). These were unmanageable in mental hospitals. Neustatter wanted nothing to do with this group. His main concern was to get rid of them – to hand them back to the courts and the penal system. However, even this was difficult:

> They do not respond to hospital discipline, they abide by none of the rules, and what is most irritating, instead of absconding and thus giving one an opportunity to hand them back to the courts, they are very disinclined to leave, and find any pretext for staying on. They like the shelter of hospital existence (Neustatter 1953: 252).

Finally, it is worth mentioning an article by W Craike (1953), which appeared in the same edition of the *Howard Journal* as Neustatter's article. Craike's article was about the psychiatric treatment of adolescent delinquent girls in an approved school. Craike was concerned to *exclude* psychopaths from the school. The inadequate type of psychopath took up too much time, whilst the admittance of the aggressive type of psychopath made it impossible to sustain the 'liberal attitude' in the school (*ibid*: 258).

CONCLUSION

At the outset of the period under discussion in this chapter, 'moral defectives' were regarded as people suffering from permanent mental disorders. In the interests of social defence, such persons had to be segregated from society, in humane conditions. The Mental Deficiency Act 1913, seemed to provide the legal powers to enable such segregation. However, psychiatrists were slow to use these powers. Far from eagerly colonising the area of behavioural problems, they seemed to want to restrict their interventions to those suffering from intellectual disorders.

During the 1920s and 1930s, there was a shift in the psychiatric outlook. Serious behavioural disorders that were previously regarded as the result of underlying physical pathology, came to be viewed more as the product of faulty upbringing and early environment. This shift was accompanied by a rise in the belief of the possibility of preventing psychopathic disorder by 're-educating' and socialising children and adolescents who presented behavioural problems. One consequence of this emphasis on young potential psychopaths and on prevention was an apparent lack of interest in the plight of the adult 'confirmed' psychopath.

By the 1940s, optimism about the prevention and treatment of psychopathic disorder was giving way to a more pessimistic attitude. The concept of psychopathy began to be applied to individuals who were considered beyond treatment and reformation, and not even manageable in mental hospitals or other institutions for disordered youths. For those running such treatment programmes, the main concern became to exclude psychopaths – to hand them back to the courts and to the penal system. It would be highly mistaken, therefore, to suggest that penal treatment professionals were, in imperialistic manner, eager to take over the problem of handling psychopathic individuals during the 1950s. In fact, the opposite was closer to the truth. This has important implications, as we shall see, for our interpretation of the inclusion of legal provision for the compulsory hospitalisation of some psychopaths in the Mental Health Act 1959.

CHAPTER 7

DISCOURSE OF PENAL TREATMENT PROFESSIONALS ON PSYCHOPATHIC OFFENDERS SINCE c 1954

INTRODUCTION

In this chapter, I look at the discourse of penal treatment professionals on psychopathic offenders from the middle of the 1950s until the present. Throughout most of this period, the law has provided for the treatment and compulsory detention of certain types of psychopathic patients. In the first section of this chapter I look briefly at the thinking behind the creation of these powers and at how penal treatment professionals have used them. I start by looking at the arguments and recommendations of the Royal Commission on the Law relating to Mental Illness and Mental Deficiency, 1954–57,[1] whose report (hereinafter the '1957 Report') led to the statutory recognition of the category of 'psychopathic disorder' in the Mental Health Act 1959. I show that the Royal Commission's proposals regarding psychopaths were often portrayed and seen as a threat to civil liberties, in that they allowed for the compulsory hospitalisation of an un-defined or hazily defined group. I do not directly challenge this view of the Royal Commission's proposals, but I do show that it is a very partial one, and needs to be balanced by a broader understanding of the Royal Commission's concerns. I emphasise that the Royal Commission were concerned in general to reduce compulsory hospitalisation, that it 'reluctantly' recommended compulsory powers with regard to psychopaths, and that it recommended compulsory hospitalisation of only certain categories of psychopaths. I also suggest that psychiatrists were far from eager to use these compulsory powers. For many treatment professionals, the problem was less one of preventing psychiatrists from abusing the power to detain psychopaths, more one of finding institutions willing to admit psychopathic offenders as patients. I also refer to studies which suggest that, in practice, libertarian fears were exaggerated (but not groundless) and that *limited* use was made of these compulsory powers.

In the second section of this chapter I look at how treatment professionals classified, made sense of, and tried to manage and treat, those they defined as psychopathic offenders during the 1960s. I start by showing that, in this period, treatment professionals developed a new conception of psychopathy. They began to regard it not – as previous treatment professionals had – as a form of mental illness or mental deficiency, but as a severe form of a more general category of personality disorder. I then turn to the explanations of this

---

1   Also known as the Percy Commission.

disorder to which treatment professionals subscribed. I show that, in their attempts to understand the roots of psychopathic personality disorder, treatment professionals turned to social-psychology and anthropology, as well as to medicine and individual psychology. They began to see the psychopathic offender, not as a product of individual psychological defect alone, but as a product of a particular type of culture. This linking of psychopathic disorder to certain features of modern culture had important implications for the treatment of psychopathic offenders. Those who dealt professionally with psychopaths became less interested in technical medical treatment and in individual psychotherapy, and increasingly pre-occupied with the idea of immersing the psychopathic offender into a humanised, communitarian culture (which differed markedly from the de-humanised, individualistic culture of modern society). However, institutional regimes were also shaped by factors other than therapeutic theory. In particular, the demands of security placed limits upon those forms of therapy which involved activity and freedom on the part of 'patients'. Treatment professionals acknowledged that, in practice, therapeutic regimes were shaped by a combination of the competing concerns of security and therapy. I conclude this section by noting the trend, towards the end of the 1960s, for psychiatrists to become increasingly reluctant to accept responsibility for the management of psychopathic offenders.

In the third section of this chapter I look at developments since the early 1970s, concentrating in particular upon the proposals of the Butler Committee on Mentally Abnormal Offenders, 1975. I show that, although the Butler Committee argued that attempts at the medical treatment of psychopathic offenders had failed, and recommended that psychopaths be sent to prisons, it would nevertheless be mistaken to regard it as initiating a move away from therapeutic interventions back to penal interventions. The Butler Committee's proposal that 'training units' be established in prisons for seriously anti-social psychopathic offenders was consistent with the therapeutic approach to crime and, in particular, with the idea of moral treatment. The section finishes by discussing briefly the shift in interest in the 1980s, towards the issue of balancing the rights of psychopathic offenders with concerns about public safety.

THE ROYAL COMMISSION AND THE LEGAL RECOGNITION OF PSYCHOPATHIC DISORDER

The Royal Commission on the Law relating to Mental Illness and Mental Deficiency, 1954–57, was appointed amidst an upsurge of public interest in the problem of mental health (see Jones 1960: chapter 12). However, the Commission itself was limited, by its terms of reference, to considering *legal and administrative issues* concerning the treatment of mentally ill and mentally deficient persons. In order to understand the nature of its recommendations with regard to psychopathic patients, it is important to understand something of the general tone of the Commission's inquiry and report. The Royal Commission was concerned to *liberalise and modernise* the law relating to the treatment of mental disorder. The tone of the Commission's report was one of enlightened progress. Its aim was to update the laws on mental health in order to register and further facilitate advances which had been made in the understanding and treatment of mental disorder. More specifically, its objective was to put interventions into the problem of mental disorder on a par with interventions into physical illness, especially by removing much of the legal formality surrounding the hospitalisation and treatment of mental pathology (1957 Report: chapter 2, para 134).

The Commission noted that public attitudes towards the mentally disordered were becoming more enlightened. Ordinary people were beginning to see the mentally disordered as sick people in need of medical care and treatment and were beginning to see mental 'hospitals' as real hospitals rather than as a sort of prison in which the 'mad' were incarcerated. However, the law relating to the treatment of mental illness was outdated. It reflected a less enlightened era, when the mentally disordered were viewed with ridicule and fear, and were locked away. According to the Royal Commission, the particularly backward feature of mental health laws as they stood was that, in order to be admitted to a mental hospital for treatment, one had to be certified as mentally ill and legally committed. This procedure reflected a time when asylums were thought of primarily as places of imprisonment and there was a perceived need to protect people from wrongful imprisonment. Provisions in mental health laws concerning the 'recapture' of 'escaped' patients symbolised all that was backward about existing mental health legislation (*ibid*: para 138). A particular concern of the Commission was to consider ways of reducing existing formalities of admission and discharge of mental patients. In particular, the Commission recommended that admission should be informal and, as far as possible, voluntary. There was no need, it argued, for legal regulation of admission procedures. The Commission was also concerned to promote community care, as an alternative to institutional treatment, in appropriate circumstances (Jones 1960: 182).

The Commission pointed out, however, that mental disorder differed from physical illness in one crucial respect: it could affect the judgment of patients so that they might not realise they were ill. In such cases the illness could be treated only against the patient's wishes at the time (*ibid*: para 136). This made it necessary to retain compulsory powers 'to override the normal personal rights of individuals in certain circumstances' (*ibid*). However, the Commission insisted, compulsory detention should be used only where treatment was deemed urgently necessary and where informal treatment was refused (1957 Report: chapter 2, paras 135–6).

The Royal Commission and psychopathic patients

The Commission recommended that the term 'mental disorder' should be used as a general one, to include three main categories: mentally ill patients, severely subnormal patients, and psychopathic patients.[2] It was suggested that the legal issues concerning these very different types of mental disorder were the same and that they could be treated as one in law (Jones 1960: 184). The main point to note about this classification, with regard to psychopathic patients, is that they were now defined as a distinct category, separate from both the mentally ill (lunatics) and the mentally subnormal (mental defectives). The long-standing tendency to regard psychopathy as a type of mental defectiveness was finally abandoned. It is also worth emphasising that although the Royal Commission defined 'psychopaths' as mentally disordered, this did not mean defining them as mentally ill. Rather, the Commission drew a distinction between mental illness and psychopathic disorder.

The Commission's definitions and descriptions of psychopaths were similar to those found in the discourse of penal treatment professionals throughout the 20th century. Using Henderson's distinction between inadequate and aggressive psychopaths, the Commission defined psychopathic patients as people with seriously aggressive characteristics or who showed pathological inadequacy in coping with the ordinary problems of life, regardless of whether these 'symptoms' were accompanied by subnormal intelligence (*ibid*: p 5). The Commission admitted that it was difficult to describe the behaviour of such persons in terms which distinguished it clearly from failings that were to some degree common to many people. Nevertheless, it indicated the type of person which it had in mind. The inadequate psychopath was a person having: '... abnormal difficulty in applying himself to any job, or controlling his spending, in planning his domestic life and in getting on with people generally' (*ibid*: para 168). The concept was also applied to 'girls and women who, though sufficiently adapted to the conventions of society in other respects, are sexually promiscuous without realising the consequences to society or to themselves or to the children' (*ibid*). Other forms of behaviour indicative of inadequate psychopathic personality included 'persistent drifting from job to job, general inability to take an interest in any form of occupation, pathological lying and swindling, drug addiction and alcoholism' (*ibid*). Aggressive psychopaths were those who were often extremely violent without apparent cause and who appeared incapable of controlling their violent tendencies (*ibid*).

What rendered these people mentally disordered, according to the Commission, was not a lack of intelligence, as ordinarily understood, but a

---

2   A fourth category of 'subnormal patients' was added in the subsequent Mental Health Bill.

lack of common sense and responsibility. Their daily behaviour showed 'a want of social responsibility and of consideration for others, of prudence and foresight and of ability to act in their own best interests' (*ibid*: para 169). Psychopaths were 'self-centred' and 'without conscience, sense of guilt or insight' (*ibid*). They lacked ordinary foresight and judgment and the capacity to learn from experience' (*ibid*).

As we have seen, the Royal Commission assumed that the vast differences between the different categories of mental disorder could be ignored by the law, since the legal issues raised by different kinds of mental disorder were the same. Hence, its main concern with regard to psychopaths was to ensure that they could be admitted for treatment 'informally', ie without being certified. But, when it came to compulsory procedures, the Commission did distinguish psychopathic patients from those suffering from mental illness or severe subnormality. The Commission seemed *reluctant* to extend the powers of detention for mentally ill and subnormal people to psychopathic patients. In keeping with its general *libertarian* tone, the Commission expressed concern that the provision of such powers would be illiberal:

> Most citizens are liable to deprivation of liberty, on grounds of behaviour, only when their behaviour offends the criminal law. If psychopathic patients are subjected to special forms of compulsion on grounds of mental abnormality which is evidenced mainly by their behaviour, this is almost equivalent to the creation of a special quasi-criminal code for them alone (1957 Report: para 30).

Hence, the Commission recommended that the powers of compulsory hospitalisation applicable to the mentally ill or subnormal should not be generally applicable to psychopathic patients. Nevertheless, the Commission did recommend compulsory powers in relation to psychopaths in a number of circumstances, and it is important to realise that this would amount to a highly significant extension of the powers of compulsory hospitalisation.

First, the Commission suggested that psychopaths under the age of 21 might be detained compulsorily, and could then be detained until they reached the age of 25 (Jones 1960: 186). The reasoning behind this was that treatment might be successful with *young* psychopaths: 'There are good arguments for providing training compulsorily when the diagnosis is made while the patient is still young, when training is most likely to be successful (1957 Report: para 31). Second, although the Commission thought that older psychopaths were unlikely to respond to treatment – and hence that there was 'insufficient justification for the detention of older psychopaths' (*ibid*) – it recommended that such psychopaths might be detained compulsorily for a four-week period for observation. Thirdly, the Commission recommended that where an adult psychopath had broken the criminal law, he or she might be detained compulsorily as a mentally disordered patient: 'If they break the law, their mental condition can properly be taken into account in determining whether special forms of medical or social care should be provided, compulsorily if necessary, instead of or in addition to normal penal measures' (*ibid*; on the subsequent use of this provision see Mitcheson 1968).[3]

Psychopathy in the Mental Health Act 1959

The Report of the Royal Commission led to the publication of a Mental Health Bill in 1958. This Bill's underlying principles reflected the liberal, modernising mood of the Royal Commission. They were: as much treatment as possible should be provided on a voluntary and informal basis; a new system of safeguards (*viz* Mental Health Review Tribunals) should be established to regulate compulsory detention where it was unavoidable; and there should be a re-orientation of health services away from institutional care towards care in the community (Jones 1960: 186–193).

The Bill defined psychopathic disorder as a persistent disorder of personality which resulting in abnormally aggressive or seriously irresponsible conduct, and which was susceptible to medical treatment.[4] In the parliamentary debates about the Bill there was much disquiet about its provisions concerning psychopaths. This disquiet was based upon two quite opposite concerns. First, there were those who were concerned about the disturbing influence which psychopathic patients would have upon other patients and the disruptive impact which they would have upon ward routines. As we saw in chapter 6, such concerns had been expressed by psychiatrists since the 1940s. In the parliamentary debates, some doctors argued that hospitals would be unwilling to admit more than a couple of 'these appalling people' (Dr R Bennett, quoted in Jones 1960: 190) and that special institutions would be necessary to deal with them. Psychopaths, in short, posed special problems of management and control which mental hospitals, especially those which were adopting modern open-door policies, were unable or unwilling to perform. Psychopaths could not easily be integrated with other mental health patients, but would have to be detained

---

3   This is important as an indication of the limits of the Commission's liberal attitude. The Commission was reluctant to recommend compulsory detention and treatment for psychopaths (unless they were children) provided they remained within the criminal law. However, once they broke the criminal law, the Commission had no hesitation about recommending that the normal penal measures could be supplemented or replaced with compulsory psychiatric detention and treatment. As we saw in chapter 2, a similar distinction was made between offender and non-offender inebriates in the late 19th century.

4   For a discussion of this definition see Walker and McCabe (1973: 219). They argued that this definition improved on that of the Royal Commission in several ways. The rationale of the treatability clause was to prevent people being detained as psychopaths for mere control purposes. A similar clause in the Mental Health Act 1983, led to recent litigation in the Court of Appeal when a Mental Health Review Tribunal refused to discharge a patient who was diagnosed as suffering from psychopathic disorder, but who had refused to cooperate in appropriate treatment – *R v Canons Park Mental Health Review Tribunal, ex parte A* (1994) 2 All ER 659–685 (see Prins 1995: 125 – I am grateful to Alan Parkin for directing my attention to this case).

and treated separately, in special institutions. Once again, we find psychiatrists resisting, rather than promoting, the psychiatrisation of this troublesome group of patients.

The second source of disquiet about the Bill's provisions for psychopaths was a small group in the House of Lords, led by the social scientist and magistrate, Lady Wootton (see Walker and McCabe 1973: 219; Ramon 1986: 232). Despite the attempts of the Royal Commission to place limits upon the powers of compulsory detention where psychopaths were concerned, this group – whose views became very influential – feared that the Bill's provisions concerning psychopaths would jeopardise civil liberties (Robinson 1966: 25–6). Wootton's position was that people who were persistently anti-social, but who did not display other signs of mental abnormality, should not be subject to compulsory powers without the protection of a trial by a criminal court (Walker and McCabe 1973: 219). Such persons should be handled as 'normal' persons; they should be interfered with only if they broke the law, in which case they should be processed as ordinary criminal justice cases (Ramon 1986: 232).[5]

The Bill, as amended, became law as the Mental Health Act 1959. The Act defined psychopathic disorder as:

> ... a persistent disorder or disability of mind (whether or not including subnormality of intelligence) which results in abnormally aggressive or seriously irresponsible conduct on the part of the patient, and requires or is susceptible to medical treatment (Mental Health Act 1959, s 4(4)).

Section 4 of the Act also provided that persons were not to be regarded as suffering from mental disorder 'by reason only of promiscuity or other immoral conduct' (see Jones 1960: 193). This provision clearly was prompted by those concerned about the implications for civil liberties of the provisions for compulsory treatment of some psychopathic patients.

The response of treatment professionals to the new provisions

Whilst civil libertarians feared that the new legislation would result in many people who behaved immorally, but were not mentally disordered, being locked up in mental hospitals without a trial, penal administrators and treatment professionals assumed that the legislation would have very little impact upon the problem of psychopathic offenders unless special institutions were built for them. Most treatment professionals actually maintained that such institutions should be established *within the penal system*. Discussing the Mental Health Bill, the author of the Howard Journal's notes of the year wrote:

---

5   See Wootton (1959: chapter 8) for her criticisms of the concept of psychopathy – discussed in the introduction to this case study.

The question is how many hospitals would be prepared to accept these often very difficult patients. Perhaps not very many. Those not accepted could be sent to prison (where they are now) and the fortunately small number of really dangerous psychopaths should in any case be kept in conditions of maximum security. The need for a special institution for criminal psychopaths within the prison system therefore remains (Anon 1959: 73).

In a somewhat similar vein, P D Scott pointed out, in a detailed discussion of the 1957 Report, that dangerous psychopaths could not be treated in hospitals without the hospital becoming something of a prison, and that it might be preferable to treat some of them within the penal system. It is worth quoting the following since it brings out the perception of the psychopath as falling between the penal and the medical domains:

> There are two ways of humanely dealing with these relatively few dangerous criminal psychopaths. Either they are admitted to a hospital which will then become something of a prison, or else they are admitted to prison which should become something of a hospital. The Commission, rightly for the majority of cases, favours the former. Yet there is more to be said for accommodating at least some ... in prison and requiring them to be under medical treatment while there, than appears at first sight (Scott 1958: 14).

The fate of this legislative provision for psychopaths

As many had predicted, the new provisions for the treatment of psychopaths were not widely used. As Kenneth Robinson demonstrated, with a study of figures on the use of the powers provided by the Mental Health Act 1959 (Robinson 1966: 27–9), psychiatrists were actually reluctant to use the powers provided. Robinson concluded his article by maintaining that the abuse of compulsory powers, predicted by some libertarian critics of the 1959 Act, did not transpire:

> There is no evidence of any of the abuse of the new compulsory powers that was feared in some quarters when the Bill was passing through Parliament. If anything, the figures suggest that the powers are still being under-used, and that psychiatrists are treading gingerly in recommending the detention in hospital of psychopathic patients (Robinson 1966: 30–31).

This conclusion seems to be confirmed by Walker and McCabe (1973) who found, in their study of the workings of the Mental Health Act, that psychiatrists were reluctant to admit psychopathic patients to mental hospitals unless they were likely to respond to treatment (*ibid*: 223). Effectively, this excluded most of those whom penal treatment professionals would have described as psychopaths because non-responsiveness to medical, penal and social interventions was one of the main things which rendered such people psychopathic in the eyes of penal treatment professionals. Psychiatrists often justified their decisions not to admit 'untreatable' psychopaths by reference to the statutory definition of psychopathic disorder which, we might recall, defined psychopathic disorder as a condition which, *inter alia*, 'requires or is susceptible to medical treatment'. Walker and McCabe argue, however, that the narrow interpretation of this definition by psychiatrists was perverse (*ibid*). They point out that 'medical treatment' was defined very broadly by the Act; it included nursing care and other types of care and training under medical supervision (*ibid*). They suggest that, even if such treatment did not improve the personalities of psychopaths, this did not mean that they did not require treatment (*ibid*).[6] Hence, according to Walker and McCabe, the narrow interpretation of the statutory definition of psychopathic disorder was peculiar and even unreasonable. However, it is easy to understand why psychiatrists interpreted the provision in this 'curiously restrictive way' (*ibid*). As I have shown, psychiatrists were reluctant to admit psychopaths to mental hospitals because they found such patients not only untreatable, but also *disruptive and unmanageable*. Their understandable concern to exclude psychopaths from mental hospitals made it likely that they would exploit (but not consciously) any ambiguity within the statutory definition in such a way.

Leaving aside the question of whether psychiatrists' interpretations of the statutory definition of psychopathic disorder were correct or even reasonable, it seems clear that the provisions of the 1959 Act, like earlier legislative attempts to establish treatment and control facilities for moral imbeciles and moral defectives, failed to achieve this objective in practice. And, the reason for this failure was that, once again, psychiatrists were reluctant, for various reasons, to take over the management of these offenders. This was one area of deviance that most psychiatrists did not wish to 'colonise' (cf Conrad and Schneider 1980). From the early 1960s on, the aim of diverting psychopathic offenders from penal to medical channels began to be replaced by the less ambitious objective of establishing special institutions, within the penal system, for the treatment of psychopathic offenders.

DISCOURSE ON PSYCHOPATHIC OFFENDERS IN THE 1960s

Before looking at how treatment professionals conceptualised, explained and tried to manage psychopathic offenders in the 1960s, it is necessary to point out that the term, as used by them, often referred to a much broader group than those formally classified as psychopathically disordered. As I have indicated, the number of persons formally labelled as psychopaths by psychiatrists or by the courts was quite small. However, as D J West pointed out, the term was often 'used purely descriptively in informal

---

6   'It makes complete sense to say that there are disorders which may not improve under nursing (or other types of care) but which *require* it: there are many examples in physical medicine of which terminal cancer is one' (Walker and McCabe 1973: 223).

communications between doctors' (West 1968: 7). In the context of this study, this informal and 'purely descriptive' use of the concept is just as important as the more formal use of the legal category. In what follows, I am concerned with the discourse of treatment professionals on all of those offenders described as psychopaths, whether or not they were formally labelled as such.

Psychopathic personality disorder

During the 1960s treatment professionals continued the long-lasting debates about the causes of psychopathic disorder and the best way of managing and treating psychopaths. What often goes un-noticed, however, was that during this period a consensus began to emerge on an important and quite novel idea. Psychopathic disorder came to be regarded as a severe form of a more general category of personality disorders.[7] For example, Dr Michael Craft (1962), who during the 1960s was regarded as a leading authority on the problem of psychopathic disorder, suggested that personality disorders could be arranged on a scale of increasing severity, ranging from the mild to the psychopathic. Those suffering from mild personality disorders could manage to remain within the boundaries of behaviour tolerated by the community but would be regarded as 'odd' (*ibid*: 47). Those afflicted by moderate personality disorders would be regarded as selfish, eccentric or cunning (*ibid*). Sufferers from severe or psychopathic personality disorders would 'make frequent court appearances' and experience some personal unhappiness (*ibid*).

Causation

During the 1960s, treatment professionals and researchers continued to disagree about the aetiology of psychopathic disorder. However, there were two noticeable trends. First, many treatment professionals adopted a combined genetic-environmental explanation of psychopathic disorder in which it was maintained that *most* cases of psychopathic behaviour resulted from a combination of genetic inheritance and faulty environment. According to this view, genetic factors predisposed certain persons to the development of psychopathic behaviour, but environmental factors actually precipitated the breakdown of social adaptation (Craft 1962: 48).

The second development needs to be looked at in a little detail. Increasingly, those who dealt professionally with psychopathic offenders turned to social-psychology, and even to anthropology and sociology, for ideas that would help them to understand those whom they were charged with managing. It is important to note that this trend was compatible with the

---

7   Previously, it had been regarded as a form of mental illness (see chapter 5), a form of mental defectiveness (see chapter 6) or as an individually distinct mental pathology (see the 1957 Report, discussed earlier in this chapter).

first trend, noted above. Those who looked for the *social* origins of psychopathic personality disorder were not necessarily committed to a purely social explanation of the phenomenon. Most of them allowed some role for biological factors. However, they seemed to believe that genetic factors could be less easily altered than environmental factors, and that alterations of the social environment therefore offered the best chance of prevention and rehabilitation.

It would be quite mistaken, therefore, to assume that, in attempting to make sense of psychopathic offenders, treatment professionals looked only to medical research and theories, or that they regarded psychopathic behaviour as a manifestation of an inborn individual pathology. As we have already seen, in chapter 6, since the 1930s those who dealt professionally with psychopathic offenders had become interested in work which dealt with methods of child-rearing. In the 1960s, this idea was pursued further by treatment professionals such as Dr Craft. In a paper on the causes of psychopathic disorder, Craft devoted considerable attention to alternative forms of child-rearing and, more generally, to alternative forms of social relations (Craft 1966). This paper started with a review of various theories about the relationship between genes and personality. Craft concluded this review by suggesting that although genetic traits had some *influence*, they did not *determine* personality and behaviour. For Craft, 'upbringing' had a larger influence upon personality and behaviour.

Craft discussed a number of studies which, he suggested, supported his view and which pointed to the kind of environmental factors that could precipitate psychopathic behaviour. One of these was Anna Freud's study of concentration camp children (Freud and Dann 1951, discussed in Craft 1966: 67–8). Freud's study was of a group of children who were rescued from a Nazi concentration camp. Their parents had been killed, but they had been kept alive. They received food, shelter and warmth but, between the ages of 2 and 4, had had minimal adult contact and had been expected to care almost entirely for themselves. Freud admitted some of these children to a Hampstead nursery and observed their initial responses to affectionate contact. She found that, initially 'they behaved very much like a group of young animals' and, in comparison to London children, were 'highly impulsive, self-centred, aggressive and demanding' (quotations from Craft 1966: 67–8). However, 'given several months of careful and sympathetic adult attention ... they turned rapidly towards the behavioural patterns expected from London children of the same age and sex' (*ibid*). Craft interprets this as indicating that these children were presenting some of the personality traits found in psychopaths. For Craft, Freud's study illustrates that a lack of affectionate contact in the early formative years can result in psychopathic personality and also that early intervention can prevent the development of severe personality disorder.

Craft also reviewed a wide range of research, undertaken between the 1940s and 1960s, which explored the connections between patterns of upbringing on the one hand, and distortions of personality and behaviour on the other (*ibid*: 68–71). The general thrust of this research was that flaws in the parental handling of children in their early formative years were a major cause of subsequent personality and behaviour disorder. Distortions of personality in general, and psychopathic personality disorder in particular, were associated with the psycho-dynamic relationships of western family life (*ibid*: 71):

> ... maternal neglect, lack of maternal affection, over-indulgence, parental mental illness, parental disinterest and over-affection, were all associated with adverse personality traits (Craft 1966: 69).

Craft went on to consider whether community, as opposed to family, rearing of children was any more successful in preventing psychopathy from developing (*ibid*: 71). He discussed J W Eaton's work, *Culture and Mental Disorders*, which was based upon a study of the Hutterite sect of 8,000 people in North America. Much of the rearing of Hutterite children was done, not by families, but by community nurseries. Compared with those of the average Western family, the child-rearing practices of these nurseries were strict and disciplinary. But, on the other hand, Hutterite children received much more affectionate adult contact. Usually, they received love and affection, not just from their parents, but from all adults in the community. One consequence of this was that Hutterite adolescents appeared less mature and independent than ordinary American adolescents. On the other hand, there was a virtual absence of delinquency and a complete absence of psychopathic personality disorder. For Craft, the studies of the anthropologist, Margaret Mead, of patterns of child rearing in New Guinea and Samoa, lent support for the finding that community child-rearing might reduce rates of crime and psychopathic disorder, but also produce people with less initiative and less invention:

> She appears to feel ... that personality distortions, neuroses, and other community misfits, are the price one has to pay for the excessive stimulation, and materialistic and educational demands of western civilisation, together with dependence on exclusive mother-child relationships arising from the typical western family. She feels that the diffusion of parent-child relationships allowed by the Samoan society also allows a gentler and more amiable mode of community life, which probably has fewer community misfits, but fewer men of action, and invention (Craft 1966: 72).

Unless Craft's views were exceptional amongst those who dealt professionally with psychopaths, we can conclude from the above that at least one of the standard criticisms of the concept of psychopathy is quite misleading. As we saw in the introduction to this case study, critics such as Ramon (1986) suggest that the concept of psychopathy is used to 'individualise' the problem of aggressive behaviour; to shift guilt for such behaviour as far as possible from the arena of collective responsibility. It seems to me, however, that treatment professionals such as Craft were quite enthusiastic about exploring the links between modern culture and psychopathic behaviour. Some regarded a certain amount of psychopathic personality disorder as the price which must be paid for a culture which produces 'strong individuals'. Indeed, Craft hints at a theme taken up by some philosophers who have explored the concept of psychopathy: that the psychopath manifests to an extreme degree traits which we often admire in people – such as emotional coolness, positiveness and aggression – when they are channelled in more valued directions (see Jensen 1979). If we want to produce people with these characteristics, Craft implies, we must be willing to tolerate a certain rate of psychopathic personality disorder.[8] To put this another way, Craft seems to be making a suggestion with which sociological critics of the concept could hardly disagree: that if we wish to prevent cases of psychopathic personality disorder we must address the cultural forms which help produce such cases. He also suggests, however, that we might not wish to live in the kind of culture which would be necessary for the elimination of the problem.

Treatment

In the 1960s, the resistance of psychopaths to all forms of treatment led, not to a move away from therapeutic responses, but to the use of the widest range of treatment methods imaginable. Since the psychopath did not respond well to any methods of treatment, no single method became dominant. Methods of 'treatment' advocated and practised included the use of drugs, psychoanalytic techniques, group therapies, educational units, psychiatric hospitalisation, confinement in special secure units, and treatment in 'penal units' such as approved schools, borstals and prisons (Craft ed: 1966; West ed: 1968).

What is quite clear, however, is that treatment professionals did not adhere to a narrow medical-somatic approach to treatment, nor even to 'individualised' forms of psychiatric treatment. In the area of psychopathy, as in the area of habitual drunkenness (see chapter 4), there was a strong move towards sociotherapeutic methods (see, in particular, Taylor 1963; id 1966; Craft 1968). The operational principles of the sociotherapeutic approach to psychopathic offenders were similar to those that guided the treatment of vagrant alcoholics in the 1960s and 1970s. A range of personal and environmental influences were employed in efforts to humanise, socialise and responsibilise the psychopathic offender. The most significant differences between the sociotherapeutic methods employed with vagrant alcoholics and those employed with psychopathic offenders were due to the need – in the case of the latter – to adjust sociotherapeutic practices to institutional settings

---

8   Cf Henderson's (1939) concept of the creative psychopath, discussed briefly in chapter 6.

in which the main objectives were to ensure internal and external security (McGrath 1966).

Towards the de-psychiatrisation of 'psychopathic' personality disorder

I indicated earlier that, in general, psychiatrists and other treatment professionals were reluctant to take on responsibility for the management and treatment of psychopaths. Towards the end of the 1960s, it seems as if many of those who initially were willing to admit psychopaths were also becoming increasingly reluctant to do so. By this time, the idea that psychopathic offenders were a medical or psychiatric problem, rather than a penal or social problem, was becoming very much a minority view amongst treatment professionals. In his introductory comment to a 1968 collection of papers on psychopathic offenders, the criminologist, D J West, argued against what he saw as the accepted view within psychiatry, that psychopathic offenders should be sent to Borstal or prison, rather than to medical institutions (West 1968: 9). He also remarked:

> Too many psychiatrists are ready to disown any responsibility and to insist that the so-called personality disorders are purely social and not at all medical problems (West 1968: 9).

As I will now show, from the 1970s, the reversal of the psychiatrisation of the problem of 'psychopathic' offenders gathered pace.

THE PROCESSING AND TREATMENT OF PSYCHOPATHIC OFFENDERS SINCE THE 1970s

During the 1970s, officials and treatment professionals decided that the existing response to psychopaths was not working and they began to explore new ways of processing and treating psychopathic offenders. The existing response to psychopathic offenders was reviewed by the Committee on Mentally Abnormal Offenders (the Butler Committee) which reported in 1975, devoting a full chapter (chapter 5) to psychopathic disorder.[9] Before looking at its recommendations on the 'treatment' of psychopathic offenders, it is necessary briefly to look at its response to arguments that the concept had no value or meaning and should be deleted from mental health legislation.

---

9   *Report of the Committee on Mentally Abnormal Offenders, 1975* (hereinafter referred to as the '1975 Report'). See also its Interim Report, published in 1974.

Dissatisfaction with the concept of 'psychopathic disorder'

By the 1970s, there was a strong move towards abolishing the category of psychopathic disorder altogether. Many of those who gave evidence to the Butler Committee argued that the references to 'psychopathic disorder' in s 4 of the Mental Health Act 1959 should be deleted. 'Psychopathic disorder' it was argued, was no longer a useful or meaningful concept (1975 Report: para 5.23). It was contended that psychiatrists disagreed fundamentally about the meaning of the term; some applied it only to dangerously anti-social offenders, others applied it to inadequate persons of all descriptions (*ibid*: para 5.20). It was also argued, *inter alia*, that the concept was circular and therefore logically defective and that labelling people as psychopaths had harmful consequences (*ibid*).

The Committee could not recommend deletion of the concept from mental health legislation as this would have affected 'civilly committed patients' who were outside its terms of reference. However, it did make its position on the issue fairly clear. It seems to have been persuaded by the arguments that psychopathic disorder was no longer a useful or meaningful concept, and that the term had become a stigmatic one which should be 'disowned' (*ibid*: para's. 5.22–5.23). However, its reasons for regarding the concept as highly undesirable were quite different to the reasons of those who wished to see the concept deleted *without replacement*. The committee did not object, as some did, to the compulsory hospitalisation and treatment of the types of person who were currently subject to compulsory powers as psychopaths. Rather, it simply wanted to replace the term with one which was in current use among treatment professionals and which was, in its view, less stigmatic. Hence, the Committee suggested that a future review should consider, not the simple deletion of the concept, but rather its substitution with the term 'personality disorder'. This would ensure that the relatively few people who were admitted to hospitals as psychopathic patients would not be denied admission because of lack of statutory authority (*ibid*: para 5.21).[10]

Recommendations of the Butler Committee on the 'treatment' of psychopathic offenders

The Butler Committee reported that, in general, psychopaths were not treatable, or at least *not treatable in medical terms* (1975 Report: para 5.34). This was in response to the drift, among treatment professionals, towards pessimism about the *medical* treatment of psychopaths. Consultant

---

10 Note that the Committee's suggestion – that the term 'psychopathic disorder' be substituted with 'personality disorder' – would have led to an *expansion* of the category. As I indicated in the previous section, the term 'personality disorder' was broader than the term 'psychopathic disorder'. The former included less severe forms of personality disorder as well as 'psychopathic personality disorder' (1975 Report: para 5.26).

psychiatrists and senior medical officers of the Prison Medical Service had stated to the Committee: 'There is no known treatment for the great majority of psychopaths and control is all that medicine has to offer'; and 'The belief that the psychopath is responsive to medical treatment has not been substantiated in the period since the Mental Health Act came into force' (*ibid*).

In a reversal of the trend – which had lasted for well over a century – towards trying to divert psychopathic offenders from penal into medical channels, the Butler Committee recommended that psychopathic offenders should be sent to prisons (*ibid*: 5.37–5.38). Crucially, however, *this did not mean a change in the objectives of intervention*. It would be mistaken to assume that the Butler Committee, in recommending the reversal of the medicalisation and psychiatrisation of psychopathic offenders, was recommending a change from therapeutic to punitive goals. It was not the view of the Butler Committee that psychopaths should be punished rather than treated. Rather, the Committee continued to define the objective of intervention into the lives of psychopathic offenders in therapeutic-rehabilitative terms. It viewed prisons as therapeutic institutions, of sorts, and claimed that, in many ways, prisons were better equipped for the task of *treating* psychopaths than were hospitals. Psychopaths were to be sent to prisons for re-socialisation, not for punishment:

> Modification of social behaviour is the essential object of the treatment of the dangerous psychopath, and whatever the difficulties confronting the penal system it is among the aims of any penal establishment to re-socialise the offender and equip him to lead a constructive life in the community after discharge. The penal system is provided with industrial workshops and educational activities of a high standard, often, indeed, superior to those available in many hospitals; these are facilities particularly relevant to the social training requirements of many psychopaths. Properly used, the prison environment can possibly provide the situation within which dangerous psychopaths can most readily be helped to develop more acceptable social attitudes (1975 Report: para 5.38).

However, the Committee were not under the illusion that prison 'training' could achieve what every other form of intervention had failed to bring about: the cure of psychopathic disorder. It regarded psychopaths as people who were very difficult to influence. However, it subscribed to the view that a treatment regime of work and social activity could encourage 'natural processes of maturation' (*ibid*: 5.39). This was in response to the suggestion, made by many of those who gave evidence to the committee, 'that the passage of time modified the behaviour of psychopaths and that there is nothing to be done but to wait for the change to take place' (*ibid*: para 5.38). The Committee agreed with the first part of this proposition but not with the second. Hence, it suggested that the phenomenon of maturation could be assisted by appropriate treatment.

The training of psychopathic offenders: a return to moral treatment

What, for the Butler Committee, was the most appropriate way of treating psychopathic offenders? It recommended that 'dangerous anti-social psychopaths should be dealt with in special institutions in the penal system' (ibid: para 5.43). These were not to be labelled as units for psychopaths but were to have a 'non-committal name' such as 'training units' (*ibid*: para 5.39). Interestingly, the Committee proposed a completely non-medical procedure for making decisions about which offenders should be sent to training units:

> We have in mind that if the trial judge considers that allocation to a training unit is desirable he should write privately to the Home Secretary to inform him of his opinion (1975 Report: para 5.43).

Admission to the units was, however, to be entirely voluntary (*ibid*: para 5.50).

The training units were to cater for dangerously anti-social psychopathic offenders aged between 17 and 35, who were willing to undertake the training offered and likely to benefit from it, and who would have a chance of employment upon release (*ibid*). As well as being for the treatment of psychopathic offenders, these units were to be places of research into personality disorder and its treatment (*ibid*: para 5.51). The main form of 'training' or 'treatment' in the units was to be 'work experience' (*ibid*: para 5.53). The proposals of the committee, and the reasoning behind these proposals, bear a striking resemblance to those of the inebriety reformers of a century earlier (see chapter 3). Psychopathic offenders were to be disciplined through the demands of work (1975 Report: para 5.53). For this to take place, work had to be productive and meaningful:

> The industrial processes carried out in the units should be realistic and demanding and should be clearly related to a useful end product. Work experience will be an integral part of the regime of the unit and the work must not be seen simply as something to give the inmates to pass the time. We hope that it may be possible for programmes of work to be fitted in to the local industry of the area where the unit is situated, and to equip the offender for future employment in the community after release (1975 Report: para 5.53).

Also, for the Committee, the *regularity* of work and the establishment of a link between productivity and remuneration, were as important, from the point of view of disciplinary training, as the actual work undertaken. The psychopathic offender was to be immersed, as fully as was possible in a secure institution, into the routines of ordinary working life:

> Workshops must be run on factory lines, geared to a production line, starting and finishing at set times and with provision for refreshment breaks. We would hope that the wages which are paid could be calculated from a basic rate with provision for incentive bonus schemes (1975 Report: para 5.53).

In addition to work, inmates of the training units were to be offered a full programme of 'social activities' ranging from educational to purely recreational (*ibid*: para 5.54). Inmates would also be subject to psychological investigation (*ibid*: para 5.55). Despite the failure, in the Committee's view, of the medical treatment of psychopathic offenders, each unit initially would be headed by a psychiatrist (*ibid*: 5.57).

The fate of the proposal for training units

Some supporters of the complete medicalisation of the problem of psychopathic behaviour would, no doubt, regard the Butler Committee's proposal to process psychopathic offenders in the penal system as regressive. However, it is necessary to remember that their proposal was, in part, a response to the failure of medical institutions to admit significant numbers of psychopathic offenders. Because of this 'failure' there was very little actual therapeutic provision for those psychopathic offenders who – in the view of the Butler Committee – should be sent to training units. In reality, being sent to a training unit would be a therapeutic alternative, not to being sent to a medical or psychiatric institution for treatment, but to being sent to a prison for punishment. The Butler Committee, far from proposing a reactionary return to a more punitive response to psychopaths offenders, were actually seeking a more realistic way of ensuring that psychopathic offenders were offered therapeutic interventions.

We can gain a fuller perspective on the character of the Butler Committee's recommendation by considering the response of the Home Office to it. As Ashworth and Shapland (1980) point out, in a comprehensive review of the ways in which adult psychopathic offenders could be disposed of, the proposal for special units in prisons to treat psychopaths was vigorously resisted by the Home Office. The response of the Prison Department contrasted sharply with that of the Butler Committee. The Prison Department's view was the more familiar one that it was wasteful to devote scarce resources to the treatment of offenders who were actually untreatable:

> There is also insufficient evidence that the regime would have the desired socialising effect. Even to launch an experimental unit would take up considerable resources, inevitably at the expense of other parts of the prison system. And these resources would be devoted to offenders who on the available evidence, seem least likely to benefit from them (The Prison Department, quoted in Ashworth and Shapland 1980: 637).

Ashworth and Shapland concluded their review by suggesting that, by 1980, the Health Service virtually had abdicated responsibility for the treatment of psychopathic offenders. Only a select few were being treated in hospitals; those whose behaviour was more bizarre or more dangerous than the norm (*ibid*: 639). Increasingly, psychopathic offenders were being sent to prisons and this trend seemed likely to continue (*ibid*). Moreover, it was unlikely that special facilities would be developed within the prison system for psychopathic offenders (*ibid*). In practice, the trend was towards processing psychopaths as ordinary offenders in ordinary prisons (*ibid*: 640).

Psychopathic offenders and public safety

Since the early 1980s, the debate over what to do with psychopathic offenders has been increasingly drawn towards the problem of balancing the rights of psychopathic offenders with the interests of public safety (see the Report of the Department of Health and Home Office Working Group on Psychopathic Disorder, 1994, para 3.5 – hereinafter referred to as the '1994 Report'). To a large extent, this issue arose as the result of the emergence, since the mid-1970s, of a campaign to promote the rights of mental patients.[11] One outcome of this campaign was that Mental Health Review Tribunals were given the power to discharge restricted patients (see the 1994 Report: para 3.4).[12] As a result of this development, the pressure to discharge psychopathically disordered offenders who might re-offend, where there were no medical grounds for confinement, was increased. Public concern was heightened by a number of highly publicised cases in which patients who had been diagnosed as suffering from psychopathic disorder, and were regarded as dangerous by many, were released from special hospitals (1994 Report: para 3.8).[13] Subsequent inquiries into what should be done with psychopathic offenders have been dominated by this concern (DHSS/Home Office 1986).

Nevertheless, the problem of finding some way of managing confined psychopathic offenders (whatever the legal framework governing their confinement) remains (Chiswick 1987). The debate about whether psychopathic offenders can be best dealt with within the medical system or the penal system continues (1994 Report). And, within each of these options, there are questions about what types of regime, and what types of approach, are most appropriate. Despite the well publicised collapse of the ideology of treatment, treatment professionals continue to contribute to this debate, and continue to do so on the assumption that psychopathic offenders are disordered people who require therapeutic rather than penal intervention (*ibid*).

---

11 See Unsworth (1987) and, for a critical assessment of this reforming campaign, Rose (1986).

12 The power was created by the Mental Health Act 1983, which followed the ruling in the European Court of Human Rights in the case of *X v United Kingdom, Application No 6988/75* (1981) 4 EHRR 181.

13 One of the most recent cases which received considerable media attention was that of Michael Buchanan, who committed a brutal killing of an ex-policeman. Buchanan was: 'a psychiatric patient suffering from a psychopathic disorder whom the top security special hospitals refused to accept and whom community health workers believed would not benefit from treatment in local hospitals' (*Guardian*, 7 November 1994, editorial).

CHAPTER 8

CONCLUSION

Since around the middle of the 19th century, reformers and treatment professionals have attempted to establish therapeutic programmes for certain types of offender, as alternatives or supplements to the penal interventions or non-intervention they would otherwise receive. These programmes are informed by, and embody, distinctive ways of classifying and making sense of offenders. In this study, I have looked in detail at the nature of some key therapeutic programmes that have been proposed (and to some extent established) and at the classifications, perceptions, understandings and explanations of offenders which inform these programmes. In doing so, I have tried to show that therapeutic programmes for offenders, and the ideas embodied in them, are much more diverse, complex and subtle than has hitherto been realised, especially by their critics who have attempted to discern the nature of these programmes by looking only at the medical model of crime.

In describing, or rather re-describing, the nature of these therapeutic programmes and discourses I have avoided evaluation.[1] In particular, I have sought neither to defend nor to discredit the therapeutic programmes and discourses which I have described and examined. Of course, at certain points my research has resulted in findings which may be useful for those who wish to discredit therapeutic-psychiatric approaches to crime. But equally, it has resulted in findings which will be of use to those who wish to defend such approaches to crime against many of the standard objections to them. My goals, however, have been to shift the focus of debate away from the advantages and disadvantages of the medical model of crime towards the advantages and disadvantages of actual therapeutic programmes and discourses and to persuade both critics and supporters that the range of therapeutic programmes and discourses under discussion is much more varied and complex than they have realised, and that they require an equally complex evaluative response. Insofar as this study contributes to the task of evaluating therapeutic programmes for, and discourses on, offenders, its contribution is an indirect one. By capturing the full range and complexity of therapeutic programmes for offenders, and of the 'ideas' which support and

---

1   In the conclusions of some chapters I have made some points about the advantages and the limitations of certain therapeutic programmes. But, as I explained, the purpose of doing this was to demonstrate how my re-description of these programmes could affect our assessment of them, not to undertake a comprehensive evaluation of these programmes.

inform them, I have tried to provide the basis for a better informed debate about what their consequences are and about whether these consequences are desirable.[2]

Perhaps the most important contribution of this study has been to demonstrate the 'internal diversity' of 'therapeutic approaches to crime'. In their 1983 essay on the social analysis of 'penality', Garland and Young suggested that the term 'punishment', insofar as it implied a singular entity – rather than a diverse and complex *range* of penal institutions, practices and discourses – hindered social analysis of the field of penal practices (Garland and Young 1983: 14). I make a similar point here with regard to therapeutic interventions into the lives of offenders. We need to substitute 'singular' terms which have been used to refer to these interventions, such as 'penal treatment' or the 'medical model' of crime, with a 'plural' term, such as therapeutic-psychiatric *approaches* to crime. Above all, it must be realised that such a term refers to a wide variety of programmes, which have a variety of objectives and which embody a variety of understandings and explanations of anti-social behaviours. It would be mistaken to attempt to evaluate therapeutic programmes for offenders as if they all employed the same approach, expressed a uniform ideology or philosophy, and had uniform effects. Instead, it is necessary to differentiate between very different types of therapeutic programme, and to distinguish between progressive and non-progressive objectives and methods, acceptable and unacceptable procedures, useful insights into anti-social behaviour and mere expressions of social prejudice.

One implication of this study, then, is that the range of therapeutic approaches to crime is much wider than many commentators seem to realise. For instance, the range includes medical-somatic interventions and compulsory procedures which, as the critics point out, are deeply problematic and can have harmful consequences. However, it also includes sociotherapeutic interventions and voluntary procedures, which avoid many of these problems and which are not obviously harmful to offenders. These interventions are, without doubt, problematic in other ways, but they deserve more careful analysis and consideration, from those interested in promoting progressive penal change, than they have hitherto received.

However, in this work I have proposed a stronger thesis than that the field of therapeutic interventions into the lives of offenders *includes* programmes and discourses which, until now, have been un-noticed and un-analysed by social scientists and philosophers content nevertheless to dismiss the whole idea of penal treatment as deeply flawed. I have suggested that the types of therapeutic programme and discourse which are usually discussed are the types which are least common in practice, and that the types which are

2   For a useful contribution to the debate about how we should go about the task of evaluating penal-therapeutic institutions and practices, see Nokes (1974).

usually ignored are the most common in practice. To draw out the implications of this thesis more fully, let us look at a fairly typical example of the way in which therapeutic interventions are now understood and represented by socio-legal scholars and philosophers. I shall take an example, not from the specialist literature, but from a more general work which discusses therapeutic approaches to crime in passing, since this best captures the image of therapeutic interventions which has filtered down from the specialist literature.

In their book, *Understanding Law*, Adams and Brownsword introduce briefly the issue of therapeutic approaches to crime in the following terms:

> ... if, as is the case, the present range of punishments do not prevent further offences by convicted criminals, should we consider rendering such persons mentally or physically incapable of committing again the offences for which they have been convicted? For example, should rapists be castrated, or violent people be treated with aversion therapy (see Anthony Burgess' novel *A Clockwork Orange*)? Given our ideas about human dignity ... would we be prepared to stomach this? (Adams and Brownsword 1992: 164).

I should make it clear that this is raised as an issue for reflection and discussion. The authors do not imply that such practices are common. But, since such ideas have indeed been proposed and to some extent implemented, the authors are surely quite right to alert their readers to them and to raise the question of whether such developments would be desirable. My problem with such statements, which are quite frequent in philosophical and sociological discussions of punishment and treatment, is that standing alone, as they usually do, they reflect and disseminate a quite misleading image of the true nature of therapeutic interventions into the lives of offenders.

As I have shown, in practice, the type of intervention mentioned by Adams and Brownsword, as if it were typical of therapeutic interventions into the lives of offenders, is quite rare. This is not what treatment professionals usually have in mind when they propose replacing or supplementing penal interventions with therapeutic interventions. Therapeutic interventions typically consist, not of 'hard' techniques such as surgery or some kinds of aversion therapy, but of 'soft' methods such as the use of personal, environmental, or organisational influences. Moreover, it is not usually the aim of therapeutic interventions to render people *incapable* of committing further offences, even if they should wish to do so. Rather the 'operational objectives' of therapeutic interventions are usually less ambitious in some ways and more ambitious in others. Few treatment professionals work on the assumption that they possess the capacity to stop those who are intent upon offending from doing so. Rather, their discourse suggests that they assume that they can help some of those who express some desire to stop offending to break the habit. Just as importantly, few treatment professionals would be content simply to stop offenders from re-offending. They usually seek other objectives, such as inculcating the social and other skills required to live an independent and happy life in the community. Adams and Brownsword's philosophical teaser would be more realistic, and less misleading, if they added something like the following. If the present range of punishments do not prevent further offences by certain types of offender – ie those whose conduct, while not indicating mental illness, does seem to stem from psychological problems which are usually the result of an appalling early environment – should we offer them treatment in rehabilitation hostels such as proposed and established by Tim Cook and his colleagues for habitual drunken offenders (see chapter 4), or in 'training units' in prisons as envisaged by the Butler Committee for psychopathic offenders (see chapter 7), through which they *might* acquire some capacity for autonomous, responsible, and social behaviour? Such a question requires a more complex response than arguably is required of the type of question with which we are usually posed in discussions of therapeutic responses to offenders.

BIBLIOGRAPHY

Adams, J and Brownsword, R (1992) *Understanding Law* London: Fontana Press

Allen, F (1973) 'Criminal Justice, Legal Values and the Rehabilitative Ideal' pp 172–85 in Murphy, J (ed) *Punishment and Rehabilitation* California: Wadsworth

Allen, H (1987) *Justice Unbalanced: Gender, Psychiatry and Judicial Decisions* Milton Keynes: Open University Press

Anon (1922) 'Criminal Youths', *Howard Journal* 1 (2): 16–18

Anon (1959) 'Notes of the Year: The Mental Health Bill and the Death Penalty', *Howard Journal* 10 (2): 73

Archard, P (1973) 'Sad, Bad, or Mad: Society's Confused Response to the Skid Row Alcoholic', in R Bailey and J Young (eds) *Contemporary Social Problems in Britain* Farnborough: Saxon House

Archard, P (1979) *Vagrancy, Alcoholism and Social Control* London: Macmillan

Ashworth, A and Shapland, J (1980) 'Psychopaths in the Criminal Process', *Criminal Law Review* October: 628–40

Balch, R (1975) 'The Medical Model of Delinquency: Theoretical, Practical, and Ethical Implications', *Crime and Delinquency* 21: 116–30

Bean, P (1976) *Rehabilitation and Deviance* London: Routledge and Kegan Paul

Box, S (1980) 'Where Have all the Naughty Children Gone?', pp 96–121 in National Deviancy Conference (ed), *Permissiveness and Control: The Fate of the Sixties Legislation* London: Macmillan

Branthwaite, R (1907/8) 'Inebriety: Its Causation and Control', *British Journal of Inebriety* 5 (3): 105–27

Bunton, R (1989) 'Drinking Disciplines' Paper presented to the British Criminology Conference, July 1989, Bristol Polytechnic

Burt, C (1937) *The Subnormal Mind* Oxford University Press

Burt, C (1944) *The Young Delinquent* (1st edn 1925) University of London Press

Carlson, E and Dain, N (1962) 'The Meaning of Moral Insanity', *Bulletin of the History of Medicine* 36: 130–40

Carr, C (1994) *The Alienist* London: Warner Books

Castel, R (1975) 'The Doctors and Judges', pp 250–69 in M Foucault (ed) *I, Pierre Rivière, having slaughtered my mother, my sister, and my brother* (trld F Jellinek) New York: Pantheon Books (reprinted in 1982 by Bison Books)

Castel, R (1980) 'Moral Treatment: Mental Therapy and Social Control in the Nineteenth Century' (trld P Miller), pp 248–66 in S Cohen and A Scull (eds) *Social Control and the State* Oxford: Martin Robertson

Chiswick, D (1987) 'Managing Psychopathic Offenders: A Problem that will not go away', *British Medical Journal* 295 (18 July) 159–60

Clare, A (1980) *Psychiatry in Dissent: Controversial Issues in Thought and Practice* (2nd edn) London: Routledge

Clark, D (1981) *Social Therapy in Psychiatry* (2nd edn) Edinburgh: Churchill Livingstone

Cohen, S (1971) 'Introduction', pp 9–24 in S Cohen (ed) *Images of Deviance* Harmondsworth: Penguin

Conrad, P (1981) 'On the Medicalisation of Deviance and Social Control', pp 102–119 in D Ingleby (ed) *Critical Psychiatry: The Politics of Mental Health* Harmondsworth: Penguin

Conrad, P and Schneider, J (1980) *Deviance and Medicalization: From Badness to Sickness* St Louis: Mosby

Cook, T (1969) 'Existing Facilities' in T Cook, D Gath and C Hensman (eds), *The Drunkenness Offence* Oxford: Pergamon Press

Cook, T (1971) 'The Rathcoole Experiment', app N of the Report of the Home Office Working Party on Habitual Drunken Offenders (1971) London: HMSO

Cook, T (1975) *Vagrant Alcoholics* London: Routledge and Kegan Paul

Cook, T, Gath, D and Hensman, C (eds) (1969) *The Drunkenness Offence* Oxford: Pergamon Press

Craft, M (1962) 'The Treatment of Adolescents with Personality Disorders', *Howard Journal*, 11 (1) 47–57

Craft, M (1966) 'The Causation of Psychopathic Disorder', pp 56–81 in M Craft (ed) *Psychopathic Disorders and their Assessment* Oxford: Pergamon Press

Craft, M (ed) (1966) *Psychopathic Disorders and their Assessment* Oxford: Pergamon Press

Craft, M (1968) 'Treating Psychopaths at Garth', pp 73–5 in D West (ed) *Psychopathic Offenders* Cambridge: Institute of Criminology

Craike, W (1953) 'Psychiatric Treatment of Adolescent Delinquent Girls', *Howard Journal* 8 (4): 258–62

Critchley, M (ed) (1955) *The Trial of Neville George Clevely Heath (Notable British Trials)* London: William Hodge and Co

Department of Health and Social Security (DHSS) and Home Office (1986) *Joint Consultation Document: Offenders Suffering from Psychopathic Disorder* London: DHSS and Home Office

Dicey, A V (1962) *Introduction to the Study of the Law of the Constitution* (1st edn 1885) London: Macmillan

Digby, A (1985) 'Moral Treatment at the Retreat, 1796–1846', pp 52–72 in W Bynum, R Porter and M Shepherd (eds) *The Anatomy of Madness II, Institutions and Society* London: Tavistock

Donnelly, M (1983) *Managing the Mind: A Study of Medical Psychology in Early Nineteenth Century Britain* London: Tavistock

d'Orban, P (1969) 'Habitual Drunkenness Offenders in Holloway Prison', pp 51–62 in T Cook, D Gath and C Hensman (eds), *The Drunkenness Offence* Oxford: Pergamon Press

East, W Norwood (1933) 'Summary of The Prison Commissioners' Report: The Medical Commissioners' Report', *Howard Journal* 3 (4): 59–64

East, W Norwood (1934) 'Summary of The Prison Commissioners' Report: The Medical Commissioners' Report', *Howard Journal* 4 (1)

East, W Norwood (1949) *Society and the Criminal* London: HMSO

Edwards, G, Hawker, A, and Williamson, V (1966) 'London's Skid Row', *The Lancet* 1: 249–52

Ellis, H (1891) *The Criminal* London: Walter Scott

Evans, R (1982) *The Fabrication of Virtue: English Prison Architecture, 1750–1840* Cambridge University Press

Fears, M (1977) 'Therapeutic Optimism and the Treatment of the Insane', pp 66–81 in R Dingwall, C Heath, M Reid and M Stacey (eds) *Health Care and Health Knowledge* London: Croom Helm

Ferri, E (1913) *The Positive School of Criminology* (trld E Untermann) Chicago: Charles H Kerr and Co

Figlio, K (1987) 'The Lost Subject of Medical Sociology', pp 77–109 in G Scrambler (ed) *Sociological Theory and Medical Sociology* London: Tavistock

Foucault, M (1967) *Madness and Civilisation: A History of Insanity in the Age of Reason* (trld R Howard) London: Tavistock

Foucault, M (1977) *Discipline and Punish: The Birth of the Prison* (trld A Sheridan) London: Allen Lane

Freud, A and Dann, S (1951) *Psychoanalytic Study of the Child* London: Imago

Frey, E (1948/9) 'Biology and Juvenile Delinquency', *Howard Journal* 7 (4): 225–33

Gardner, A (1928) 'Science Approaches the Lawbreaker', *Howard Journal* 2 (3): 203–7

Garland, D (1985) *Punishment and Welfare: A History of Penal Strategies* Aldershot: Gower

Garland, D (1994) 'Of Crimes and Criminals: The Development of Criminology in Britain', pp 17–68 in M Maguire, R Morgan, and R Reiner (eds) *The Oxford Handbook of Criminology* Oxford: Clarendon Press

Garland, D and Young, P (1983) 'Towards a Social Analysis of Penality', pp 1–36 in D Garland and P Young (eds) *The Power to Punish* London: Heinemann Educational Books

Gath, D (1969) 'The Male Drunk in Court', pp 9–26 in T Cook, D Gath and C Hensman (eds), *The Drunkenness Offence* Oxford: Pergamon Press

Gillespie, R (1930) 'The Service of Psychiatry in the Prevention and Treatment of Crime', *Howard Journal* 3 (1): 22–28

Glatt, M (1964) 'Crime, Alcohol and Addiction', *Howard Journal* 11 (4): 276–84

Goff, D (1969) 'The Legal Position in the USA', pp 89–95 in T Cook, D Gath and C Hensman (eds), *The Drunkenness Offence* Oxford: Pergamon Press

Goffman, E (1968) 'The Medical Model and Mental Hospitalisation', in his *Asylums* Harmondsworth: Penguin

Gould, S (1981) *The Mismeasure of Man* London: Penguin

Greenwood, V and Young, J (1980) 'Ghettos of Freedom: An Examination of Permissiveness', pp 149–74 in National Deviancy Conference (ed) *Permissiveness and Control: The Fate of the Sixties Legislation* London: Macmillan

Gunn, J, Robertson, G, Dell, S, and Way, C (1978) *Psychiatric Aspects of Imprisonment* London: Academic Press

Gusfield, J (1980) 'Foreword' pp v–x in P Conrad and J Schneider, *Deviance and Medicalization: From Badness to Sickness* St Louis: Mosby

Halleck, S (1979) 'The Future of Psychiatric Criminology', pp 139–58 in C Jeffery (ed) *Biology and Crime* Beverly Hills, California: Sage

Hamblin Smith, M (1922) *The Psychology of the Criminal* London: Methuen

Hamblin Smith, M (1926) 'Review of Report of the Prison Commission 1924–25', *Howard Journal* 2 (1): 38–44

Hamilton, J, Griffith, A, Ritson, B and Aitken, R (1978) *Detoxification of Habitual Drunken Offenders* Edinburgh: Scottish Home and Health Dept

Harding, C and Wilkin, L (1988) '"The Dream of a Benevolent Mind": The Late Victorian Response to Inebriety', *Criminal Justice History* 9: 189–207

Harrison, B (1971) *Drink and the Victorians* London: Faber and Faber

Haynes, S (1864/5) 'Clinical Cases Illustrative of Moral Imbecility and Insanity', *Journal of Mental Science* 10: 533-49

Healy, W and Bronner, A (1936) *New Light on Delinquency and its Treatment* New Haven: Yale University Press

Hearnshaw, L (1987) *The Shaping of Modern Psychology: An Historical Introduction* London: Routledge and Kegan Paul

Henderson, D (1939) *Psychopathic States* New York: Norton

Henderson, D (1944) 'Psychopathic Constitution and Criminal Behaviour', pp 105–121 in L Radzinowicz and J Turner (eds) *Mental Abnormality and Crime* London: Macmillan

Hirst, P and Woolley P (1982) *Social Relations and Human Attributes* London: Tavistock

Honderich, T (1971) *Punishment: The Supposed Justifications* Harmondsworth: Penguin

Ingleby, D (1985) 'Professionals as Socialisers: The "Psy Complex"', *Research in Law, Deviance and Social Control* 7: 79–109

Ingram-Smith, N (1969) 'Prospects for the Future in the Community', pp 161–4 in T Cook, D Gath and C Hensman (eds), *The Drunkenness Offence* Oxford: Pergamon Press

Jayewardene, C (1963/4) 'The English Precursors of Lombroso', *British Journal of Criminology* 4: 164–70

Jensen, O (1979) 'The Mask of Psychopathy', in D Weisstub (ed) *Law and Psychiatry II* New York: Pergamon Press

Johnstone, G (1991) 'Between Permissiveness and Control: Community Treatment and Penal Supervision', *Law and Critique* 2 (1): 37–61

Johnstone, G (1996) 'From Experts in Responsibility to Advisers on Punishment', in P Rush, S McVeigh and A Young (eds) *Criminal Legal Doctrine* (forthcoming) Oxford University Press

Jones, K (1960) *Mental Health and Social Policy, 1845–1959* London: Routledge and Kegan Paul

Jones, K (1972) *A History of the Mental Health Services* London: Routledge and Kegan Paul

Kelynack, T (1904/5) 'Medico-Legal Aspects of Inebriety', *British Journal of Inebriety* 2: 117–29

Kendell, R (1979) 'Alcoholism: A Medical or a Political Problem', *British Medical Journal* 10th Feb: 367–71

Kessell, N and Walton, H (1965) *Alcoholism* Harmondsworth: Penguin

Kittrie, N (1973) *The Right to be Different: Deviance and Enforced Therapy* Baltimore, Maryland: Penguin

Laycock, T (1862) 'The Antagonism of Law and Medicine in Insanity, and its Consequences. An Introductory Lecture', *Journal of Mental Science* 8: 593–7

Laycock, T (1869) 'Suggestions for Rendering Medico-Mental Science Available to the Better Administration of Justice and the More Effectual Prevention of Lunacy and Crime', *Journal of Mental Science* 14: 334–45

Leigh, D (1961) *The Historical Development of British Psychiatry I: 18th and 19th Century* Oxford: Pergamon

Light, R (1986) 'Policing Skid Row: Criminal Justice and the Habitual Drunkard', *Policing* 2 (2)

Lowerson, J and Myerscough, J (1977) *Time to Spare in Victorian England* Hassocks, Sussex: Harvester Press

McCord, W and McCord, J (1956) *Psychopathy and Delinquency* New York: Grune and Stratton

McGrath, P (1966) 'Methods of Care: The English Special Hospital System', pp 135–44 in M Craft (ed) *Psychopathic Disorders and their Assessment* Oxford: Pergamon Press

MacIntyre, A (1985) *After Virtue: A Study in Moral Theory* (2nd edn) London: Duckworth

McLaughlin, P (1985) 'Police Management of Public Drunkenness in Scotland', *British Journal of Criminology* 25 (4): 344–64

MacLeod, R (1967) 'The Edge of Hope: Social Policy and Chronic Alcoholism, 1870–1900', *Journal of the History of Medicine* July: 215–45

Maudsley, H (1873) *Body and Mind* London: Macmillan

Maudsley, H (1874) *Responsibility in Mental Disease* London: King and Co

Menninger, K (1968) *The Crime of Punishment* Viking Press (republished in 1977 by Penguin Books)

Mercier, C (1917) 'Moral Imbecility', *The Practitioner* 99 (October): 301–308

Mill, J S (1859) *On Liberty* London: John Parker and Son

Miller, M (1975) *Evaluating Community Treatment Programs* Lexington, Mass: Lexington Books

Miller, P and Rose, N (eds) (1986) *The Power of Psychiatry* Cambridge: Polity

Mitcheson, M (1968) 'The Use made of Section 60 of The Mental Health Act for the Treatment of Psychopathic Offenders', pp 23–30 in D West (ed) *Psychopathic Offenders* Cambridge: Institute of Criminology

Moran, R (1978) 'Biomedical Research and the Politics of Crime Control', *Contemporary Crises* 2: 335–57

Moran, R (1980) 'Medicine and Crime', chapter 8 of P Conrad and J Schneider, *Deviance and Medicalization: From Badness to Sickness* St Louis: Mosby

Mort, F (1987) *Dangerous Sexualities: Medico-Moral Politics in England since 1830* London: Routledge and Kegan Paul

Murphy, J (1979) *Retribution, Justice and Therapy: Essays in the Philosophy of Law* London: D Reidel

Murphy, J (1979b) 'Moral Death: A Kantian Essay on Psychopathy', in his *Retribution, Justice and Therapy: Essays in the Philosophy of Law* London: D Reidel

Neustatter, W (1953) 'Problems of Probation with a Condition of Residence at a Mental Hospital', *Howard Journal* 8 (4): 251–55

Nimmer, R (1971) *Two Million Unnecessary Arrests: Removing a Social Service Concern from the Criminal Justice System* Chicago: American Bar Foundation

Nokes, P (1967) *The Professional Task in Welfare Practice* London: Routledge and Kegan Paul

Nokes, P (1974) 'The Evaluation of Penal Systems', pp 68–82 in L Blom-Cooper (ed) *Progress in Penal Reform* Clarendon Press: Oxford

Nye, R (1984) *Crime, Madness, and Politics in Modern France: The Medical Concept of National Decline* Princeton, NJ: Princeton University Press

O'Connor, P (1963) *Britain in the Sixties: Vagrancy* Harmondsworth: Penguin

O'Donovan, K (1984) 'The Medicalization of Infanticide', *Criminal Law Review*, May: 259–64

Pearson, G (1975) *The Deviant Imagination: Psychiatry, Social Work and Social Change* London: Macmillan

Peddie, A (1860) 'Dipsomania: A Proper Subject for Legal Provision', *Transactions of the National Association for the Promotion of Social Science*, 538–46

Penton, J (1946/7) 'Lessons from the Army for Penal Reformers: Selection of Personnel Applied to Delinquency', *Howard Journal* 7 (2): 81–85

Phillimore, P (1979) 'Dossers and Jake Drinkers: The View from One End of Skid Row', pp 29–48 in T Cook (ed) *Vagrancy: Some New Perspectives* London: Academic Press

Pichot, P (1978) 'Psychopathic Behaviour: A Historical Overview', pp 55–70 in R Hare and D Schalling (eds) *Psychopathic Behaviour: Approaches to Research* Chichester: Wiley

Pick, D (1989) *Faces of Degeneration: A European Disorder, c 1848–c 1918* Cambridge: Cambridge University Press

Pittman, D and Gordon, C (1958) *Revolving Door: A Study of the Chronic Police Case Inebriate* Glencoe, Ill: The Free Press

Pollak, B (1969) 'Rathcoole House – An Experiment in Rehabilitation', pp 109–114 in T Cook, D Gath and C Hensman (eds), *The Drunkenness Offence* Oxford: Pergamon Press

Porter, R (1987a) *Disease, Medicine and Society in England, 1550–1860* London: Macmillan

Porter, R (1987b) *Mind Forg'd Manacles: A History of Madness in England from the Restoration to the Regency* London: Penguin (originally published by the Athlone Press)

Prichard, J C (1837) *A Treatise on Insanity and Other Disorders Affecting the Mind* Philadelphia: Haswell, Barrington and Haswell (reprinted in 1973 by Arno Press, New York)

Prichard, J C (1847) *On the Different Forms of Insanity in Relation to Jurisprudence* London: Hippolyte Ballière

Prins, H (1980) *Offenders, Deviants, or Patients* (1st edn) London: Tavistock

Prins, H (1995) *Offenders, Deviants, or Patients* (2nd edn) London: Routledge

Radzinowicz, L and Hood, R (1990) *The Emergence of Penal Policy in Victorian and Edwardian England* (1st edn 1986) Oxford: Clarendon Press

Ramon, S (1985) *Psychiatry in Britain: Meaning and Policy* London: Croom Helm

Ramon, S (1986) 'The Category of Psychopathy: Its Professional and Social Context in Britain', pp 214–40 in P Miller and N Rose (eds) *The Power of Psychiatry* Cambridge: Polity

Raphael, D (1973) 'Moral Sense', pp 230–35 in P Wiener (ed) *Dictionary of the History of Ideas: Studies of Selected Pivotal Ideas III* New York: Charles Schribner's Sons

Rees, J (1933) 'The Causes and Cure of Crime: From the Psychologist's Standpoint', *Howard Journal* 3 (4): 28–34

Report of the Select Committee on Habitual Drunkards (1872) *Parliamentary Papers*, vol 9

Report from the Departmental Committee on the Treatment of Inebriates (1893/4) *Parliamentary Papers*, vol 17

Report of the Departmental Committee appointed to Inquire into the Operation of the Law Relating to Inebriates and to their Detention in Reformatories and Retreats (1908), *Parliamentary Papers*, vol 42, cd 4438

Report of the Royal Commission on the Care and Control of the Feeble-Minded (1908b), *Parliamentary Papers*, vol 39, cd 4202

Report of the Mental Deficiency Committee being a Joint Committee of the Board of Education and Board of Control (1929) London: HMSO

Report of the Royal Commission on the Law Relating to Mental Illness and Mental Deficiency (1957), Cmnd 169 London: HMSO

Report of the Home Office Working Party on Habitual Drunken Offenders (1971) London: HMSO

Report of the (Butler) Committee on Mentally Abnormal Offenders (1975), Cmnd 6244 London: HMSO

Report of the Department of Health and Home Office Working Group on Psychopathic Disorder (1994) (Chairman: Dr John Reed) London: Department of Health and Home Office

Robinson, K (1966) 'Law and Practice of Psychopathic Disorder in England and Wales', pp 23–31 in M Craft (ed) *Psychopathic Disorders and their Assessment* Oxford: Pergamon Press

Rose, N (1985) *The Psychological Complex: Psychology, Politics and Society in England 1869–1939* London: Routledge and Kegan Paul

Rose, N (1986) 'Law, Rights and Psychiatry', pp 177–213 in P Miller and N Rose (eds) *The Power of Psychiatry* Cambridge: Polity

Rose, N (1989) *Governing the Soul: The Shaping of the Private Self* London: Routledge

Rothman, D (1971) *The Discovery of the Asylum: Social Order and Disorder in the New Republic* Boston: Little Brown & Co

Rotman, E (1990) *Beyond Punishment: A New View on the Rehabilitation of Criminal Offenders* New York: Greenwood Press

Rubington, E (1967) 'The Half-way House for the Alcoholic', *Mental Hygiene* 51 (4)

Scott, P (1958) 'The Psychopath: An Examination of the Recommendations of the Report of the Royal Commission on the Law Relating to Mental Illness and Mental Deficiency, 1954–57', *Howard Journal* 10 (1): 6–17

Sedgwick, P (1982) *Psycho Politics* London: Pluto Press/New York: Harper and Row

Silkin, S (1969) 'Foreword' pp xiii–xv in T Cook, D Gath and C Hensman (eds), *The Drunkenness Offence* Oxford: Pergamon Press

Sim, J (1990) *Medical Power in Prisons: The Prison Medical Service in England 1774–1989* Milton Keynes: Open University Press

Simmons, H (1978) 'Explaining Social Policy: The English Mental Deficiency Act of 1913', *Journal of Social History* 3: 387–403

Skultans, V (1975) *Madness and Morals: Ideas on Insanity in the Nineteenth Century* London: Routledge and Kegan Paul

Smart, C (1989) *Feminism and the Power of Law* London: Routledge

Smith, Robert (1978) *The Psychopath in Society* New York: Academic Press

Smith, Roger (1981) *Trial by Medicine: Insanity and Responsibility in Victorian Trials* Edinburgh University Press

Stedman Jones, G (1971) *Outcast London: A Study in the Relationship between Classes in Victorian Society* Oxford University Press

Stocking, G (1973) 'From Chronology to Ethnology: James Cowles Prichard and British Anthropology', Introductory essay to J Prichard, *Researches into the Physical History of Man* (1st edn 1813) University of Chicago Press

Stonham, Lord (1969) 'Introductory Address', in T Cook, D Gath and C Hensman (eds), *The Drunkenness Offence* Oxford: Pergamon Press

Sullivan, W (1924) *Crime and Insanity* London: Edward Arnold

Symonds, J (1864/5) 'Remarks on Criminal Responsibility in Relation to Insanity', *Journal of Mental Science* 10: 273–5

Szasz, T (1972) 'Bad Habits are Not Diseases: A Refutation of the Claim that Alcoholism is a Disease', *The Lancet* 2: 83–4

Szasz, T (1974) *The Second Sin* London: Routledge and Kegan Paul

Taylor, F (1963) 'The Treatment of Delinquent Psychopaths', *Howard Journal* 11 (2): 84–92

Taylor, F (1966) 'Methods of Care: The Henderson Therapeutic Community', pp 105–115 in M Craft (ed) *Psychopathic Disorders and their Assessment* Oxford: Pergamon Press

Tether, P, and Robinson, D (1986) *Preventing Alcohol Problems* London: Tavistock

Thomson, J B (1867) 'The Effects of the Present System of Prison Discipline on the Body and Mind', *Journal of Mental Science* 11: 340–48

Thomson, J B (1870) 'The Hereditary Nature of Crime', *Journal of Mental Science* 15: 487–98

Thomson, J B (1871) 'The Psychology of Criminals', *Journal of Mental Science* 16: 321–50

Todd, A (1983) 'Women's Bodies as Diseased and Deviant: Historical and Contemporary Issues', *Research in Law, Deviance and Social Control* 5: 83–95

Tredgold, A (1917) 'Moral Imbecility', *The Practitioner* 99: 43–56

Unsworth, C (1987) *The Politics of Mental Health Legislation* Oxford: Clarendon Press

Walker, N (1968) *Crime and Insanity in England I: The Historical Perspective* University of Edinburgh Press

Walker, N and McCabe, S (1973) *Crime and Insanity in England II: New Solutions and New Problems* Edinburgh University Press

Watson, S (1988) 'The Moral Imbecile: A Study of the Relations between Penal Practice and Psychiatric Knowledge of the Habitual Offender', PhD thesis, University of Lancaster

West, D (1968) 'Psychopaths: An Introductory Comment', pp 7–11 in D West (ed) *Psychopathic Offenders* Cambridge: Institute of Criminology

West, D (ed) (1968) *Psychopathic Offenders* Cambridge: Institute of Criminology

Wiener, M (1990) *Reconstructing the Criminal: Culture, Law and Policy in England, 1830–1914* Cambridge University Press

Williams, K (1991) *Textbook on Criminology* London: Blackstone

Winslow, F (1843) *The Plea of Insanity in Criminal Cases* London

Wiseman, J (1970) *Stations of the Lost: The Treatment of Skid Row Alcoholics* University of Chicago Press

Wootton, B (1959) *Social Science and Social Pathology* London: George Allen and Unwin

INDEX